Japan's Big Six

Case Studies of
Japan's Largest Contractors

Sidney M. Levy

McGraw-Hill, Inc.

New York   San Francisco   Washington, D.C.   Auckland   Bogotá
Caracas   Lisbon   London   Madrid   Mexico City   Milan
Montreal   New Delhi   San Juan   Singapore
Sydney   Tokyo   Toronto

Library of Congress Cataloging-in-Publication Data

Levy, Sidney M.
    Japan's big six : inside Japan's construction industry / Sidney M.
Levy
       p.   cm.
    ISBN 0-07-037522-4
    1. Construction industry—Japan. I. Title.
    HD9715.J22L47 1993
    338.4'7624'0952—dc20   93-12550
                                            CIP

1 2 3 4 5 6 7 8 9 0 DOC/DOC 9 9 8 7 6 5 4 3

ISBN 0 -07-037522-4

*The sponsoring editor for this book was Larry Hager, the editing
supervisor was Caroline Levine, and the production supervisor was
Suzanne W. Babeuf. This book was set in Century Schoolbook by
McGraw-Hill's Professional Book Group composition unit.*

Printed and bound by R. R. Donnelley & Sons Campany.

Contents

Preface

About six years ago, I stumbled upon a construction site in the Union Square section of lower New York City. What was unusual about this site was the Japanese lettering on the blue plywood pedestrian fence surrounding it. The lettering announced the name of the construction manager—Kumagai Gumi.

My interest piqued, I began to investigate, and discovered that Kumagai Gumi was one of a select group of billion-dollar contractors known in Japan as the Big Six. Digging a little further, I discovered that each of the other five members of this group—Kajima, Taisei, Shimizu, Obayashi, and Takenaka, had maintained branch offices in the United States for almost a quarter of a century.

Why did these builders come to this country and what were their plans for the future? Are we experiencing foreign intrusion into yet another basic American industry, and if so, will these contractors prove as successful in their endeavors as Japanese automobile manufacturers and consumer electronics makers have been in capturing significant portions of the American market?

It appears that the Big Six and somewhat smaller Japanese builders, such as Aoki, Mitsui, Daiwa, Toda, Fujita, and Sumitomo, have been setting up branch offices in the United States, ostensibly to service their long-time clients who are expanding their North American manufacturing and distribution facilities. Given the political pressure exerted by the U.S. Trade Commission on the Japanese government to open their domestic markets to more American firms, it is not surprising that these Asian builders have endeavored to maintain a relatively low profile in developing branches in the United States.

But what if trade barriers between these two governments are lowered, or continue to crumble, as they have been? Will Japanese contractors feel free to aggressively pursue construction work in America and ultimately garner a larger portion of the construction market? This is a question that is yet to be answered, but one thing is clear: We do live in an ever-shrinking world, economically speaking, and the mobility of industrial firms and service organizations is increasing rapidly. We need, more than ever before, to think globally, to promote technology transfer, and to encourage the free exchange of ideas.

Events in eastern Europe during the past few years have resulted in the creation of entirely new economic entities, and the maturing of the European Economic Community (EEC) could result in the creation of a trade-barrier-free marketplace of gigantic proportions. Companies from all over the world will be free to seek a portion of this market, but only those companies versed in the workings of that commercial arena can hope to gain a respectable share.

Let's turn to Asia, on the other side of the globe. If the industrial prowess of Japan and South Korea becomes linked with the untapped resources of the People's Republic of China and India's huge pool of potential workers, an economic force comprising 47 percent of the world's population will have been created.

Even if the overwhelming majority of general contractors, specialty trade contractors, architects, and engineers in the United States never come in contact with any foreign builders, in particular Japanese contractors, the lessons learned by studying them can only add to one's storehouse of knowledge.

A recent article in *The New York Times* pointed out the growing trend of cross-breeding between Japanese and American managers as Japanese firms try to assimilate more closely in the American market and U.S. firms seek closer ties to their customers in Japan. If and when this process becomes more commonplace in the design and construction community, we will need to prepare ourselves to face the challenges that these opportunities present. Getting to know Japan's Big Six may be a start in that direction.

Sidney M. Levy

This Shrinking World

THE GLOBAL COMMUNITY

We think nothing of squeezing our morning orange juice from fruit grown in Israel or lacing up our Taiwanese-made sneakers before going to the store to replenish our supply of Columbian coffee. The world has become incredibly small in the past 50 years or so, and our daily lives have become inextricably bound up in the ebb and flow of the rest of the world lapping against our shores. And we in the United States continue to beam our cultural and economic signals around the world; just inquire about Louie Armstrong in Vienna, or ask for a Coca-Cola in Sri Lanka, or watch the Caterpillar tractors at work in Rwanda. *Globalization* is the word to describe what's happening in the world today—one huge marketplace where survival of the fittest, economically speaking, prevails.

For those of us associated with the construction industry in the role of client, architect, engineer, contractor, or equipment and material manufacturer or supplier, globalization opens the door to opportunity—either lost or found. It might be the $400 billion U.S. construction market, the projected expenditure of $3.3 trillion for public works project in Japan in the next decade, the $500-billion-plus market in 11 other Asian countries between now and 1999, the construction generated by the $4 trillion purchasing power of the European Economic Community, or the almost unlimited demand for projects of all kinds once the Eastern European situation settles down. There are six contractors headquartered in Japan which undoubtedly will share in these markets.

THE BIG SIX

The Big Six—Kajima, Kumagai Gumi, Obayashi, Shimizu, Taisei, and Takenaka—are Japan's largest constructors, and their aggregate net sales volume and orders backlog in 1991 exceeded $190 billion. Collectively, they employ more than 85,000 engineers, architects, and construction specialists, and they engage in business activities that range far and wide. Although construction is the main thrust of these builders from the Orient, it is by no means their only business. One firm owns the largest bookstore in Japan and operates a subsidiary that produces documentary movies. Another builder has devoted a major portion of its corporate energies to researching construction in outer space, while another Big Six contractor employs a staff of biologists to conduct basic research on human and plant-cell structures.

Takenaka traces its origins back to 1610, making it the oldest operating construction company in the world. Two other contractors are more than 150 years old. Not content to rest on their laurels, each of these Big Six builders constantly strives to improve its operations and seek new records for itself and the industry. One company established a new record for underwater tunnel construction; another built the longest suspension bridge in the world; and a third is set on winning the title "Builder of the World's Tallest Building," surpassing the current record holder by 1800 feet.

These six Japanese construction companies share another common trait—a strong commitment to research and development. Their individual R&D facilities contain sophisticated laboratory and testing equipment and are staffed by hundreds of engineers dedicated to pursuing new construction techniques and products while they continue to test and improve the existing ones. Innovative and complex engineering designs, along with space-age technology, flow from these research institutes as each builder pursues a competitive edge both in its domestic market and the international arena.

The Kajima Corporation, founded in 1840, built Japan's first skyscraper, Kasumigaseki, in 1963, and recently constructed what is reputed to be the world's most acoustically perfect concert hall, Suntory Hall, nestled in Tokyo's Ark Hills complex. The Kajima Group includes such seemingly disparate subsidiaries as Kajimavision Products Co., Ltd. (a producer of documentary films), the Yaesu Book Store (Japan's largest), and the Kajima Foundation for the Arts.

The Obayashi Corporation, established in 1890, recorded a $9.76 billion sales volume in 1990. The current chairman of the board, Mr. Yoshiro Obayashi, is proud of the fact that 6000 of the company's employees have advanced degrees in the physical sciences and engineering disciplines. Obayashi is equally proud of its sophisticated shield-tunneling machines and the wide array of construction robots included in its $100-million-plus equipment inventory. The Corporation recently completed a bridge connecting the Akashi Straits in Japan, establishing a new world record for this 5838-foot-long suspension bridge, exceeding the Humber Bridge in the United Kingdom, the previous record holder, by more than 1200 feet.

Shimizu Construction Company, Ltd., has been involved in residential construction in a big way in recent years. It built 4390 housing units in the Kawson Hawthorden project in Malaysia and 2300 units in Iraq, with a total floor area of 3.76 million feet. More recently, Shimizu completed Anatepe New Town in Turkey, a development of 26,000 housing units designed to accommodate 100,000 residents. In 1987 Shimizu formed a space projects division to engineer and construct space-based structures with related earthbound support systems.

One of Takenaka Corporation's outstanding achievements may be just the fact that the company, founded in 1610 by Takenaka Toh-bei Masataka, is now being run by his direct descendant Toichi Takenaka some 381 years later. The company's unique designs appear throughout Asia and include the National Theater in Japan and the Nagshima Tropical Gardens, a collection of space-frame glassed atriums encompassing 300,000 square feet. Takenaka, acting as a general contractor in the tough Manhattan construction market, recently designed and built the sleek Nippon Club building on West 57th Street in New York City. Its most daring project to date may be Sky City 1000, planned for completion in Japan in the next century. This structure will be the world's tallest building, reaching 3280 feet into the sky and surpassing the current record holder, the Sears Building in Chicago, by almost 1800 feet.

Kumagai Gumi is a relative newcomer to the construction scene, having been founded in 1938. A pioneer in fast-breeder nuclear-reactor construction, it completed "Monju," the first of its kind in Japan. Kumagai Gumi may be best known in the eastern United States for its affiliation with New York developer William Zeckendorf, Jr., in such projects as Worldwide Plaza in Manhattan.

Taisei ended 1991 with a sales volume of $14 billion, and with all of its affiliates and subsidiaries boasts a total employment of 24,000. Taisei was Japan's first constructor of bridges and tunnels for the then revolutionary *shinkanses*—bullet trains. The company also joined the ranks of world record holders when it constructed the longest sub-sea tunnel in existence, connecting mainland Honshu with the island of Hokkaido. This Seikan Tunnel is 33 miles long, with the undersea portion 14.5 miles in length.

How did these world class builders and designers rise out of the devastation of postwar Japan to become major international competitors in today's construction industry? Is this the case of "Japan, Inc.," intent on monopolizing yet another important global industry, or is it merely a case of these builders being in the right place at the right time? To get to know and understand these constructors a little better, a short discussion about Japan, its geography, history, and culture, will help pave the way.

JAPAN—THE COUNTRY

Japan is an archipelago consisting of 3922 islands, the four main ones being Honshu, Hokkaido, Kyushu, and Shikoku. These islands extend more than 1744 miles from northeast to southwest, and comprise a total land area of 143,574 square miles, slightly less than the state of Montana (145,392 square miles). Much of Japan is not easily habitable, what with its mountainous terrain and deep valleys, not to mention its 60 more or less active volcanoes. With a population of approximately 123 million people spread over such a restricted land area, it is no wonder that the population density of the country is 857 people per square mile, in sharp contrast to the 68 people per square mile in the relatively wide-open spaces of the United States. Fourteen percent of the country's total population, 17,833,000 people, live in just five cities—Tokyo, Yokohama, Osaka, Nagoya, and Sapporo. The fact that the Japanese live in such close quarters has often been advanced as one of the reasons for their consensual approach to life.

JAPAN—ITS HISTORY

Just as America's strong individualism is rooted in its early settlers' desire to be set free from tyranny and oppression, so could Japan's national character have been forged in the furnace of past events. Japan is an ancient country, one in which myths and facts exist side by side. The country can trace its history back to 600 B.C. when it is said that the first emperor Jimmu, descendant of an earlier sun-goddess, established the country's capital in the ancient city of Yamato. Recorded history in Japan did not really begin until contact had been made with China's much more advanced society sometime in the fifth century. Japanese culture draws heavily upon Chinese heritage, not only in its written language and its sharing of religion and administration of state affairs, but even in how the country's name was derived.

In the first century A.D., the kingdom of Yamato was also known as Nihon (origin of the sun), an apt name for an island empire poised on such a far-eastern location. Its near neighbors, China and Korea, were told by the inhabitants of Yamato that the name Nihon or Nippon was also acceptable, but scholars from those other Asian countries pronounced the name as *Jih-pen* which later evolved into Japan. Even today, all three names are interchangeable and used by corporations—Nihon Johnson Control, Nippon Steel, All Nippon Airlines (ANA), and Japan Air Lines.

In the sixth century, Chinese and Korean monks brought Buddhism to Japan, supplanting its indigenous religion Shintoism, "The Way of the Gods," a belief that stressed and revered the beauty and bounty of nature above all else.

Japan's civilization had been very undeveloped before this Chinese influence arrived. The country had no written literature to speak of, no documentation of historical events, and no legal structure. Buddhism changed the way the Japanese viewed life—and death. Shintoism had stressed man's dependence upon nature, and when an individual died it was thought that all of his worldly wealth should accompany him to the new subterranean world of the after-life. But with the introduction of Buddhism a very important new religious concept was introduced into Japan: the need to incorporate art and architecture as necessary to feed man's soul.

Before the introduction of Buddhism, the only structures of note in Japan were huge earthen mounds that served as tombs for the wealthy, in much the same manner that the pyramids of Egypt were built to serve as final resting places for the great pharaohs. Buddhism, with its emphasis on the spiritual nature of man, saw these earthen tombs give way to the beautiful winged-roof temples and soaring pagodas that have come to epitomize Japanese architecture.

The Japanese government embraced the building of Buddhist temples during that period, and architects, artisans, and craftsmen were actively designing and building the types of intricately carved wooden structures that can be seen all over Japan today. Possibly this was the first alliance between government and industry that carried forth to this day, creating the "Japan Incorporated" image pervading the world of trade.

Japan had been relatively isolated since the time the sun-goddess was thought to have descended to earth; even to today, no conquering army has ever invaded its shores. The last such threat came in the thirteenth century when the Mongol fleets of Kublai Khan were turned back from Japan's shores by a disastrous typhoon, referred to in Japanese history as a "divine wind"—a Kamikaze, a name familiar to World War II buffs. During this period of time, and extending into the sixteenth century, Japan became a country ruled by a succession of warring dictators.

With the introduction of the matchlock rifle to Japan in 1543, the method of waging war in that country changed dramatically. Feuding warlords could no longer depend upon nature's forests and mountains to provide protection against antagonists, and thus they began to build elaborate castles and other sturdy fortifications. This triggered the need to develop the engineering and construction skills required to build these complex structures.

In the sixteenth century Japan briefly flirted with cultivating international relationships, but then suddenly cut itself off from all economic, cultural, and diplomatic contacts with the rest of the world. The country remained in seclusion until the arrival of Commodore Matthew Perry in 1853, when his four "black ships" sailed into Tokyo Bay requesting, or possibly more accurately, demanding, that the country open its ports to trade. Perry brought with him some gifts, including a working telegraph and a fully functioning miniature steam locomotive that fascinated the dignitaries he met. It became readily apparent to the Japanese that these Americans were "people to learn from."

THE MEIJI RESTORATION

The Emperor Meiji, whose reign encompassed the period from 1868 to 1912, was the ruler responsible for opening Japan to the rest of the world. His "Meiji Restoration," as that period was called, saw artisans, architects, and engineers from all over the world being invited to Japan and being welcomed to share their accomplishments with the Japanese people. World commerce and industry had their origins under Emperor Meiji's rule, and the era of modern-day Japan had begun. During the first half of the Meiji Era, government investment in river and road work shifted to the construction of a national railway system which eventually would consume between 40 and 50 percent of all public works expenditures for a period of 40 years before it ended in 1920.

As it developed diplomatic relationships with the West during those years, Japan began to fear that it would fall under the thumb of colonialism, as did China, Indo-China, and several other East Asian countries. But by the use of adroit diplomacy, accompanied by a rapid build-up of its military establishment, Japan began to create a defensive shell around itself, while at the same time adopting the best from its foreign suitors. From the United States and France, Japan patterned its educational system; from Great Britain it began to develop what would soon become a formidable navy; and from Germany, several political and medical institutions were copied.

JAPAN'S ENTRANCE INTO THE TWENTIETH CENTURY

As the end of the nineteenth century approached, Japan began to feel that its emerging industrial economy was becoming increasingly dependent upon the supply of critical raw materials from other nations. It seems rather ironic that, while Japan abhorred the spread of colonialism by the Western powers at that time, the military establishment within the country became more dominant, and after a major build-up of forces, looked around to flex its new-found muscles.

In 1882, Japan cast covetous eyes at China, and Korea, its arch enemy, and by 1895 had sent troops into both countries under the guise of protecting Japanese diplomats and resident business interests. The Japanese navy rather rapidly and quite decisively routed the Russians in the 1905 Russo-Japanese War, and the entire world suddenly took notice of this new Asian Power who was fast shedding its Buddhist image and emerging as a nation whose behavior began to be patterned after the Bushido credo, "The Way of the Warrior."

The worldwide depression of 1929 strengthened the argument within Japan's military establishment that the country's fragile economic condition must be bolstered by a strong military presence in East Asia. In 1931, at the insistence of the military, railroad construction assumed a national priority once again, and by 1940 accounted for 30 percent of all government infrastructure expenditures.

Right-wing elements in the country gave support to the creation of the Greater East Asia Co-Prosperity Sphere, a thinly veiled movement to invade and conquer neighboring nations, an adventure that ultimately led to Japan's entrance into World War II and the almost complete destruction of the country by 1945.

POSTWAR JAPAN

General Douglas MacArthur had been designated *Supreme Commander for the Allied Powers* (SCAP) after the surrender of Japan, and his mission was to mold the "new" Japan into a Western-style democracy. A new constitution called the Peace Constitution was adopted, patterned after the U.S. Constitution; a bicameral legislative body, the Diet, was established, consisting of an upper house called the House of Councillors and a lower house, the House of Representatives.

Article 9 of the new constitution pledged the abandonment of war as an instrument of national policy, a development that in later years would free the government from diverting massive sums of money away from the country's economic growth to defense uses. Unions, which had been outlawed during the war, were now legalized and encouraged to prosper, and many other social changes were effected that would ultimately chart the future course of postwar Japan.

The end of the war had witnessed the abolition of the *kangokubeya* system of debt bondage of immigrant or forced labor construction work gangs that had been assembled whenever and wherever workers were in short supply. At one point in pre-war Japan as many as 20,000 workers had allegedly been conscripted into a labor bondage system in the construction industry and made to work long hours under the absolute control of the gang boss.

The *zaibatsu,* giant holding companies composed of corporations from 20 to 30 basic industries such as steel, shipping, construction, and insurance, had been clustered around a powerful bank and had been active in Japan prior to the war. MacArthur declared these zaibatsu illegal, and they were broken up in much the same manner as the robber barons' cartels were disbanded in the United States in the early twentieth century.

In 1949 Joseph Dodge, a Detroit banker, was dispatched to Japan to perform major surgery on its economy, and out of his dynamism and wisdom the Dodge Plan was created. Government aid was cut off from thousands of small and medium-size businesses, resulting in scores upon scores of bankruptcies. The Dodge Plan employed seemingly draconian measures at the time, resulting in an economic purge that eventually turned Japan into a free-market economy.

In 1948, the Ministry of Construction was established, and one year later the Construction Contractors Law was enacted to help the country's building industry get back on its feet. Construction projects at that time were focused on food production facilities, flood control projects to offset the effects of severe deforestation created by wartime lumber demands, and, of course, work for the U.S. Armed Forces.

Japan was given massive doses of foreign aid during those all-important postwar years as she struggled to survive. The U.S. military bases that were established on Japanese soil during the Cold War also kept the money flowing.

The outbreak of hostilities in Korea and America's ultimate involvement there brought an unexpected bonanza to the Japanese economy as factories sprang up in support of the war effort. Japan became a marshalling yard and staging area for U.S. troops and supplies enroute to South Korea. In 1952 alone, the United States spent some $750 million to support its military bases on Japanese soil. Between the years 1951 and 1955, the United States and other United Nations peacekeeping forces pumped $3 billion into the Japanese economy.

The United States at that time was deeply concerned about the survival and revival of the Japanese economy in order to ensure a stable country that would remain staunchly pro-Western and anticommunist in a critical area of the world. President Dwight D. Eisenhower, in a June 1954 speech, stated, "Japan cannot live and Japan cannot remain in the free world unless something is done to allow her to make a living." Secretary of State John Foster Dulles, in a meeting with Japanese Prime Minister Shigeru Yoshida later that year, also reiterated the need to get Japan back on its feet. However, Secretary Dulles stated that trade with Southeast Asian countries was probably a better prospect for Japan than trade with the United States. To prove his point he held up a brightly patterned flannel shirt made in Japan of a cheap material. "This shirt," he said, "is an exact copy of one made in America of substantially better quality cloth." He chided the Japanese, and told them that their focus on copying but producing a copy of lesser quality would be a major stumbling block in expanding their trade. Oh, if Mr. Dulles were alive today!

In the late 1950s, the rapidly emerging Japanese economic miracle was gaining momentum. Japan's gross national product in 1957 was a mere one-sixteenth that of the United States, but was growing by leaps and bounds. According to government statistics in Japan, in April 1959, industrial plant construction had increased 40 percent over the previous month, and an astounding 82 percent over the previous 12-month period. By the end of calendar year 1959 industrial production in the country had risen 24.2 percent, and by the end of fiscal year 1959 (March 1960), Japan's *gross national product* (GNP) had increased 20.6 percent from the previous period. At about that time Prime Minister Ikeda Hayato unfolded his government's income doubling plan with a stated goal of increasing the country's GNP from $36 billion to $72 billion in 10 years, while increasing per capita income from $300 to $579.

Japan's GNP increased 450 percent, from 16.2 trillion yen in 1960 to 72.4 trillion yen in 1970, and it continued to increase by extraordinary rates, reaching 274.8 trillion yen by 1979. The year 1960 saw industrial production take another spectacular leap ahead, closing out the period 26.3 percent above the previous year. By fiscal year 1960, Japan's GNP had reached $40.736 billion and was surpassed only by the United States, Great Britain, West Germany, and France, in that order.

As if the activity on the economic front was not enough to keep a Japanese contractor busy, the building boom created by the 1964 Olympics to be held in Tokyo and Sapporo was like hauling coal to Newcastle. New sports facilities had to be constructed for both the summer and winter games, older stadiums had to be renovated and enlarged, and an Olympic Village started from scratch. The Japanese government conceded that it would have to spend about one-quarter billion dollars just to build new roads and repair existing ones for these events.

THE JAPANESE PEOPLE

As difficult and dangerous as it is to characterize a nation's people, perhaps the Japanese make this task somewhat easier. The Japanese word *wa* means harmony, and harmony is an important part of Japan's culture and its people. The need for harmony may harken back to feudal days, when villages were isolated from each other and the country as a whole was isolated from the rest of the world. Daily life demanded reliance upon each other, and harmony was a requisite within the village. The association with one's village and one's family has always been of great importance to the Japanese, and there is a special holiday in the country commemorating both ancestors and the ancestral home.

Toward the end of the second week of July, the holiday of *O-bon* (Homage for the Dead) is celebrated. Many businesses close completely, while others maintain substantially reduced staffs so that employees can return to their ancestral villages, and pay respects to their forebears. Woe be it to any visitor to the country at that time who wishes to make a reservation on the famed *shinkanses* (bullet trains), because they are crowded to the gunwales with O-bon travelers.

THE INFLUENCE OF THE VILLAGE

The villager never strayed too far from the village concept; it was merely transferred to one's school, university, or place of employment. The practice of lifetime employment is centered upon the village concept of commitment to one's community and seeking security from that community in return. The concept of lifetime employment echoes these tenets: "Come work with us. Devote your working energies toward the welfare of the corporation and the company, in return, will watch over you." The almost selfless concern for the collective well-being of the group may well be the foundation for the Japanese economic miracle.

Consider the secretary who remains at her desk long after quitting time so that she can proofread her boss's letters before placing them on his desk the next morning. Or consider the group of engineers who voluntarily decide to work late into a weekend night because they feel an obligation to complete and thoroughly recheck their design in order to meet a tight proposal-submission deadline. Or consider the project manager who takes only four or five days vacation each year even though he is entitled to three weeks. His reasoning? "My group would have to work harder to make up for my absence, and that's not fair; and besides, if I take too much time off, my supervisors will feel that I do not have enough interest in my company."

Because employees of Japanese companies plan to devote their entire career to one company, the company in return invests a great amount of time and money to train and educate its staff. In-house training sessions are conducted periodically, and it is not at all uncommon for a construction company to send some of its key people back to school for advanced degrees.

THE CONSTRUCTION INDUSTRY IN JAPAN

The Ministry of Construction

Similar to cabinet posts in the United States, the various ministries of Japan include Finance, Foreign Affairs, Commerce, Education,

International Trade, and Construction. The *Ministry of Construction* (MOC) is the government agency charged with the overall control of the construction of public works projects, reconstruction and maintenance projects in the public sector, and it supervises all infrastructure and government building construction. The MOC has such diverse functions as overseeing the award of billion-dollar domestic building projects and providing arbitration services to individual citizens who may have a dispute with their local builder. The Ministry employs more than 25,000 people and has six major divisions: Housing, Roads, Rivers, City Bureau, Economic Affairs, and the Secretariat. It maintains literally hundreds of offices and facilities around the country.

Ever since the Korean War, when the construction industry contributed so heavily to Japan's GNP, the MOC has remained a very influential agency within the government, and while it may not be as powerful as the Ministry of International Trade and Industry (MIT), it ranks in the top echelon of government ministries, receiving a larger than proportionate share of the country's annual budget. Between 1981 and 1989, construction investment as a percent of GNP in Japan ranged from a high of 19.34 percent in February 1981 to a low of 15.4 percent in 1985, leveling out at 18 percent in fiscal year 1989. As a means of comparison, in 1990 the value of all construction activity in the United States accounted for 9.6 percent of the country's GNP.

The ratio of private to public work is 2:1 in Japan, and the ratio of building construction to civil engineering construction also is 2:1. One-half of all private construction work is residential. The position of Minister of Construction is a much sought-after post, not only for its obvious "pork barrelling" potential, but also for the political contributions that the office can attract and pass on to the ruling Liberal Democratic Party campaign coffers.

The acts as a catalyst for *research and development* (R&D) in Japan, which it regards as primary to the health of the construction industry. Not that much government-sponsored R&D is conducted, as compared to that in private industry, but the policies of the MOC do encourage private sources to develop new products and technologies. The MOC funds and operates two research institutes, the Building Research Institute and the Public Works Research Institute, both located in Tsukuba Science City. Together, these two facilities have annual budgets approximating $73 million.

Building Codes in Japan and the Building Center of Japan (BCJ)

Unlike the United States, with its myriad local and state building codes, Japan's Building Law effectively establishes guidelines for construction throughout the country, including life-safety requirements, building-height restrictions, and set-back requirements. Although engineering standards and methods, as well as approved building materials, are specified in the law and its accompanying ordinances and MOC modifications, new products and construction techniques can be approved on a case-specific basis.

The Building Center of Japan (BCJ).   A privately funded organization whose mission it is to review and evaluate new construction technologies, BCJ is unique in its functions. It acts as a focal point where government and private research activities meet, are collated, and are disseminated to the industry. The Building Center of Japan conducts educational seminars, publishes various types of research papers, and performs evaluations on research and development projects submitted to it by owners and contractors, all of which provide the Center with the more than $10 million it requires annually for its operating budget.

The process by which new construction products and technologies are approved in Japan affords some insight into the ways in which private R&D efforts permit a builder to create a special product and sharpen its competitive edge. When a contractor develops a new product or construction method not specified in the Building Law, in order to consider using this new product or method, the company must first make application to the BCJ, submitting all substantiating documentation to support its use. A committee at BCJ reviews the submission and then interviews the contractor to learn more about the product or procedure. If the committee deems the application worthwhile, a subcommittee is formed to conduct further studies. When it becomes necessary to have an independent laboratory conduct tests, BCJ engages an MOC-approved facility to perform the work.

After BCJ has completed its investigation, it issues a finding, along with its bill, and if the Center has given the builder's proposal its stamp of approval, the contractor then forwards his request to the Ministry of Construction for its final review and the authorization to use the new product or process. The Building Law does provide the MOC with the authority to accept a new material or method of construction, or rule on a product, being equal to one stipulated in the law. However, the liability for performance is borne by the designer and the contractor. For that reason alone, it is no wonder that contractors proposing these innovative products perform exhaustive tests prior to implementation. Premature or unexpected failure not only can create a major financial liability, but would seriously damage a contractor's reputation and cast aspersions on the quality and thoroughness of its entire research and development organization.

Contractors and Subcontractors

At present there are about 525,000 contractors licensed to do business in Japan under the provisions of the Construction Contracting Law, a law containing terms that regulate the construction industry in the country. About 150 of these contractors are general contractors as we know them in the United States, and the balance are subcontractors. The great majority of both general contractors and subcontractors are small concerns. Only 1.9 percent of all contractors are capitalized at more than $362,000 and only 17.7 percent are capitalized at more than $72,000. Yet one-third of all general contractors attain a yearly volume in excess of $70 million.

Subcontracting in Japan

Subcontracting is more prevalent in Japan than in the United States, and there are more tiers of subcontractors than American general contractors are accustomed to dealing with. For instance, a carpenter subcontractor may subcontract rough framing to a second-tier subcontractor who, in turn, might subcontract roof joists to a third-tier subcontractor who, in turn, may hire a fourth-tier subcontractor to distribute the joist.

It is common practice to pay a subcontractor monthly for all labor expended. However a general contractor may present a subcontractor with a 120- to 150-day note for materials and equipment furnished that month. If the subcontractor is in need of immediate cash, he merely takes the general contractor's note to the bank and discounts it.

Japanese general contractors tend to work with the same nucleus of subcontractors and vendors for years and years, providing not only work for these companies, but training and education as well. General contractors from time to time will conduct training sessions for various subcontractors to introduce them to new methods of assembling components, or new tools or procedures in the marketplace, or even instruct them in basic management skills. As a result, their subcontractors become more knowledgeable, and their increased efficiency passes through to the general contractor and ultimately benefits the client.

The Construction Contract in Japan

Relations between client, contractor, and designer are team-oriented, and adversarial confrontations are avoided like the plague. One has only to look at the format of a typical Japanese construction contract with its sparseness of restrictive language (Fig. 1.1) to note how mutual trust must play a major role in client-builder relationships. Even contracts in the public sector reflect the Japanese penchant for brief con-

The Owner..

and the Contractor...

have entered into this Contract for the performance of the work

entitled...

in conformity with the following clauses, the annexed General Conditions,

............sheets of the Design Drawings and............volume(s) of the Specifications.

1. Place of Work...

2. Term of Work

   Commencement: on the............day of............ in the year 19..........,

          or within............days from the date of the Contract

   Completion : on the............day of............ in the year 19..........,

          or within............days from the date of the Commencement

3. Time of Delivery : Within............days from the date of Completion.

4. Contract Price : ....Yen

5. Payment of Contract Price:

   Advance Payment : at the time of signing the Contract.................

   Partial Payment(s) : ....

   The closing date for demand of each partial payment:..................

   At the time of delivery:.................................

6. Other Matters:

この契約の証として本書2通を作り、当事者および保証人が記名押印して、当事者がそれぞれ1保有する。

本語と英語との間に解釈について相違がある には日本語の本文による。

In witness whereof, this Contract has been prepared in duplicate and the parties hereto and the guarantors have hereunto put their respective seals and names. Each of the parties hereto shall keep its respective copy of this Contract.

In case of any discrepancy of interpretation between the Japanese and English Texts, the Japanese Text shall prevail.

Date:

召和　　　年　　　月　　　日

注　者
Owner

保証人
Surety

負　者
Contractor

保証人
Surety

I have hereunto put my seal and name to assume the responsibility of the Supervisor.

理　者
Supervisor

Figure 1.1 A typical Japanese construction contract.

14

Form of Agreement

1. Name of the Work _____

2. Place of the Work _____

3. Time for Completion _____

4. Contract Sum _____

5. Payment of Contract Sum: Advance payment _____
   Partial payment _____
   Final payment _____

6. Name of the Arbitrator _____

7. Other matters _____

For the execution of the above-mentioned Work, the Owner and the Contractor have entered into the Contract in conformity with the annexed General Conditions and Supplementary General Conditions.

The Surety shall be responsible for fulfillment of obligations under this Contract in case of the Contractor's failure of performance of the Contract.

In witness of the Contract, the parties thereto shall prepare _____ scripts of the Contract, and each shall keep one with the signatures and the affixing seals.

The Owner	Address Name	The Seal
The Contractor	Address Name	The Seal
The Surety	Address Name	The Seal

Figure 1.2 Standard form of contract for government building and civil engineering projects.

tract language. The Standard Form of Agreement for Government Building and Civil Engineering Projects (Fig. 1.2) consists of only one page. However it is accompanied by the 46-paragraph General Conditions Contract patterned in many areas after the American Institute of Architects A201 document, General Conditions of the Contract for Construction. Both negotiated and competitively bid projects in the private sector often use simple contracts; a bill of quantities contract is sometimes used, a format reflecting Britain's previous colonial influence in Asia.

Bill of Quantities Contract

The bill of quantities contract is one in which a detailed count of each component of construction in included in the bid document. At times, this list of materials, the bill of quantities, can occupy hundreds of pages and will list the exact number of doors, steel studs, square feet of sheetrock, number of electrical outlets, lighting fixtures, and so forth to be incorporated into the building. As the project progresses, the client will hire a quantity surveyor to count the actual number of each item being set in place, and after the project has been completed an adjustment of contract sum may occur if more or fewer items than originally contracted for have been installed.

Contractors' Licensing Requirements

In Japan both general contractors and subcontractors must be licensed in order to work on anything but very small construction projects. Licenses are issued by the Ministry of Construction to those contractors who will be operating throughout the country, and local prefecture governments issues licenses to contractors working in only one prefecture. In order for a general contractor to obtain a license, it must show proof of financial stability, certify that it employs qualified managers and qualified full-time engineers, and present proof of having successfully and satisfactorily completed certifiable contracts.

PUBLIC WORKS PROJECTS AND THE CONTRACTOR RATING SYSTEM

In the public works sector of the Japanese construction industry, a system of government ratings or rankings has been established; this is a prequalification process whereby only those contractors with acceptable ratings and experience on comparable projects will be invited to bid on designated projects.

The government rating system involves a sophisticated process that takes into account the contractor's financial condition, funding ability, credit line, paid-in capital, management and organizational structure, past history of similar projects, statements of client satisfaction, and the history of the contractor in completing previous projects on time and with high quality-levels. Architectural and engineering design capabilities and research and development activities all play a part in the government's annual rating. One or two substandard projects may be just enough to lower a contractor's rating, thereby disqualifying the company from bidding on the larger, more complex projects; conversely, outstanding performance, strong financial status, and excellent management and engineering skills can raise the contractor's rating.

FACTORS IN RANKING OR RATING

The government annually reviews each contractor's rating based on the results obtained from a complex formula. Contractors are asked to provide the following information, which will determine the outcome of their yearly rating:

1. Annual average value of completed construction works in the field of interest to the firm
2. Net worth
3. Number of staff members engaged in the construction business
4. Business conditions
   a. Profitability (ordinary ratio of profit to volume of completed construction works, ordinary profit ratio of total liabilities and net worth, ratio of break-even point)
   b. Liquidity (current ratio, quick ratio, month of processing working capital)
   c. Productivity (logarithm of value of completed construction works per capita; logarithm of added value per capita; logarithm of total liabilities and net worth per capita)
   d. Stability (fixed ratio, ratio of fixed liabilities to net worth)
5. Number of technical staff members
6. Number of years in business
7. Construction performance
8. Experience in special construction
9. Safety performance in construction
10. State of labor welfare

Each of these factors is weighted and becomes part of a formula which produces the ultimate contractor rank.

The formula: $(1) \times \dfrac{(2) + (3)}{70} + \dfrac{(4)}{40} + \dfrac{(5) + (6)}{55} + (7) + (8) + (9) + (10)$

The range of values for each item is as follows:

(1) 178–14	(2) 120–60	(3) 60–30	(4) 184–0	(5) 200–26
(6) 50–10	(7) 675–300	(8) 200–0	(9) 0–15	(10) 5 – 15
				(a + b)

where a = the number of cases of unpaid wages by the firm and
b = the number of unpaid wages by a subcontractor where the firm (prime contractor) is responsible **Note:** Another case of the nurturing atmosphere between general contractor encouraged by the government.

Occasionally, the government will encourage the submission of joint-venture proposals in an attempt to give smaller contractors an opportunity to work on more complex projects with larger, more experienced general contractors. The successful completion of these joint-venture alliances permits the smaller contractor to improve its company's over-all performance and possibly raise its annual rating, thereby improv-ing its chances to work on larger projects. This "nurturing" concept appears to pervade the industry.

ADVANCE PAYMENTS AND BONDS

Clients in both the private and public sectors customarily provide the general contractor with an advance payment that may vary from 20 to 40 percent of the total contract sum. The purpose of the advance is to allow the contractor to purchase materials for the project up front and to distribute advance payments to subcontractors for the same pur-pose. This practice appears to have originated in the late 1940s when postwar contractors had no capital to speak of and needed funds to start a project. A glance through any Japanese contractor's annual re-port will reveal some rather large numbers included on the "liability" side of the balance sheet indicating receipt of advance payments. Some of the largest construction firms list total advances for the year rang-ing from $3 billion to $5 billion.

The writer met with a distinguished panel of Japanese construc-tion professionals touring the United States in late 1991, few of whom could speak English, so all questions and answers were passed through an interpreter. When asked where all of the advance pay-ments ended up, there was some polite laughter among the Japanese builders before the interpreter responded. "The money goes to our subcontractors, and of course some of it stays with the general con-tractor for mobilization costs." Perhaps quite a bit stays with the general contractor.

Bonding Requirements in Japan

The Japanese word for bond is *bondo* and while the concept and word may be similar to American terminology and practices, there are sig-nificant differences between the two countries' use of this instrument of surety. Bonds are furnished by Japanese contractors to ensure that they will meet three types of obligations:

1. Performance on public works projects within Japan

2. Performance on private works projects within Japan

3. Requirements of the overseas market

Public Works Bonds

Advance payment bonds. Prior to the receipt of an advance payment, the contractor receiving an award on a public works project must submit an advance payment bond issued by one of only three surety companies currently registered with the Ministry of Construction. These surety companies issue no bonds other than advance payment bonds. In case the contractor does not complete the project satisfactorily, or if the public works agency cancels the project before it is scheduled to start, these bonds ensure the return of the advance payment.

Bid bonds not a requirement.   In the public sector, the use of a bid bond actually is preempted by the government's selective tendering system, where nonperformance carries with it the threat of having one's annual ranking lowered to such a degree that participation on future projects is questionable.

Performance bonds.   Section 5 of the General Conditions for Government Building and Civil Engineering Construction (Fig. 1.3) contains provisions for three types of bonds that may be required by owners of public works projects:

Surety for pecuniary liability.   A guarantee to cover damages arising from the default of a contract

Surety for completion of the work.   An instrument where a contractor names another contractor as guarantor of the project completion, a rather unique situation in which another builder will agree to complete the project rather than providing an insurance policy via a bonding company to arrange for successful completion

Performance bond.   A performance bond that guarantees only 10 percent of the contract sum, not the full contract sum

Labor and material payment bonds.   These bonds are not mandatory for public works projects. The Ministry of Construction's watchdog function, enhanced by various laws and regulations, is to police the industry to ensure that payments are made to subcontractors. Late payments or nonpayments will also have a negative effect on the contractor's annual rating.

Private Sector Bonding

There are no laws requiring contractors to submit bonds on private work, and the requirement for a bond is a matter of negotiation between contractor and client. In actuality, the use of bonds in private-sector work is extremely rare.

Overseas Bonding Requirements

Each foreign country may have its own bonding requirements, and Japanese contractors working overseas must comply with them; they

*   *   *

5* (A) Surety for Pecuniary Liability

(1) The Contractor shall give the surety for pecuniary liability who shall guarantee the payment for the amount of damages arising from any default under the Contract on the part of the Contractor.

(2) The aforesaid surety shall be selected by the Contractor in accordance with the conditions established by the Owner.

5* (B) Surety for Completion of the Work

(1) The Contractor shall give another contractor as the surety for completion of the Work, who shall guarantee himself to carry out and complete the Work in succession to the Contractor, should the Contractor fail to complete the Work.

(2) The aforesaid surety shall be selected by the Contractor in accordance with the conditions established by the Owner.

5* (C) Performance Bond
The Contractor shall effect the performance bond of an Insurance company to be jointly and severally liable with the Contractor in a sum not less than ten percent of the Contract Sum for the due performance of the Contract.
The aforesaid insurance policy shall immediately after the execution of the Contract be deposited to the Owner.

6 Succession of Rights and Obligations

(1) The Contractor shall not assign to any third party or let him succeed to his rights or obligations arising from this Contract without the written consent of the Owner.

(2) The Contractor shall not assign or lend to any third party, or place for mortgage or any other security, the Work objective or the confirmed construction materials for partial payment in accordance with clause 33 (2) (including manufactured goods at shops, as provided hereinafter for the same) without the written consent of the Owner.

*As the case may require, strike out clause 5(A), (B) or (C).

Figure 1.3 Section 5 of General Conditions of Contract for building and civil engineering construction with bonding requirements.

may include bid bonds, payment and performance bonds, advance payment bonds, and maintenance bonds. In such cases, the contractors either obtain these bonds from insurers in the foreign countries or from Japanese insurance companies.

Bonding Sources

Unlike the United States where insurance underwriters are the main source of construction bonds, in Japan regional bonding companies, or sureties, as they are called, are established by a group of contractors in a given region. Each of the members contributes to the funding of the surety company, and individual bond premiums are paid by the contractor to the surety. Not only are bonds rarely used, but, as one 32-year construction veteran stated, "In all my years in the construction industry, I have never seen a bond called. If the contractor runs into trouble, the other builder members of that surety company will intercede and help him out."

THE DARKER SIDE OF THE INDUSTRY

The word *dango* is anathema to any Japanese contractor. Dango, in simple terms, means collusion. Both government and industry have been accused of practicing dango in awarding public works projects. A contractor who has made a substantial cash contribution to a politician's campaign, or has supported an elected official in subtle or not so subtle ways, could be expected to receive some consideration in kind; it might be an outright award of a competitively bid project because the other contractor's bids have been manipulated in some way or another, or a favored contractor might receive some inside information allowing him to gain knowledge that other bidders do not have.

Dango is alleged to take place when a consortium of contractors meets in some resort area to determine whose turn it is to win that next big contract; all builders participating in this collusive exercise receive either a cash payment or a profitable portion of the job when it has been awarded to the predesignated "low-bidder."

Some Japanese journalists several years ago estimated that as much as 60 percent of all contributions to the ruling Liberal Democratic Party came from the coffers of construction companies. Dango is said to operate like a giant siphon, picking up construction industry funds and transferring them back to the politicians who promise to keep the pipeline full.

AMAKUDARI

The Japanese word *amakudari* is frequently heard in the construction industry. Translated as "descent from heaven" it refers to post-retirement employment of government bureaucrats by large contractors. The retirement age in Japan is 55, affording ample time for a second career, particularly where such employment can speed the flow of information back and forth between industry and government agencies. The *National Personnel Authority* (NPA) requires a two-year waiting period before a former government administrator can obtain a position in private industry, but waivers of this rule are often obtained from NPA. The construction industry seems to provide especially good opportunities for those officials descending from heaven. In 1991, as in 1990, the construction field led all other types of industries by placing 50 ex-government officials in managerial posts with builders in the private sector.

It is refreshing to know that dango and amakudari are practiced solely by the Japanese construction industry, and that these concepts are totally foreign to U.S. contractors.

JAPANESE EXPERIENCE IN OVERSEAS CONSTRUCTION WORK

Japanese contractors are well versed in operating outside of their country. As early as 1897 Japanese builders could be found working in Korea and Formosa as those countries began to expand their railway systems. Japan's military-backed colonialism during the late-nineteenth and early-twentieth centuries saw more railroad construction being completed on the Asian continent, culminating with the establishment of the South Manchurian Railway Company in the puppet state of Manchuria.

In the early 1930s Japanese contractors were busily building hydroelectric power plants and mining development facilities in Manchuria and North Korea. In 1937 a consortium composed of Shimizu, Obayashi, Takenaka, and Hazama formed an enterprise named Kyoei-Kai, and ventured to Mexico to build a 37-mile stretch of highway between Veracruz and Jalapa, a job that lasted seven months. By the time war broke out in Asia in 1940, Japan's builders were undertaking projects of a primarily military nature from northern to southern China as well as in other close-by Southeast Asian countries.

Following the close of World War II, the U.S. occupation forces sought to rejuvenate the Japanese construction industry, encouraging Japanese contractors to join in the massive amounts of reconstruction work under way and to participate in the effort to build new American military bases in Asia. Japanese contractors were allowed to bid on military installation work on Okinawa in 1950, and construction activity in the region accelerated with the outbreak of the Korean War, creating work for more than 25 Japanese firms on that island.

It was on Okinawa that Japanese builders were introduced to the joint-venture concept when four U.S. contractors, Morrison Knudsen, Bechtel, Pomeloy, and Kewitt joined with Kajima, Takenaka, and Obayashi on one major project. At that time these Japanese companies possessed significantly less prowess and expertise than their American counterparts, and this joint-venture opportunity allowed them to learn a great deal about mechanization and the site management techniques required to run large projects.

Reparation work by Japanese contractors in Asia began with the building of the Baruchan HydroElectric Power Plant No. 2 in Burma in 1954; various other infrastructure work in Indonesia, Vietnam, and Hong Kong kept them active for the next 12 years. Commercial projects overseas were not pursued with any great success until the later part of the 1960s, when Japanese contractors began to seek work in India, South America, and North Africa. By 1974, overseas construction contract awards by Japanese constructors reached $666 million. Ten years later this total had climbed to $37.4 billion as the petro-dollar-rich Arab nations went on a building spending binge. Shimizu was contracted to build a huge urban development in Baghdad, and Taisei was busy constructing hotels and hospitals, along with other buildings, in Iraq. The Fujita Corporation was awarded a major deep-water pier project, and Mitsubishi began to build schools in the latter country.

When the Middle East construction market began to slow down around 1985, Japanese contractors began to make a greater effort to obtain work in North and South America. They also ventured into Europe, at the same time increasing the sales volume in their prime marketing area, Asia.

During the years 1955 through 1983, Kumagai Gumi, Kajima, Shimizu, Taisei, and Obayashi remained at the forefront of all Japanese contractors as far as volume was concerned. Only Takenaka was temporarily displaced from the Big Six, having been forced into eighth position by Penta Ocean and Aoki Construction.

JAPANESE BUSINESS PHILOSOPHY

Personal relationships play a major role in business dealings in Japan, and many of these relationships have remained in place for hundreds of years as feelings of mutual trust became deep-rooted and firmly established.

The role of lawyers in the preparation and finalization of contracts is limited, and perhaps that is one of the reasons there are less than 15,000 full-practice attorneys in the entire country, as compared to 700,000 in the United States. As one major contractor stated rather simply, "If we bring a lawyer to the negotiating table, our client will get the impression that we are incapable of handling our own affairs."

The basic philosophy of Japanese business in general seems to favor holding a market share rather than making an immediate profit or a high return on investment in the short run. The philosophy of Japan's major contractors mirrors this concept, and while they are just as profit-oriented as builders the world over, they are equally concerned about market share, and rationalize that profits may be somewhat lower than normal while market share is being acquired. This long-term approach toward establishing a strong market position is probably one of the contributing factors behind the Japanese builder's commitment of large sums of money to construction research and development.

A glance at four Big Six annual reports and comparison of them with those of two U.S. contractors, the giant Fluor Corporation of Irvine, California, and the Turner Corporation, headquartered in New York, reveals some interesting disparities. Table 1.1 displays, among other things, the substantial amounts of advance payments received by Kumagai Gumi, Kajima, Shimizu, and Taisei. These Japanese contractors appear to retain more of their annual profits rather than distribute them to the shareholders. Their cash on hand and marketable securities position reflects the longer-term philosophy approach, where there is less pressure to instantly reward stockholders when profitable years occur.

The pursuit of market share is not a theoretical one either; witness the following standings published by McGraw-Hill's *Engineering News Record Magazine,* first in 1982 and then again in 1991, almost ten years later:

1982 top international contractors	Billion $	1991 top international contractors	Billion $
1. Brown and Root	10.74	1. Fluor Daniel	18.056
2. Fluor Corporation	10.60	2. Shimizu	17.85
3. The Parsons Group	10.24	3. Kajima	16.29
4. Bechtel	10.11	4. Taisei	15.91
5. Kellog Rust	6.70	5. Takenaka	15.26

while Big Six volume in 1982 was   and volume of U.S. firms in 1991 was

Taisei	4.521	M.W.Kellog	12.9
Kajima	4.494	Bechtel	12.003
Kumagai Gumi	2.89	The Parsons Group	11.7
		Brown and Root	7.39

In slightly less than ten years, the Japanese contractors have entered that rarified atmosphere of the top five international construction companies.

JAPANESE RESEARCH AND CONSTRUCTION

The ten largest construction firms in Japan annually spend about $300 million, in the aggregate, to fund their research institutes. The Ministry of Construction also operates the sophisticated Building Research

TABLE 1.1 Financial comparatives—Japanese and international U.S. contractors, for the year 1990

	Kumagai Gumi	Kajima	Shimizu	Taisei	Fluor Corp.	Turner Corp.
Net sales	$6.47 billion	$8.986 billion	$8.898 billion	$10.568 billion	$7.446 billion	$3.258 billion
New orders awarded	$7.836 billion	$12.208 billion	$12.836 billion	$13.471 billion	$7.632 billion	$3.42 billion
Backlog at years end	$12.66 billion	$15.916 billion	$12.051 billion	$13.257 billion	$9.447 billion	$4.740 billion
Net income	$94.9 million	$177.8 million	$163.6 million	$130.3 million	$146 million	($10.77 million)
Cash dividend per share	$.06	$.07	$.07	$.057	$.24	$1.00
Total assets	$10.6 billion	$12.986 billion	$11.9 billion	$14.182 billion	$2.475 billion	$782 million
Net worth	$2.126 billion	$1.854 billion	$1.67 billion	$1.954 billion	$863 million	$35.7 million
Per share	$3.14	$3.69	$2.13	$1.92	$5.29	$7.33
Number of shareholders	71,413	50,140	59,166	99,145	16,300	not available
Number of employees	8341	13,173	10,612	12,101	22,188	not available
Cash on hand	$1.283 billion	$1.64 billion	$1.46 billion	$1.89 billion	$229 million	$47 million
Marketable securities	$120 million	$742 million	$383 million	$810 million	$41.3 million	$-0-
Advances on projects	$4.01 billion	$5.196 billion	$5.03 billion	$3.363 billion	$271 million	$-0-

Institute and Public Works Research Institute in the research city of Tsukuba, about 45 miles north of Tokyo. Japanese universities conduct little research, in sharp contrast to institutes of higher learning in the United States, where 60 percent of all basic research is conducted, backed heavily by the federal government. The intense R&D activities of Japan's builders is unmatched in the United States, and according to a study released by the Japanese Management and Coordination Agency in February 1992, construction research in that country increased 24 percent between 1988 and 1989. Publications reviewed by the U.S. Embassy in Tokyo indicate that this trend will continue. Industrial research in Japan appears to be funded at higher levels than in the United States. In 1989 their industrial research funding amounted to $85.4 billion, versus $71.11 billion in the United States, according to National Science Foundation findings. The level of construction research in the United States has been calculated at 0.1 percent of gross sales, which would equate to between $400 and $434 million, although some experts in this country put the actual figure at more like half of that amount. Major contractors in Japan routinely commit 0.5 percent of gross sales to R&D, which would translate into $2 to $2.5 billion.

Japanese contractors freely admit that they have learned a great deal from the U.S. construction industry, and this blend of American knowledge and Japanese culture has produced a strain of formidable, internationally recognized constructors. The odds appear to be that one or more of the Big Six Japanese contractors will remain in the elite group of world-class contractors well into the twenty-first century. The following chapters may shed some light on why these expectations may come to fruition.

Chapter 2

Kajima Corporation

A Century and a Half of Integrity

In 1990, Shoichi Kajima, president of the construction company that still bears his family name, presided over ceremonies celebrating the corporation's 150th anniversary. Not only has Kajima persevered through the normal trials and tribulations foisted upon it over the last century and a half, including a war that totally devastated its country's economy, but it now ranks as one of the largest construction companies in the world.

CORPORATE HISTORY

The Early Years

Iwakichi Kajima, son of an ancestral wealthy farmer, sought to make his own way in the world in 1840 and he apprenticed himself to a master carpenter so as to learn the trade. By the age of 25, Iwakichi had attained the skills required to qualify as a master carpenter, and he set out to become an independent contractor. Young Iwakichi gained the patronage of Lord Matsudiara, who ruled over an area now known as Toyama Prefecture, in the northern portion of Honshu that borders on the Sea of Japan. Kajima gained a reputation as a first-class craftsman at about the time that Japan was beginning to open its doors to the West. Yokohama, a city possessed of a natural harbor on Tokyo Bay, was hurriedly expanding into a major port city where several British firms were already located and other Western nations were anxious to become established.

Iwakichi Kajima was befriended by an Englishman named William Keswick, who was the manager of Jardine, Matheson & Company, Ltd., a British trading house, and in 1860 Kajima was awarded a contract to construct *Ei-Ichiban Kan* (British No. 1 House). This was a Western style structure, which was being designed as a symbol of modern-day Japan. After Kajima had completed what was then the first Western-style structure in the entire country, the U.S. firm of Walsh Hall and Company was so impressed by the quality and speed of Kajima's construction that it hired the company to build American House Ichiban.

Walsh, in turn, recommended Kajima to other businessmen locating in the Yokohama area, and this fledgling construction company, now known as Kajima Kata, was off and running. When Kajima's first son Iwazo was born, it appeared that the lineage of the business would continue, but as the boy grew into manhood he forsook the construction business and apprenticed himself to a tortoise shell shop, anticipating a future in commerce.

A few years later, due in part to his father's failing health and in part to his inability to make a living in buying and selling turtle shells, Iwazo joined Kajima Kata, bringing with him the business acumen he had acquired from his dealings in the world of commerce. Iwazo looked upon the construction company as a business, not just a craft. When Kajima saw an opportunity to generate more profits by buying a local gravel company, he did so, and he began selling aggregate to Takashima, a company engaged in building Japan's first railway running from the Shimbashi district in Tokyo to nearby Yokohama. This relationship led to Kajima's entry into the railroad construction business at a time when Japan was rapidly expanding its rail system. In order to handle this new, rather specialized form of construction, a separate civil engineering company was spun off at Kajima Kata in 1880 and named Kajima Gumi; the term *gumi* roughly translates as "group or gang."

Between 1882 and 1904, Kajima successfully built a significant portion of the railways in Japan, and the company traveled to Korea to build the first rail line between the port city of Inchon and Seoul. During the Russo-Japanese War of 1905, Kajima was hired to repair damaged rail lines in Manchuria, and at the end of that war started to build a double-track line for the South Manchurian Railway, miscellaneous warehouse buildings, and housing for railroad employees. Railway construction remained an important adjunct of Kajima's construction business well into the twentieth century, until World War I interrupted many of these foreign projects. In those years preceding the First World War, Kajima became involved in the then new field of hydroelectric power construction, and the company proceeded to build the Shishidome Power Plant on the Katsura River, completing the project in October 1912.

The Next Generation

It was not uncommon in Japan for a successful family to adopt a son if it was incapable of producing its own, and Iwazo adopted Seiichi, a young man from the Iwate Prefecture about 300 miles up the coast from Tokyo, not too far away from the northernmost island of Hokkaido. Seiichi, a graduate of the Civil Engineering Department of Tokyo Imperial University, had come courting Iwazo's first daughter Itoko, and ended up not only marrying the girl but assuming the Kajima family name after adoption. Iwazo could not have made a better choice of a son. Seiichi was not only a fine engineer, but he had an intuitive business sense. When in 1912 his adoptive father died and he assumed the presidency of the company, he established a rule, "One business for one man," supposedly the United States equivalent of "Shoemaker know thy last." He began to consolidate many of the business operations created by his predecessor, sold off property, both business and personal, and put the money in the bank. When financial panic gripped Japan after the conclusion of World War I, Kajima Gumi's considerable capital in the form of cash on deposit at the Daiichi Bank, gave the firm a substantial edge over its competitors, many of whom could not survive those difficult times.

PRE-WAR ACTIVITY

The period 1916–1917 saw construction activity in Japan on the increase, and Kajima Gumi, in a joint venture with a local company, was commissioned to build the Tanna Tunnel, a project being touted at that time as the largest construction project of the century. Begun in 1918, this project became a nightmare. Although originally scheduled for completion by 1924, the project took 16 years to complete, partially due to geological faults and vast amounts of underground water. In those days there was no such thing as conducting geological surveys prior to commencing work; a contractor just plowed ahead and dealt with problems as they occurred. An enormous cave-in occurred when workers had burrowed to the 4687-foot mark. It took almost five years to remove the debris, stabilize the tunnel walls, and advance another 60 feet. As work progressed to the 7878-foot mark, a blasting operation released a flood of water from an underground spring. The water and the mud, ooze, and black sand that were released required another three-and-a-half years to clean up, and the reappearance of another major source of underground water after the Izu earthquake struck in 1930 resulted in cave-ins, the exposure of more faults in the rock strata, and a delay of another two years.

From 1912 to 1926, hydroelectric power came into its own in Japan, and Kajima's experience in this type of construction gained the company a contract to construct the first high concrete dam in the country, the Ujigawa Dam, a structure 101-feet tall, 298-feet long, and requiring 52,316 cubic yards of concrete. The successful completion of the Ujigawa Dam was followed by the Mabechi River hydroelectric project, the Hananuki dam, and a waterworks project for Yoshima Hydroelectric in 1918. Kajima continued to be awarded similar projects and built the Otake Steam Power Station in 1919 and a second power plant for Ujigawa Electric the following year.

Because of its involvement in so many of these kinds of projects, Kajima established an electric department in 1928, and by 1931 had completed 16 similar structures, ending with the Marunuma Dam, at that time the highest of its type in Japan. With their considerable expertise in power plant construction, Kajima ventured overseas and built the 100,000-kw Sun-Moon Lake power station in Taiwan in 1934.

A newly created building construction department, formed in 1919, was also active at this time, and scores of industrial, commercial, and retail buildings were being completed by Kajima in Japan during the 1920s.

History repeated itself when Seiichi adopted a son, Morinosuke, the fourth child of Toshio Nagatomi, a member of a family that traced its lineage back to the thirteenth century. Morinosuke, a graduate of the law school at Tokyo Imperial University, had embarked on a civil service career when he met and married Ume Kajima, Seiichi's daughter. The academic leaning of Morinosuke would have a profound effect on the path the company would take when he assumed the presidency of Kajima in the late 1930s. His training in the law caused him to gravitate to political office, and in 1953 he also entered politics and gained election to the House of Councillors, an office similar to that of a U.S. senator.

Seiichi continued to guide the company through good times and bad, and in 1946 he also entered the political arena and was appointed to the House of Peers as a representative of the construction industry. Six months later, at the age of 72, he suddenly became ill and passed away, and the presidency of the company was transferred to his son Morinosuke.

Upon assuming command of Kajima, Morinosuke stated that construction was a "people business," and he proceeded to hire engineers, teachers, and bookkeepers, and instituted many organizational changes. He felt strongly about the role his employees should play in the company, and considered them family, not just workers. He announced that even though sales volume dropped from time to time, there would be no reduction in personnel, thereby establishing a policy of lifetime employment. After he had twice won reelection to a national political office, in 1957, he was appointed to the office of Minister of State in charge of the Hokkaido Development Agency. Before assuming that position Morinosuke appointed his wife Ume to the presidency of the company, a post she held for ten years. Even though she was the daughter of a former president of Kajima, the idea of a woman being placed in such a high corporate office was a bold one at that time. Even today, women's role in Japan is considered to encompass only household financial matters and raising a family, not being active in the corporate world.

Ume Kajima stayed on as president until 1966, when she turned the office over to Takeo Atsumi. Besides being an able administrator, Ume is remembered as a humanitarian, and older corporate executives still talk about the time she donated a power plant to a grade school without electricity on Amami Island, a remote speck of land half-way between Japan and Okinawa. She even sent along several cases of movies for the students to enjoy once their new power plant was operational.

THE WAR YEARS

The years between 1941 and 1945 were tense ones for Kajima as the Japanese economy concentrated on supporting Japan's war effort. The larger construction companies in the country were pressed into service to build all kinds of industrial and military projects. Sumitomo Metal Industries ordered Kajima to immediately begin construction on its Shizuoka factory complex in November 1942. Its site covered 35.5 million square feet, 834 acres in all. In 1943 Hitachi Ltd., directed Kajima to build Shimizu City, the largest munitions factory in the Orient at that time. This immense factory was located on a 316-acre site. Kajima built a major facility at the Etajima Naval Academy, barracks and aircraft hangers for the Takeyama Marine Corps. The company was also commissioned to build massive aboveground and underground air-raid shelters for the Imperial Chamber. The Japanese government anticipated that the final stage of the war would see the Japanese islands being attacked, and in 1944 several of these large underground structures were hurriedly ordered built, in frenzied anticipation of an invasion by the Allied Forces. About 90 percent of the work had been completed by the time Japan surrendered.

POSTWAR ACTIVITIES

The key to Kajima's future would lie in its ability to shake off the past and enter the dynamic era of growth that began to appear over the horizon. During the war years Kajima had expanded operations into Taiwan, Korea, Manchuria, French Indochina, Thailand, Malaysia, Singapore, and Java; by the war's end in 1945, its substantial investment in these countries had been totally destroyed. Kajima estimated its losses at 36 million yen, not easily converted into today's dollar equivalent, but at that time a sum representing three times the company's paid-in capital.

In the years before the war, contractors in Japan did not enjoy high social status; they were primarily suppliers of pools of skilled and unskilled labor. Clients furnished all of the equipment and most of the materials required for a project, and at times even instructed the contractor in the technologies necessary to complete various phases of construction.

As part of the postwar reforms, General Douglas MacArthur, *Supreme Commander of the Allied Powers* (SCAP), suggested that the Japanese government enact the Employment Security Law in 1947, a bill that prohibited a company from operating a labor-supply business. This law had a telling effect on many construction companies, drastically changing the method by which they could operate. Another law, the Law Concerning the Prevention of Requesting the Government Payments by Unjust Means, was meant to curb black-market prices, which were becoming rampant in the construction business in Japan. Unfortunately, larger companies came under closer government scrutiny, while many smaller builders could slip through the net. These two laws had a dampening effect on the efforts of larger builders who were trying to reorganize and remobilize. But the star that occasionally shone over Kajima reappeared in 1949. Enter the Age of Construction Technology.

THE AGE OF CONSTRUCTION TECHNOLOGY

The Institute of Construction Technology had been established in Japan in June of 1945, just before the end of the war. A government agency at that time called the Control Association of the Japanese Construction Industry had been created to assist in fulfilling Japanese armed forces construction needs.

Seiichi Kajima had been appointed chairman of this association when it was founded, but it became moribund at the time of Japan's defeat two months later. In 1949 Mr. Toh-emon Takenaka of Takenaka Corporation, and Dr. Seion Utsumi, a director of the former institute, approached Morinosuke Kajima requesting that his company provide the necessary funds to reactivate this research facility. Mr. Kajima, envisioning a dream come true, took over the operations of the Institute in April 1949, revived it, and renamed it the Kajima Institute of Construction Technology.

One of the first research projects to be pursued at the Institute involved the field of geotechnics—soils, the composition of soil, and the ways to modify soils in order to improve their quality and stability. The research that came out of the Institute at that time enabled Kajima to gain a dominant position in the construction of steel mills in Japan. Rebuilding the country's steel industry required buildings with massive foundations to support the huge blast furnaces. Seaside industrial areas were springing up all over Japan, and locating steel mills in these areas would be highly beneficial. Ocean-going ore and coke carriers could unload their essential materials into silos directly adjacent to the steel mills, and scrap iron from abroad could be brought directly into processing areas within those buildings.

Kajima received a contract from Yawata Iron and Steel (later to be renamed Nippon Steel Corporation) to build structures to house Blast Furnaces Nos. 1, 2, and 3, at that time the world's largest, with the capability of producing 2000 tons a day per furnace. Kajima's success in building these structures on soft, reclaimed land was directly attributable to the projects carried out in their research institute. Subsequent contracts from Fuji Iron and Steel, Sumitomo Metal Industries, and Japan Steel and Tube quickly followed. The wisdom and foresight of Morinosuke Kajima paid off rather quickly.

POSTWAR WORK WITH THE U.S. GOVERNMENT

U.S. construction companies began to move into the Pacific Rim at the end of World War II at the behest of the American government when the construction of several U.S. armed forces bases was announced. One of the first such projects was on the island of Okinawa, where a major air base and support facilities were to be built. The General Headquarters of the Allied Forces in Japan wisely invited some Japanese contractors to participate in some of these projects.

Kajima immediately recognized the value of working with U.S. builders so that their engineers could learn the most up-to-date construction methods. Kajima joined with Obayashi and Takenaka, two other old-line firms, and joint-ventured with U.S. Morrison Knudsen Company to build military barracks and ancillary buildings on Okinawa. In 1950–1951, Kajima, having been instrumental in introducing the joint-venture concept into postwar Japan, teamed up with Kumagai Gumi to construct a new U.S. Army barracks at Camp Fuji in Japan. The Japanese government quickly saw the virtue in these joint ventures and in March 1952 published *Guidelines for Joint Venture Practices* to assist other contractors who wanted to participate in these kinds of ventures. Kajima began to be recognized in Japan as a construction innovator.

**Kajima's Battle With U.S. Government
Red Tape**

Relationships with the U.S. forces were not always rosy for Kajima and other Japanese contractors. When Kajima had completed about 70 percent of its contract on the Itazuke Air Field job in 1947, the U.S. officer-in-charge abruptly, and apparently without reason, kicked the company off the job. Morinosuke Kajima, although extremely uneasy about a direct confrontation with his client, appealed directly to Colonel Hawkins of the Eighth Army in Yokohama. Hawkins rescinded the order and put the company back to work. On another occasion an inspecting officer at the Atsugi Air Base project, where Kajima was working, arbitrarily rejected the aggregate that was being proposed for the concrete mix design, even though no tests on the material had been made to determine its acceptability.

Kajima first became aware of the concept of "claims" when it was counseled by Morrison Knudsen managers and was told that U.S. firms would be quick to file a claim against their government if they felt they had been wronged. For what may have been the first U.S. construction concept to be absorbed by Japanese contractors, and one that took great fortitude in facing one's conquerors, Kajima filed a claim against the U.S. government after 95 percent of its requested change orders were denied by the Atsugi Air Base project administrator.

Kajima pressed the claim, and was able to recoup 40 percent of the original amount, which was promptly transferred to its Institute of Construction Technology. Neither the amount of the claim nor the amount recovered was as important as the message this settlement conveyed. Kajima was elevated in the eyes of the industry, and this action by one of their own helped to place Japanese contractors on a more or less equal footing with the arm of the U.S. Occupational Forces administering construction contracts.

THE ENSUING BOOM

The first in a series of economic booms took place in Japan in 1950 during the initial stages of the Korean War. The U.S. government announced plans to spend at least $340 million that year on procurement projects in Japan related to the war. Hundreds of millions of dollars would be spent over the next five years as Japan became a staging and marshalling area for U.S. and United Nations Forces fighting in South Korea. Japanese contractors, Kajima included, would garner several large U.S. government construction contracts during that time.

The second construction boom in Japan came about in 1956 and lasted one year, as plant equipment investment in the country experienced explosive growth. Kajima's soils and substructure research played a significant role in creating the dominant position that the Japanese steel industry would achieve in the world's steel market.

The Japan Atomic Energy Research Institute and the Japanese Atomic Energy Commission were established in 1955, and in 1956 Kajima, in a joint venture with Shimizu, built the Tokai Nuclear Power Plant, the country's first, albeit rather small, a 50-kw research-type reactor.

The third construction boom arrived in 1959 and lasted until 1960 as industrial expansion continued to increase dramatically. This period of intense industrial activity was followed in 1963 by the construction work that began to focus on the upcoming Tokyo Olympic Games. The year 1967 was known as the Three C Boom in Japan as cars, cooler air conditioners, and color TVs were manufactured and exported in record numbers.

KAJIMA IN THE SIXTIES

In 1961 Kajima went public, offering shares of stock, and as Japan's economic growth accelerated, so did Kajima's. By the end of 1961, Kajima had become the largest contractor in Japan; in 1962 it was ranked second in the world; and in 1963 rose to the position of No. 1 among international contractors. Just one look at the company's after-tax profit during these years and later, reveals its phenomenal growth.

Year	After-tax profit (in million yen)
1960	1.1
1961	2.1
1062	2.8
1963	3.5
1964	3.9
1965	4.2
1966	4.4
1967	4.7

The frequent revaluation of the yen and the dollar makes conversion to dollar figures over the years difficult. For example, the dollar was worth 220 yen in 1981, 180 yen in 1986, before fluctuating between 140 and 127 yen to the dollar between 1987 and 1991. However, a 400 percent plus increase in after-tax profit in seven years in any stable currency is an impressive achievement.

This trend toward increasing net income continued through the late 1970s and into the 1980s, witness the contract awards and net income for the years 1979 to 1983. Of particular interest is the increase in total assets and net assets, even though contract awards decreased in 1982 and 1983:

	FY* 1979	FY 1980	FY 1981	FY 1982	FY 1983
	(Figures in million yen)				
Contract awards	744,648	904,105	1,011,381	1,003,805	906,279
Net income	13,503	14,340	16,048	19,107	17,076
Total assets	854,128	979,890	1,086,537	1,187,871	1,090,722
Net assets	149,269	156,963	166,808	179,644	189,802

*FY represents *fiscal year*.

In FY 1983 contract awards fell slightly below those of 1980, but net income increased 19 percent above 1980 levels. Total assets over this five-year period increase by 28 percent and net assets increased 27 percent.

KAJIMA'S SALES ACTIVITY IN 1991

At the end of FY 1991, on March 31, 1991, Kajima had received $16.24 billion in new contract awards during that fiscal period. Its revenue, or billings, for that period were $12.068 billion, on which the company derived $325,028,000 in net income. At fiscal year end, Kajima had a $22.192 billion backlog. Some of its major construction projects in Japan included Tokyo Metropolitan Building No. 2, a 501,728-square foot advanced pharmaceutical manufacturing plant, the 138-foot-high Utena Dam in Ehime Prefecture, foundation work for the 12,824-foot-long Akashi Straits Bridge project, major subway expansion in Tokyo, and a state-of-the-art intelligent combined office building–residential hotel complex in Tokyo.

Overseas, the company completed a major hospital complex in Egypt, the Meese Tower and a 55-story 841-foot-high intelligent office building in Frankfort, Germany, Europe's tallest building. Kajima built the Sherwood Hotel in Taipei, the Shanghai Center in China, a Sony VCR factory in Malaysia, and is participating in the 350-acre Stockley Park Heathrow development in the London suburbs, a project that will contain low-rise intelligent buildings on 100 acres, the balance of the site being devoted to a golf course, playing fields, and a park.

Figure 2.1   The Sabikawa Power Station underground construction work in progress.

Kajima has constructed nine underground power stations in recent years, excavating more than 1.3 million yards of material in the process. Figure 2.1 shows the Sabikawa Power Station under construction; it is a 900,000-kw plant, 167 feet high, 541 feet long, and 92 feet wide, carved out of the rock lying beneath the picturesque mountains in central Japan's Tochigi Prefecture. Figures 2.2 and 2.3 illustrate two of Kajima's recent building projects with unusual architectural features. Figure 2.4 is the award-winning design for the renovation of Tokyo's Ochanomizu railway station; Kajima won another design competition to build a domed sports facility in Izumo City (Fig. 2.5). The supports under the fabric dome are delicately shaped wood members.

Mr. Taro Kawano of Kajima's International Division says that Kajima much prefers to negotiate work rather than obtain contracts by the open-bid method. Fifty percent of its work is obtained via the negotiated contract, and 45 percent is awarded by clients who have placed Kajima on selected bidder's lists, and these awards are not necessarily made to the lowest bidder. Only 5 percent of its work comes from open, competitive budding in the private market, and most of their negotiated work is obtained in Japan.

In Japan, the joint-venture (JV) concept is very popular, according to Mr. Kawano, and although the bidding market is highly competitive, this JV approach is very much in line with Japanese society and its desire to create harmonious relationships and share the work.

Figure 2.2   The Hitachi Civic Center.

Figure 2.3   An art complex in Mito.

Figure 2.4 Ochanomizu Station in Tokyo, which has won top awards.

The government encourages joint ventures whenever it publishes notices to bid on public works projects.

KAJIMA'S WORLDWIDE OPERATIONS

Kajima's world headquarters building is located on Motoakasaka 1-chome in the Minato Ward of Tokyo. Its sleek, modern aluminum skin contrasts sharply with the traditional Japanese architecture behind the row of new skyscrapers that Kajima counts as its neighbors (Fig. 2.6).

Like the other members of the Big Six, Kajima maintains overseas district offices on all five continents. In Europe, Kajima district offices can be found in Great Britain, France, Spain, and Germany. The Middle East and African construction markets are serviced by offices in Egypt, Turkey, and Kenya. There is a South American branch in Chile and one down under in Sydney, Australia, to service clients in southeast Asia. The Asian market is covered by district offices in Beijing, China; New Delhi, India; Jakarta, Indonesia; Taipei, Taiwan; Hong Kong; Singapore; Kuala Lumpur; Malaysia; Bangkok, Thailand; and Manila, in the Philippines. In addition to these overseas construction offices, Kajima owns 26 affiliate companies in Japan with such diverse activities as road building, chemical grouting, leasing services, documentary film production, real estate, retail book sales, resort management, and book publishing.

In the United States, the company's principal subsidiary is Kajima International, Inc., known simply as KII.

(a)

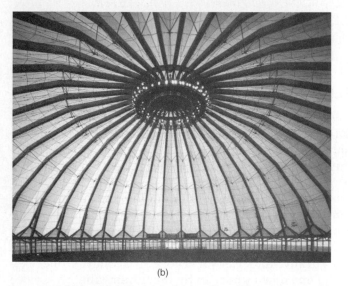

(b)

Figure 2.5   Mokumoku Dome in Izumo City. (*a*) aerial view, (*b*)
view of the fabric dome from inside, with its delicately shaped
wooden structural support members.

KAJIMA INTERNATIONAL INC. (KII)

Kajima's presence in the United States began in 1964 when the company designed the Japanese Village at San Diego's Sea World amuse-
ment park. Three years later the company undertook the first major
development project by a Japanese firm when it built the New Otani
Hotel and Garden and the Weller Court Shopping Center in the
Little Tokyo section of Los Angeles. By 1975 Kajima had expanded

Figure 2.6 Kajima's world headquarters, framed by traditional Japanese architecture.

operations to the East Coast and established an office in New York City. One of its first projects was to complete the interior design for the Bank of Tokyo project at 100 Broadway.

In 1979, the company entered the Georgia construction market and built a plant for TDK Magnetic Tape in Peachtree City. A Dallas, Texas, office was opened in 1983, and Kajima proceeded to build three office buildings in that state. Although Kajima did not open its Florida office until 1986, it had already built the 627,000-square foot Seawinds Condominium complex on Singer Island, just north of Palm Beach, three years earlier. This project was followed shortly thereafter by Martinique 2, another condo in North Palm Beach.

The newly established Process Mechanical Division afforded Kajima the opportunity in 1985 to build its first large turnkey industrial project in this country, an auto assembly plant for Mazda

Motors. This job was followed quickly by a similar endeavor for Diamond Star Motors and Subaru-Isuzu Automotive, Inc. When Kajima started construction on the first phase of the Los Angeles World Trade Center at Long Beach in 1988, it marked the first of four phases of what will be Kajima's largest commercial development project in this country.

By 1991 Kajima's U.S. subsidiary KII had attained an annual sales volume of $400 million, quite a respectable figure despite a year in which construction activity in the United States took a decided downturn. KII's sales volume reached an all-time high of $513 million in 1990 when it could count many major Japanese and American firms on its list of clients:

Goodyear Tire and Rubber Company	Hitachi
Mazda Motor Manufacturing Corporation	Diamond Start Motors
Pioneer Industries	Yamaha
American Airlines	Kidder Peabody
Fuji Bank	Trammel Crow

Design-Build and KII

KII is striving to be recognized as one of the nation's foremost design-build firms specializing in turnkey projects. In 1990 its sales volume was split: 54 percent design-build and 45 percent general construction work. That same year, McGraw-Hill's *Engineering News Record* magazine listed KII in the No. 24 spot among all U.S. design-build firms and No. 32 in ENR's listing of general building contractors.

This company is well-suited to the design-build concept, as a tour through the Englewood Cliffs, New Jersey, corporate headquarters building will reveal. KII headquarters houses a general building construction group and separate architecture and engineering design groups. Recognizing the inherent differences between interior work and general construction, KII also maintains an interior design section at Englewood Cliffs along with a companion interiors construction group.

One of the company's leading design firms, Hellmuth, Obata & Kassabaum, Inc., (HOK) of St. Louis, Missouri, participated in several projects with Kajima in the late 1980s, and during the course of their association, both firms got to know each other better, and according to King Graf, HOK's Vice Chairman, a loan was arranged between the two companies.

In 1990, Kajima advanced $22 million to HOK in the form of a loan which can be converted into a 35 percent share of the designer's stock. Questions immediately arose within the architecture/engineering/construction community as to the purpose of this "loan." Was this an attempt to purchase HOK? Would HOK become a captive designer to Kajima and further KII's capabilities and market share in the design-build field? Not much is being said by either KII or the Kajima Corporation about any of these possibilities, but the principals of HOK circulated the following letter to all of its employees:

Dear Fellow Employee:

Since HOK was founded in 1955, we have become recognized as one of the top design firms in the United States. As we build on our past success, we are positioning HOK for the future—to take advantage of the unprecedented political and economic change occurring throughout the world and to compete more effectively in today's global marketplace.

We are very pleased to inform you that HOK's shareholders are being asked to approve a strategic alliance with Kajima Corporation of Japan, one of the world's largest design and construction firms. If approved by the shareholders, the strategic alliance will become effective on July 1, 1990.

This represents an exciting opportunity for HOK and for all of our employees:

- First, it will immediately elevate HOK into a more effective global competitor—better able to take advantage of new opportunities in the Pacific Basin and to compete more effectively in key markets around the world, including Middle Eastern and rapidly evolving European markets.
- Second, it offers an expanded capability to pursue new, major international projects that require more of a total "turnkey" approach of financing, design and construction.
- Third, and most important, it enables HOK to attain new levels of growth without losing sight of our fundamental values—design quality, client service and personal dedication.

Under the proposed agreement, Kajima will provide HOK with a $22 million loan. These funds will be applied toward HOK's expansion—be it a new office on the European continent or the acquisition of an environmental engineering firm, just to cite two possibilities. In return for this investment, Kajima will share in the growth of HOK by taking a minority position at a later date.

We want to emphasize that *HOK will remain an independent firm* with the highest standards of quality, service and professionalism.

We know that you recognize the confidential nature of the proposed agreement and therefore ask that you limit your discussion of this matter to persons directly associated with HOK. Please direct any outside inquiries you might receive to Dana Collins in Corporate Communications at 314/421-2000. We welcome you to direct your own questions to us or any member of the Board of Directors.

It should give all of us great pride that Kajima recognizes HOK's growth potential and shares our enthusiasm about the firm's future. We are confident that the alliance will provide all of our employees with significant professional development opportunities into the next century.

Very truly yours,

| Gyo Obata | Jerry Sincoff | King Graf | Bob Stauder |

The HOK-Kajima relationship came to the fore in March 1992 when Kajima announced that it would break ground on a $500 million "smart" office building on the water in Tokyo. Although Nippon-Sogo architects were the original designers of this 21-story Telecom Center, the firm of Hellmuth, Obata, and Kassabaum was brought in as a team member in 1989. Kajima invited another American team member, Schal Associates of Chicago, Illinois, to join with joint-venture partner Taisei Corporation to build this 1.7-million-square-foot project.

KII's Business Philosophy

Marvin Suomi, an 11-year veteran of KII and now its senior vice-president and a company director, stated his corporation's goals. "We are an American construction company, and we deal in the marketplace like any other U.S. contractor. Our 545 employees represent a mix of both Japanese and American professionals and, of course, we deal with U.S. subcontractors and suppliers as we work around the country. Our ability to perform in-house architectural and engineering services permits us to bring more control into the construction process, since we are less dependent upon outside forces to produce the quality product we demand and our clients expect."

Suomi went on to state, "Kajima is a company with incredible integrity. If we had to rely upon 'hard bidding' against the crowd, only to have to find ways to recoup enough money to build the project, this is not the way our company wishes to make a living." As if to reinforce his statement about integrity, he pointed to KII's decision to complete a project on Florida's Singer Island after its French developer had pulled up stakes when the condominium market softened a few years ago. KII felt it had a moral obligation to complete the work, which it did, turning it over to the bank upon completion.

In 1990, 22 percent of KII's business originated within the manufacturing sector, and the company's Process Mechanical Division played a crucial role in obtaining those contracts. When KII was invited to build Mazda Motors auto assembly plant in Flat Rock, Michigan, in 1984, the newly formed Process Mechanical Division was assigned the responsibility for the coordination and installation of all the production equipment for the facility. Not only did this division coordinate the design of all electrical and mechanical rough-ins, concrete bases, and equipment foundations, but its engineers were also presented with the task of converting metric measurements to U.S. inch-foot equivalents for certain equipment being purchased overseas.

Marvin Suomi says, "What is so vitally important in a manufacturing facility is what goes on inside the facility, and not so much what happens to the shell. Most manufacturers are less concerned with the building envelope than they are with getting the equipment installed and up and running on schedule. With our Process Mechanical Division people, we stay with the owner from start to finish and effectively coordinate every aspect of the setting up of the production lines. At times we may even purchase some of the equipment and machinery, and of course we are there during the critical start-up and test period. This process gives us a tremendous edge over our competition, because it can become the ultimate in single-source contracting from the client's perspective."

Where does KII's future lie? One has to only look at some of its past accomplishments to predict its future; with the company's unlimited bonding capacity, it is free to go where others fear to tread. Dr. Shoichi Kajima, president of the Kajima Corporation, visited KII in 1989 on the occasion of its 25 years in the United States; he discussed Kajima's formidable lead in many aspects of construction research at its institute in Japan, but said little about its application in the American marketplace.

Mr. Koji Hayashi, executive Vice President of *Kajima Engineering and Construction, Inc.* (KEC), based in Los Angeles, California, can however attest to the fact that Kajima's research and development activities can play an important role when the company wants to expand its market share: "Back in 1983, a consortium of companies in the Unites States initiated a plan to construct a high-speed train line between Los Angeles and San Diego based upon the Japanese bullet-train system. Having played a major role in the construction of Japan's bullet-train system, Kajima saw the project as an opportunity to expand its heavy construction business to the U.S. market, and in 1984 I was dispatched to Los Angeles to investigate this opportunity, and determine how to set up our heavy construction operation."

Unfortunately, the Los Angeles–San Diego train venture never came about, but Mr. Hayashi saw other areas where KEC could offer something new to the marketplace. KEC's parent company and an affiliate, Kajima Road Co., Ltd., had just developed a specially curved-surface asphalt paving system, and they used this unique equipment to win a contract to build a high-speed automobile test track for Nissan in Arizona. Since that time KEC has built six golf courses in various western states, and by 1990 had been awarded contracts totaling $160 million. According to Mr. Hayashi, the company's revenues for 1991 were projected to double, which is quite an achievement from a company that ostensibly came to this country to bid on a project involving their high-speed train technology but stayed on to capture other heavy construction contracts.

With such dramatic results stemming from R&D efforts in Japan, does Kajima plan to expand on its considerable achievements in advanced construction technology to capture other segments of America's construction market? Could a significant transfer of technology take place between Japan and the United States? Dr. Kajima says, "It is my hope that one day there will be an American Research Group within the Kajima Institute that will deal specifically with U.S. construction needs." But in the meantime, a well-financed U.S. design-build firm with top-flight managers and a deep-seated desire for perfection appears to have a bright future.

KAJIMA CORPORATION TODAY— CELEBRATING ITS 150TH ANNIVERSARY

The commitment to R&D begun by Morinosuke Kajima is not only being kept alive by Dr. Shoichi Kajima, but it is being substantially enhanced in Japan and elsewhere. The two Kajima technical research institutes (KaTRI) located in the Nishi-chofu and Tobitakyu sections of Tokyo today employ 440 researchers, engineers, and support staff. The entire corporation has an R&D budget of $180 million, $72 million of which goes directly to KaTRI. The research dollars over the years have led to the development of a wide range of construction robots: concrete-floor-finishing robots, wall-tile integrity-testing robots, shotcreting and spray-painting robots, and rebar-placing robots. These research dollars have brought an exciting new product, carbon fiber reinforced concrete, from the laboratory to commercial production. And these research dollars have permitted the company to develop a whole list of new construction techniques and technologies, such as:

1. A high-pressure abrasive-water-jet cutting machine capable of cutting through thick steel plate and foot-thick reinforced concrete

2. Balanced cantilever long-span precast concrete bridge construction

3. Prestressed concrete cable-stayed bridges

4. Shield tunneling machines, including one of the world's largest, which is almost 46 feet in diameter

5. Advances in the production and placement of roller-compacted concrete

6. New building framing methods using steel beams and reinforced-concrete slabs that permit clear spans of up to 65 feet.

7. Three-dimensional carbon fiber and aramid fiber concrete-reinforcing systems

8. Concrete crack image-scanning systems

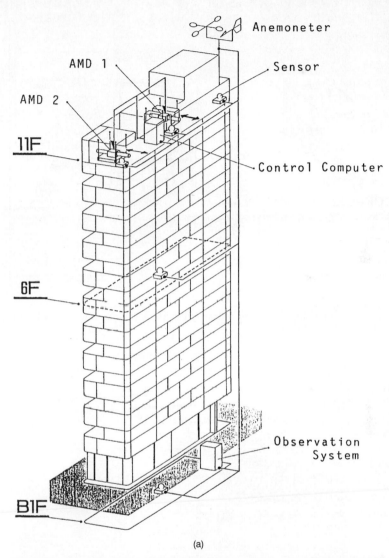

Anemoneter

AMD 1

AMD 2

Sensor

11F

Control Computer

6F

Observation
System

B1F

(a)

Figure 2.7 The Kyobashi Seiwa Building's active mass damper system. Vibrations picked up by computer are evaluated, and instructions are forwarded to the active mass dampers to move in a way that will counteract the vibration forces on the structure. (*a*) AMD composition concept of the building, (*b*) equipment composition, with AMD 1 and 2, and the hydraulic power system that activates them.

9. A wide array of earthquake-resistant and tremor-isolation devices including base isolation, honeycomb damper and joint damper systems, and the world's first active mass damper installation, used in the Kyobashi Seiwa Building in Tokyo (Fig. 2.7)

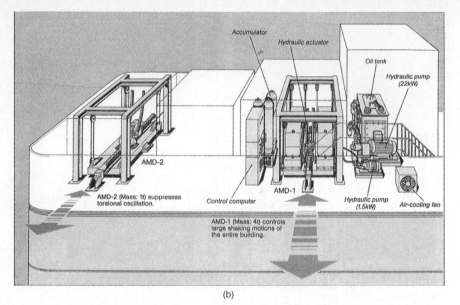

(b)

Figure 2.7 (*Continued*) (*b*) equipment composition, with AMD 1 and 2, and the hydraulic power system that activates them.

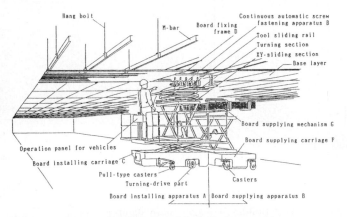

Figure 2.8 Automatic ceiling board installation machine.

10. An automatic ceiling-board-installation machine (Fig. 2.8)

11. An all-weather enclosure that creates a factory environment at the construction site (Fig. 2.9)

Kajima is sharing its R&D wealth with the United States on both the East and West Coasts.

(a)

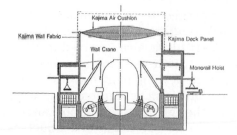

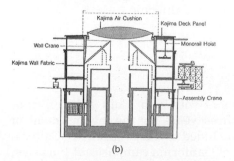

(b)

Figure 2.9 Kajima's all-weather enclosure. (*a*) roof being lowered, (*b*) two configurations of all-weather enclosures.

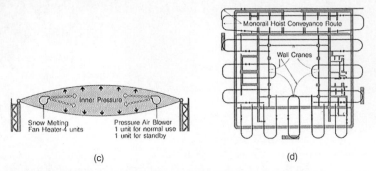

Figure 2.9 (*Continued*). (*c*) ice-melting roof. (*d*) monorail system to provide lifting capability.

THE KOBORI RESEARCH COMPLEX, INC.

Founded in 1986 as an affiliate company of Kajima, Kobori Research Complex, Inc., is headed by President Takuji Kobori, a distinguished doctor of engineering and past professor at Kyoto University. Dr. Kobori is a past president of the Architectural Institute of Japan, chairman of the Council for Nuclear Energy Technology for the Japanese government, winner of the Grand Prize of the Architectural Institute of Japan, and was nominated for the *Engineering News Record* 1990 Construction's Man of the Year Award.

The Kobori Institute devotes its energies to investigation, R&D, design analysis, and consulting work relating to aseismic and seismic-response control systems. The Institute is also involved in R&D and consultation pertaining to special structures such as nuclear energy facilities and ocean and aerospace development facilities. The Kobori Institute presently is involved in a joint research project with Princeton University working on earthquake ground-motion analysis, reliability and damage assessment of buildings, and liquefactions of soils. The Kobori Institute is also working on eight projects of a similar nature at the University of California.

CALIFORNIA UNIVERSITIES FOR RESEARCH AND EARTHQUAKE ENGINEERING—CUREE

Kajima has signed a unique agreement with eight California universities to provide $3.2 million over three years for the advancement of earthquake engineering research. Included in the program are Caltech, Stanford, USC, and the University of California campuses at Berkeley, Davis, Irvine, Los Angeles, and San Diego. Begun in 1990 and scheduled to run until 1993, the program provides for not only research funding, but also for an exchange program whereby personnel from the U.S. universities will spend some time at Kajima's research labs in Japan, and some of Kajima's researchers will visit the United States. The program will create a unique opportunity for engineers, designers, and researchers from both countries to work together on projects of interest and concern to Japan and the United States.

KAJIMA EVOLUTION 21—KE-21

On April 1, 1991, reflecting upon its 150 years as a construction company, top management determined that a major restructuring of the corporation was in order to meet the challenges of the next 150 years, and KE-21 was announced.

Corporate President Akira Miyazaki and CEO Shoichi Kajima, along with Chairman Rokuro Ishikawa, announced the formation of four interconnected but autonomous units within the company. Each of these entities are independently managed, and operate under the corporation's overall strategy and master plan named Kajima Evolution 21. These four new groups—the Construction Group, the Architectural and Engineering Design Group, the Development Group, and the New Business Group act as profit centers working toward Kajima's basic strategy—diversification, globalization, and federated management.

Diversification: Deepen construction activities, respond to the wider needs of the Architectural/Engineering (A/E) business, obtain a higher return on equity in the development business, develop a strategic plan for new business ventures while maintaining autonomous operations of the four groups.

Globalization: Individual groups are to look outside Japan's domestic market for new opportunities. They must respond to Japan's emerging open-market policy, which would include increased activity on joint ventures of all kinds within the country. Each group should pursue its own search to acquire subsidiaries and affiliates to reinforce its global position.

Federated management: Autonomous operations of individual groups are to be enhanced by assistance from headquarters. Management integration of each business group, including its subsidiaries and affiliate companies, is to be achieved.

Kajima's headquarters organization is to act as a synergizing agent to plan and establish strategies for the entire Kajima group. This new organizational structure for KE-21 is presented in Fig.

2.10. Mr. Akira Iwabuchi, whose Office of Corporate Strategy is located at Kajima's Motoakasaka world headquarters in Tokyo, explains that KE-21 is designed to create the optimum working environment for the group worldwide.

Each of these four new groups will be operating as a profit center. For example, Mr. Iwabuchi says that the Architectural/Engineering Group may decide to offer its design services to clients that may not wish to use Kajima's Construction Group as their contractor. As an example of the trend toward globalization, Kajima's recent associa-

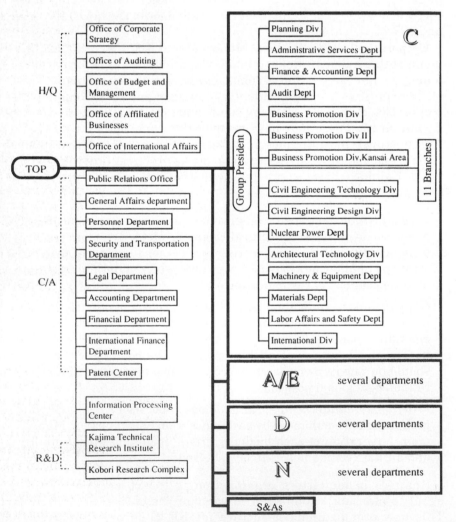

Figure 2.10   KE-21 corporate structure after KE-21 was initiated.

tion with the U.S. architectural/engineering firm of Hellmuth, Obata, and Kassabaum (HOK) has been beneficial. He says that HOK has excellent facilities management capabilities that have been put to good use in Kajima's own organization. HOK gave Kajima valuable computer software, and the company's two computers are connected by modem. HOK's local Japan offices are working with Kajima on a number of projects.

Mr. Iwabuchi sees the environmental market as a lucrative one, and one that fits Kajima's corporate philosophy. The coming years should produce substantial profits from participation in waste and water treatment projects, air pollution control systems, and the general greening programs of global industrial corporations. He sees many joint-venture opportunities worldwide, since Kajima's expertise, financial base, and personnel assets, although substantial, are limited.

KE-21's New Business Group is on the cutting edge of diversification activity, according to Mr. Iwabuchi, and Kajima affiliates, which probably are more non-construction-related than construction-related, should grow considerably in the next century.

In the next century another goal of KE-21 will be to seek growth in the development activities of the group, since these ventures have been profitable in the past, and because development utilizes all of the group's strengths to best advantage. Kajima's global expansion can be witnessed in Hong Kong with the announced start of construction of the 68-story Tregunter Towers on Old Peak Road. When it is completed, this will be the tallest residential building in Asia. The developer is Allied Kajima, Ltd., with offices in the Allied Kajima Building on Gloucester Road, Hong Kong. An advertisement in the May 27, 1992, *South China Morning Post* newspaper announced the sale of luxury apartments ranging in size from 2020 to 3798 square feet for the duplex units. Prices started at $932,000 (U.S.), and of the 187 units planned, one-half are already sold. For anyone interested, a deposit of $67,567 to $135,175 will hold one of the remaining 93 units.

When asked whether KE-21's creation of individual profit centers might emphasize profits at the expense of other corporate values, Mr. Iwabuchi responded, "Quality is the hallmark of the Kajima groups. Each group will pursue profits—but not at the expense of quality."

Mr. Shiochi Kishimoto, a manager in the Architectural Planning Department of the corporation's Planning Division discusses another aspect of Kajima's policies and the unique Japanese way that may affect how the company copes with the future:

The differences between U.S. and Japanese construction companies can be seen in their relationships between designers and clients. The line between architectural companies and construction companies in Japan is very vague. Historically, society in Japan conducts itself in a vague manner. In order to promote harmony and cooperation between all parties, everyone talks and discusses what they want to accomplish before arriving at a consensus of opinion. We don't tend to rely on the written word the way you do in the West. The relationship between contractor, designer, and client mirrors Japanese society itself.

The level of completeness of the design documents in our two countries is readily apparent. Drawings prepared by U.S. architects are working drawings, but when Japanese contractors receive drawings from Japanese architects they re-draw them. And in the process, the builders find many areas where they can improve details and may find errors that they are expected to correct.

And when asked about the role of Japanese contractors in the European Economic Community, Mr. Kishimoto continues:

We may follow our Japanese clients to Europe and assist them in building their new plants, like we did in the U.S., but we will find it difficult to participate in their public works projects and other domestic projects because of our unfamiliarity with local market conditions.

I don't know what the next century will bring—perhaps more reliance on the written contract as Japan adjusts to Western ways. But we must still be able to keep the uniqueness that is Japan.

KAJIMA'S PERSONNEL POLICIES AND COMPANY BENEFITS

"We liken the project manager to the position of president of a small company," says Mr. Taro Kawano of the Construction Group's International Division. "In Japan, the project manager is responsible for project quality, scheduling, profits, subcontractor selection to a significant degree, safety, client relations, business development, and assuring a harmonious relationship with the project's neighbors," continues Mr. Kawano.

The company needs to acquire top-flight people to carry out these overall responsibilities effectively, and successful candidates can look forward to salaries of $70,000 by the time they reach their late thirties, and as high as $120,000 by age 50.

Kajima offers lifetime employment to its employees and, like many other Japanese corporations, wage and fringe-benefit packages increase with seniority. For example, vacation time increases with seniority, and when asked about the number of vacation days offered to a long-time employee, the answer was, "We have 150 vacation days a year." With raised eyebrows, the writer replied, "I never realized your policy was so liberal, considering the well-advertised Japanese propensity for work and little or no play." "Well," the manager went on to explain, "this 150-vacation-day policy includes Saturdays and Sundays (that's about 104 of the 150 days). There are 13 national holidays in Japan, and it is traditional to take possibly five days away from work during the summer O-bon Festival when families unite at their ancestral home. Then there is the five-day holiday between Christmas and New Year's when many businesses are closed." That leaves the four-week company vacation policy for long-term employees, but when asked how many actual vacation days are taken, the answer was, "The norm would be about 5 days."

Mr. Kawano said that company policies dictate working hours, which begin at 8:30 A.M. and end at 5:15 P.M., daily, five days a week. The company's yearly total working hours per employee are designated as 1840 hours a year, but Kajima office workers actually work about 2000 hours a year, and field personnel work between 2200 and 2300. But when vacations are taken, they can be spent at one of 10 company-owned resort areas where the employee pays an average of $9.25 a day per person for a room and two meals.

Housing is very expensive in and around Japan's major cities, and Tokyo is one of the most expensive. A tiny (400 square-foot) two-bedroom apartment with a living-dining room combination may cost $1,200 a month, and not in a prime location, either. So the company provides its employees with housing subsidies. Employees working in the Tokyo office are provided with a $650 a month subsidy. In other, lower-cost-of-living areas, the subsidy is less.

At Kajima's new KI (Kajima Intelligent) Building across town in Tokyo, its design group is housed in a structure conceived with employee amenities in mind, from its beautifully landscaped atrium (Fig. 2.11a), to its rooftop garden (Fig. 2.11b), to its fully equipped and staffed restaurant (Fig. 2.11c), where a delicious lunch can be purchased for about 600 yen ($4.50), a bargain by Tokyo standards.

A feature not likely to be found in any U.S. company is the cocktail lounge adjacent to KI's cafeteria. Company employees are encouraged to socialize so as to get to know each other better, and all throughout the downtown areas, after normal working hours, groups of "salarymen" from companies all over town can be seen gathered together in bars or restaurants, having a beer or two. The cost of beer and hard liquor in these places can be rather high, depending upon the location, popularity, and prestige factor, and a $7.00 beer or a $12.00 scotch is not uncommon in the fancy places. Because of this, the company provides a place where employees can gather after work, have a few drinks at reasonable prices, and get to know each other better.

(a)

Figure 2.11 KI (Kajima Intelligent) Building details. (*a*) atrium.

(b)

(c)

Figure 2.11 (*Continued*) (*b*) rooftop garden, (*c*) serving area of full-service restaurant.

Retirement at Kajima, except in special cases, is mandatory at age 60, and the company offers employees a lump-sum payment based upon multiples of their last year's salary and length of service. These lump-sum payments average about $300,000.

QUALITY CONTROL—A BULWARK OF THE CORPORATION

In the 1950s and 1960s, companies built as rapidly as possible because economic expansion warranted it. Get it up and get it up fast, was the word of the day. But gradually, both contractor and client realized that quality was a necessary requirement for the long term, and the construction company that could not adapt to this new ethos would not survive in the coming years.

In 1987 Kajima President Shikawa introduced CWQC (*company-wide quality control*) to create an "enhancement of spirit" and to provide the roots for a scientific management system. Quality at Kajima is interpreted as: meeting the standards imposed by the client at a *cost* of construction that is reasonable; *delivery* of the building on time; and the operation of a *safe* working environment. The letters QCDS become a part of the CWQC program. Kajima developed a four-pronged approach to quality control:

1. *Make a plan* (PLAN).   Decide on the objectives; establish the methods.

2. *Implement the plan* (DO).   Educate and train; carry out the plan.

3. *Check the work* (CHECK).   Check the work to see if it conforms to the plan.

4. *Take action* (ACTION).   Take the necessary corrective action if the work is substandard.

The letters *PDCA*—Plan, Do, Check, Action—become a key element of the program. Every element of work has its own PDCA, whether in an operation or a safety program. The PDCA program, when applied to daily management at the site, can be illustrated in a typical program involving concrete work:

Plan.   Fix a target, working hours, level of quality in placing concrete, and so on. Take into consideration the location of placement, volume and quality of concrete; prepare a manual for concrete placement, stating placement of workers, appliances to be used, arrangement of any platforms, delivery schedule for materials, placement of reinforcing, curing time, and so forth.

Do. Explain the manual to the foreman and make certain that everything is understood. Place concrete.

Check. Check according to QC manual. Pay special attention to overall balance of each part and any discrepancies in the working requirements.

Action. If any abnormalities are detected in the progress of concrete delivery, placement, and so forth, take appropriate countermeasures at once and, to determine causes, try to completely understand why things did not go as planned. Were the provisions of the manual followed? If not, did this mean they weren't understood? Was there a problem with the quality of a worker or workers? Was anything overlooked in the planning stages?

After the operation is completed a thorough review must be made with all QC members to determine what went right and what must be corrected so that it will function properly the next time.

There are three targets in the QC Program:

Target 1. Elevate the problem-consciousness of each individual, based on his or her own assignment and duty. Elevate company morale through motivation. Launch a company-wide participation, open-door management policy.

Target 2. Improve control mechanisms through a thoroughgoing program to check over all phases of company activities. Utilize PDCA circles effectively, and implement a more comprehensive and integrated control system.

Target 3. Elevate profitability and competitiveness by realizing optimum operational efficiency, lower cost, and a quality assurance scheme. Fortify, optimize, and expand the sales organization through more intensive computerization. Promote R&D and expand new peripheral business fields. Kajima's *Company-Wide Quality Control Program* encompasses more than 41 pages in its introductory form. Figure 2.12 depicts the quality assurance flowchart during the design stage, and Fig. 2.13 is the construction-phase flowchart.

The system is neither complex nor simple. It involves a great deal of planning, indoctrination, and implementation, backed up by a total commitment by management at all levels. Kajima made its declaration to introduce *total quality control* (TQC) in 1978, and through intelligent planning, excellent communications, perseverance through the initial stages of development, and tenacity in its implementation, Kajima was able to win the coveted Deming Prize in 1982.

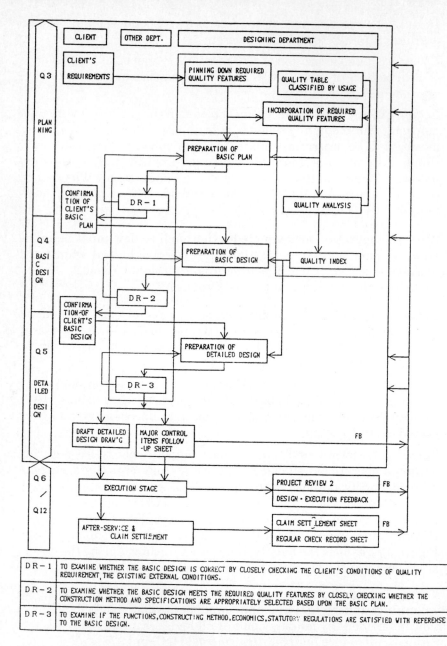

D R — 1	TO EXAMINE WHETHER THE BASIC DESIGN IS CORRECT BY CLOSELY CHECKING THE CLIENT'S CONDITIONS OF QUALITY REQUIREMENT, THE EXISTING EXTERNAL CONDITIONS.
D R — 2	TO EXAMINE WHETHER THE BASIC DESIGN MEETS THE REQUIRED QUALITY FEATURES BY CLOSELY CHECKING WHETHER THE CONSTRUCTION METHOD AND SPECIFICATIONS ARE APPROPRIATELY SELECTED BASED UPON THE BASIC PLAN.
D R — 3	TO EXAMINE IF THE FUNCTIONS, CONSTRUCTING METHOD, ECONOMICS, STATUTORY REGULATIONS ARE SATISFIED WITH REFERENSE TO THE BASIC DESIGN.

Figure 2.12 Kajima's QC flowchart for design phase.

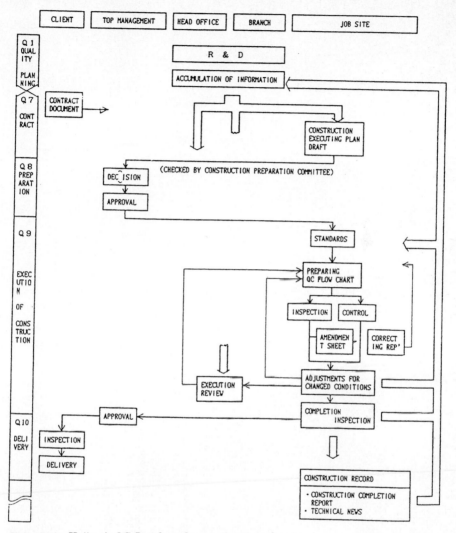

Figure 2.13 Kajima's QC flowchart for construction phase.

The twenty-first century looms just over the horizon, and Kajima awaits its coming with much anticipation, confident that it is fully prepared to meet any challenges that this new era will demand.

3

Takenaka Corporation

A Japanese Dynasty

Having been founded in 1610, Takenaka Corporation can proudly boast of being the oldest, continuously operating construction company in the world. Even more unusual is the fact that after 381 years, a direct descendant of Takenaka Toh-bei Masataka, the founder, is still at the helm of this international construction company, which achieved a 1991 sales volume of $14.47 billion. (In Japan it was customary to have one's family name precede one's given name; hence Takenaka, the family name, is followed by Toh-bei, the given name. This practice is still followed in many instances.)

Mr. Toichi Takenaka, the current president of the corporation, reiterates his ancestor's credo, "A building is not a product, but a work of art." Whether Takenaka Corporation is completing its work on the Imperial Palace in Tokyo, paving the runways at the Singapore Changi International Airport, or obtaining the certificate of occupancy for the Nippon Club Building on West 57th Street in Manhattan, the company strives for perfection in both design and construction.

IN THE BEGINNING

The Kingdom of Wa, as Japan was called in the third century, was a land of emperors and empresses, and as the centuries sped by, warrior dynasties led by their shoguns (generals) came to power and subverted the authority of some of these regional monarchs.

Early builders in Japan were likely to have among their clients either active or deposed emperors or shoguns, who often acted as sponsors. Takenaka Toh-bei Masataka was no exception. When he started his carpentry business in the early 1600s, his first benefactor was the military leader Oda Nobunaga, for whom the young Takenaka built a palace and numerous shrines, a company tradition that continued to grow after the founder's death.

Toh-bei was a *toryo,* master carpenter, who created the Osumi style, a new building technique that incorporated elaborately carved patterns into the decorative and structural members of the building. The master carpenter in those days also assumed the role of architect, designing the entire structure and the detailed carvings that put his individual stamp on the project. The Taiho Shrine, located in Shiga Prefecture and completed in 1847 by Takenaka, is an excellent example of the intricate carvings for which the company became famous. Figure 3.1 is a photograph of elaborately carved joints and brackets at one of the shrine's roof corners, and Fig. 3.2 is a photograph of the Tohfukuji Shrine in Kyoto, one of several buildings constructed by Takenaka in 1819.

Years after Toh-bei's demise, generations of skilled Takenaka carpenters continued to specialize in both palace and shrine construction projects, bringing with them the specialized designs and techniques of the intricate Osumi-style carvings. The roots of the modern company, however, were not to be formed until 1899, a period when Japan began to open its doors to the world following Commodore Perry's voyage into Tokyo Bay. The Emperor Meiji accelerated Japan's desire to absorb Western culture, and his efforts planted the seeds for the industrialization of Japan. Thus began the growth of Takenaka and other major Japanese contractors who would be part of the industrial and infrastructure construction activity that characterized Japan's frenetic attempt to achieve Westernization.

On February 2, 1899, Toh-emon Takenaka, of the fourteenth generation of builders from that venerable firm, left his older brother in charge of the family business where it had been founded in Nagoya. He struck out for the newly opened port city of Kobe and established a branch office there in order to participate in the modernization of the city that was just beginning. Fascinated by Western design techniques, Toh-emon began to meet and exchange ideas with university-trained architects and scholars from the nearby Kyoto Imperial University, gaining much valuable experience by working with these professionally trained designers.

In 1909, the family business in Nagoya closed, and operations were consolidated in Kobe, where its name was changed to Takenaka Komuten, the term *Komuten* meaning, literally, "construction work premises." Toh-emon was intent upon providing his clients with not only quality construction work, but the design for these projects as well, a master builder concept that dated back to ancient times in Japan. This design-build approach had begun to diminish at that time as independent architects set up practice in the country at the turn of the century. Toh-emon liked to think of his young company as a "design office with a construction department." This concept was to carry

(a)

(b)

Figure 3.1 Elaborate Osumi-style carvings by Japan's carpenter artisans. (*a*) design detail, (*b*) intricate wood-carved beams at the corner of a Takenaka-constructed shrine.

(a)

(b)

Figure 3.2 The temple at the Tohfukuji Shrine in Kyoto built by Takenaka in 1819.
(*a*) outside view of temple, (*b*) entranceway showing intricate, carved details.

through to the present day, when one of the other Big Six competitors referred to Takenaka as "a design firm with construction capabilities."

During the first decade of the twentieth century, the company received a commission for one of its first major projects. Mitsui, one of Japan's great trading houses, contracted with Takenaka to build 4 one-story tiled-roof buildings. The total floor area of the entire project would be 45,000 square feet; when completed, this project gained the company considerable recognition and elevated Takenaka to the status of a major constructor.

In 1912 Takenaka constructed what was probably the first reinforced-concrete structure in the country for the Takashimaya Department Store in Kyoto. This structure was designed by Tadahiko Hibi, of the Kyoto Imperial University Department of Engineering, who at that time was considered a pioneer in these kinds of structures, as was his co-designer Toshikata Sano, of Tokyo Imperial University's Architecture Department. The tradition of marrying the best designers to the construction process had begun.

Toh-emon's fierce determination to learn as much as he could from sophisticated designers led him to lure several outstanding engineers and architects to Takenaka in order to increase his company's ability to obtain contracts for more complex projects. This desire to attract the most promising designers of their day to enhance the company's reputation has become a Takenaka tradition down through the years.

During those early years of the twentieth century, large masonry buildings with steel frames and concrete structures were beginning to proliferate in Japan, and Takenaka wanted his firm to gain as much experience as possible in these kinds of projects. He wanted to become a leader in the construction of what were then the very sophisticated projects. His opportunity arrived when he was requested to build a private residence for Ryuhei Murayama, president of one of Japan's largest newspapers, the *Asahi Shimbun*. Murayama had been pleased with the results of Takenaka's work for other clients, so he also commissioned the firm to build his new newspaper plant. Reasonably experienced in reinforced-concrete structures, Takenaka convinced the industrialist to build his new office and printing plant of reinforced concrete, even though it would be more expensive than the brick buildings that were rising all around. The main building was to be four stories high, and the printing plant itself was to be three stories. The showpiece of the complex was to be a clock tower soaring 131 ft into the air, with a 9-foot-diameter Swiss clock on each of its four faces. When the building was completed in October 1917, it was one of the largest newspaper plants in the world.

The disastrous Kanto earthquake of 1923 destroyed one-third of Tokyo and most of nearby Yokohama, and resulted in more than

140,000 deaths. One of the casualties of this tragic event was the Tokyo office of *Asahi Shimbun*. Now a steady client, the newspaper asked Takenaka to rebuild its headquarters, and Kikuji Ishimoto, one of Japan's leading architects at the time and leader of the Secession Movement in Japanese architecture, was engaged to do the design. His masterpiece broke entirely with the traditions of the day, with its rounded concrete facade and parabolic arched windows, reminiscent of German Expressionism. Ishimoto arranged to have a brilliant yellow and blue band painted beneath the building's cornice, a complete departure from the austere designs of the times.

Fifty-six years later, in 1979, Takenaka was once again called upon to build a brand-new building for *Asahi Shimbun*, to accommodate its offices in the Tsukiji district of Tokyo. This time the building was a 15-story yellow-ocher ceramic-tile-clad design that would accommodate the sophisticated technologies that were now required to produce modern newspapers.

Takenaka's reputation as an innovative builder seeking the most expressive designs was becoming well known, and by 1927 the firm's design staff had increased to 50, to keep up with its expanding work load. In 1931 Jun Ichiro Ishikawa, the head of the design department, made bold use of three new building materials—stainless steel, aluminum, and curved glass—when he designed the award-winning Yokohama Asahi building, a 10-story modernistic structure in the international style.

Takenaka, like other large construction companies in Japan, participated in many major projects during the reconstruction of the country after World War II, but the firm concentrated its business activity in the private sector, shying away from any significant government projects. In fact, in 1985 government business accounted for only 7 percent of Takenaka's annual construction revenues.

According to company historian Toru Yamanaka, the company's reluctance to become heavily involved in public works projects probably dates back to the early 1870s. When Takenaka was still located in Nagoya, the company was commissioned to build a Western-style regimental army barracks. While construction was under way, Takenaka was subjected to some rather high-handed dealings by the military. Toh-emon Takenaka was so upset that he considered legal action, something almost unheard of in those days. After due deliberation he decided that he would not be capable of facing down the powerful military, so he persevered and finished the job, but vowed not to become involved in these kinds of projects ever again.

Mr. Keisuke Shobu, assistant general manager of Takenaka Corporation, says that this tenet still holds forth today, in that 85 percent of the corporation's sales volume in 1991 was in the private sector, and the company does virtually no civil work. Although this may be true, the statement is somewhat paradoxical, since Takenaka owns the Takenaka Civil Engineering Company, which has 1500 employees; in 1991, the Takenaka Civil Engineering Company's sales volume was $1.07 billion.

THE POSTWAR PERIOD

The company's concentration on design-build projects after the war continued, and in 1960 the Building Contractors Society (BCS) in Japan, an organization composed of 50 of the country's top contractors, initiated a program of annual merit awards for outstanding design. In the 23 years that have followed, 328 buildings have received the BCS award, and Takenaka was the recipient of 41 commendations. Except for 1973, the company received at least one award each year. But the one they are most proud of came in 1968. That was the year that a design was being sought for the National Theatre to be built in Tokyo, and the design competition evolved into the biggest contest of its kind since the war. Contractors with design departments, architectural firms, and even architects teaching at some of Japan's most prestigious universities entered the contest. Takenaka's Hiroyuki Iwamoto won out over 307 entries, and the company went on to build this much-acclaimed structure (Fig. 3.3).

In 1973 the Ministry of Construction sponsored a competition to design and construct a new city on 50 acres of reclaimed land in Hyogo Prefecture. The rules for the competition stipulated that 3400 high-rise apartments were to be built, and the proposal was to include provisions for the maintenance of these buildings as well as lease-up responsibility. The applicants were also to include construction of the required support facilities for the complex. Takenaka teamed up with Nippon Steel, Takasago Thermal Industries, Matsushita Kyosan, and Matsushita Electric to win first place from among the 22 other proposals submitted. For its efforts, the Takenaka group won the renowned Architectural Institute of Japan Prize in 1980. This award-winning Ashiyama Heights housing complex, shown in Fig. 3.4, is interesting, not only in its scope, but also for the magnificent ocean view it affords its occupants.

Not limiting its endeavors solely to Japan, Takenaka entered the international competition for the new Paris Opera House in 1983 and placed highest of all the entries from Japan. In 1987 Takenaka was honored by Shinkenchiku-Sha, publisher of *The Contemporary Japanese Architects Series* of books, when the Eleventh Edition was devoted to *the design works of Takenaka Komuten*.

(a)

(b)

Figure 3.3 Takenaka's award-winning National Theatre in Tokyo. (*a*) outside elevation, (*b*) interior view of theater.

TAKENAKA AT AGE 381

Takenaka's head office is located in the Chuo Ward in Osaka, with its main offices in Tokyo and regional offices in Sapporo, Sendai, Yokohama, Chiba, Nagoya, Kobe, Kyoto, Takamatsu, Hiroshima, and Fukuoka. As of January 1991, the company employed 8650, a number that includes 5724 architects and engineers. The company's organiza-

Production System
An 'industrialized production system'
was adopted that made the most effective
possible use of all sub-systems such as
factory production, transportation and
site production, and allowed for the
smooth progress of the whole job.

Figure 3.4 Ashiyama Heights housing complex—another award winner.

tional structure is rather straightforward, as displayed in Fig. 3.5.
What may be somewhat unusual in a corporation such as this is the
line of reporting. The construction field office reports directly to the
general manager of the regional branch, which has direct access to the
senior managing director, the managing director, and to the executive
vice president and president of the corporation. It is apparent that the
construction process remains a critical and important part of
Takenaka's corporate philosophy.

Worldwide operations are handled through the company's many
overseas branch offices. European operations are funneled through a
series of offices located in England, France, Spain, Germany,
Amsterdam, and Belgium. Middle East construction is controlled
through Takenaka Iran, Ltd., in Tehran. In the Far East and Pacific
Rim, branches in Bangkok, Thailand; Jakarta, Indonesia; Singapore;
Kuala Lumpur; Taiwan; Hong Kong; and China handle the work.

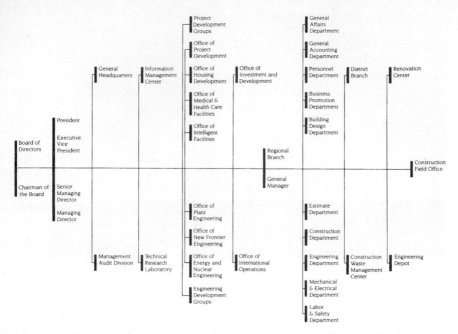

Figure 3.5   Takenaka's organizational chart with unusual direct line to field office.

Figure 3.6   The Tokyo Dome—the Big Egg.

TAKENAKA'S MAJOR WORKS TODAY

A great number of Takenaka's construction projects are designed by its architectural group, and they collaborate with other local or international design firms when the occasion arises. One such project is the Tokyo Dome, better known as the Big Egg, an example of collaborative work with Nikken Sekkei. Home of the Yomiuri Giants baseball team, this inclined, low-rise, cable-reinforced, air-membrane-roofed structure has become a Tokyo landmark (Fig. 3.6). The roof membrane is a dual layer of Teflon-coated fiberglass fabric weighing about 400 tons. The total floor area of the Big Egg is 1,239,778 square feet and it has hosted a wide range of events, ranging from sports, to rock concerts, to grand opera. The Big Egg has a number of computer-controlled support systems such as roof-level sensors, heat-radiation-scanning fire detectors, roof-movement sensors, and pressure-adjustment dampers.

Takenaka designers and constructors have worked together on other types of recreational facilities, public buildings, educational facilities, temples and shrines, industrial and commercial projects, hotels, and housing and transportation facilities, but some of their most spectacular work can be seen in their office building design. The Shibaura Square Building (Fig. 3.7) is a 547,953-square foot 21-story office building in Tokyo. The Toho Hibiya Building (Fig. 3.8) and the headquarters of Mutoh Industries (Fig. 3.9) are also located in Tokyo. The Kobe New City Hall (Fig. 3.10) is a more classic design. The Shin-Kobe Oriental City C3 building (Fig. 3.11) is nothing less than spectacular. Located at the base of the mountains that provide a backdrop for this seaport city, the soaring reflective glass spires of the 37-story hotel, set against those ancient forests, bring primitive and modern Japan together in one frame.

About 93 percent of the company's current sales volume is generated within Japan, and for the foreseeable future Takenaka sees the overseas market increasing from its present 7 to 8 percent of its yearly volume to just about 10 percent.

Mr. Takashi Hara, the general manager in charge of research and planning, said that in 1992 the Japanese government announced a plan to set aside 430 trillion yen over the next 10 years for various proposed public expenditures. Based upon the current exchange rate of 130 yen, this is an astounding $3.3 trillion, or $330 billion per year over the projected life of the program. With economic conditions in Japan taking a decided downturn, the government may have second thoughts about instituting such a grandiose scheme, but even in a watered-down fashion, domestic construction activity certainly will be increased, and Takenaka stands to obtain a reasonable portion of the work.

Figure 3.7 Shibaura Square office building designed by Takenaka.

Figure 3.8 Another Takenaka design—the Toho Hibiya Building.

Figure 3.9 The headquarters for Mutoh Industries in Tokyo.

KOBE'S HARBOR LAND WATERFRONT REVITALIZATION PROGRAM

The company is involved in a few mega-projects right now. One is Kobe Harbor Land (Fig. 3.12), involving the revitalization of the Kobe waterfront, one of Japan's prime deep-water harbors. Kobe Harbor Land will encompass a major portion of the downtown area southwest of the Hanshin Expressway Nishinomiya Kobe Line and will contain 2.05-million square feet of office, commercial, and retail space. Currently there are 1000 construction workers at Kobe Harbor Land working on the building for Matsuzakaya Department Store, a 380-year-old client (Fig. 3.13), and several other retail establishments (Fig. 3.14). The number of workers will increase as various finishing trades are brought on the site. Takenaka has been commissioned as developer, designer, and contractor for this 10-year project valued at $2.31 billion in today's dollars.

There are a number of major construction projects, both planned and under way in Osaka, and Takenaka is getting its fair share of work there, including the N-6 Project, which incorporates a new fireproof steel-structure concept involving concrete-filled steel-tube columns. Takenaka says that the increased loading capacity of these new columns is such that spacings can be increased, making this design

Figure 3.10   The Kobe New City Hall—a collaborative effort.

cost-effective, because the higher cost of the concrete-filled steel will be offset by the use of fewer columns.

The company recently completed the Hokkaido Housing Supply Corporation project in Sapporo, an 11-story residential building encompassing 630,750 square feet and a 169,000-square-foot covered promenade.

In 1987 Takenaka entered an international design competition for a second National Theater in Japan. This theater would be used as an

Figure 3.11　Shin-Kobe Oriental City C3.

opera hall and will be located in the Shinjuku section of Tokyo, an area that is becoming home to most of the city's new skyscrapers. The company was recently advised that it was selected as the design winner, and construction should commence in the near future. Although Takenaka saw fit to engage a German designer with opera house experience, its own acoustical research activities are truly impressive. In Takenaka's specially designed acoustical chamber (Fig. 3.15) the sound replicating qualities of some of the world's outstanding symphony halls can be produced. Seated in a concert hall chair in the middle of this chamber, a technician proudly announces that visitors will be treated to Mozart's *The Marriage of Figaro* as though they were seated in the orchestra, center stage, of Vienna's famed Philharmonic Hall. The

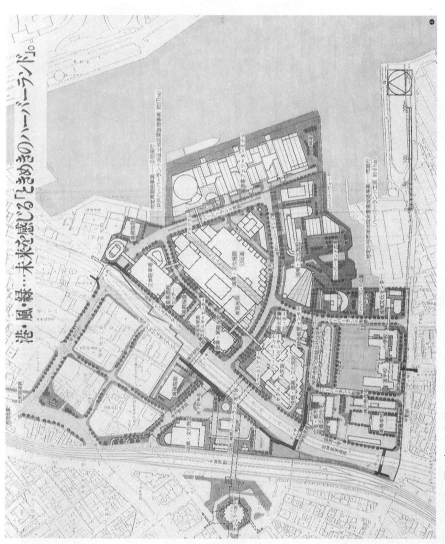

港・風・緑…未来を感じる「ときめきのハーバーランド」104

Figure 3.12 The $2.31-billion Kobe Harbor Land project, showing construction-line limits.

Figure 3.13   Building for 381-year-old client Matsuzakaya at Kobe Harbor Land.

Figure 3.14   Other construction activity at Kobe Harbor Land.

Figure 3.15 Takenaka's acoustical chamber.

house lights dim and the rousing strains of Mozart fill the room. The technician then advises visitors that if their ear is trained, they will next hear the same work as though played in Amsterdam's Concert Hall. The performance is repeated again, reproducing the acoustical qualities of the Osaka Symphony Hall. And then, possibly in deference to Takenaka's American visitor, Seiji Ozawa conducts the Boston Symphony in a rendition of Mozart's *Marriage of Figaro* as it would sound in Symphony Hall. All without leaving that one chair.

TAKENAKA IN THE UNITED STATES

Takenaka International (U.S.A.), Ltd., was established in 1960 in San Francisco and has since expanded to a New York office which controls branches in Chicago, Illinois; Indianapolis, Indiana; Lexington, Kentucky; and Atlanta, Georgia. California supports a regional office in Los Angeles and there is another regional office in Honolulu. Takenaka's U.S. clients are the equivalent of *Fortune* 500 companies, and include projects for the American branches of Japan's major banks and distribution centers such as Kubota, Kawasaki, Richo Corporation, Makita, and Matsushita Electric.

The Takenaka Total Package System (TPS) is a solution to design and construction on a global scale. The TPS relieves clients of involvement in the details of planning, budgeting, and scheduling, and lets them focus on strategic issues such as overall project management and critical requirements.

The TPS anticipates the client's needs with a highly integrated turn-key system that takes care of every aspect of a project, from initial feasibility studies through management and maintenance of the completed work. The net result is a work that meets the client's requirements at a fraction of the cost and time needed by more traditional methods.

With the Takenaka Total Package System, a single contract designating sole responsibility for both design and construction can be made alter the basic planning and design stage, and construction work can begin during the preparation of contract documents. The result is a considerable saving in total project time and reduction of total project cost. In addition to these advantages, the availability of construction expertise during the design phase allows the architects to consider fully questions of constructibility and cost.

The TPS makes it possible for us to apply our Total Quality Control (TOC) to all stages of design and construction. TOC is a systemized program that was initiated by Takenaka in design and construction industry, and has been successfully used in all our design-build projects. The combination of Total Package System and Total Quality Control, simply means a higher quality building in shorter construction period and lower cost, and enables us to extend our service to the clients even after the construction work has been completed.

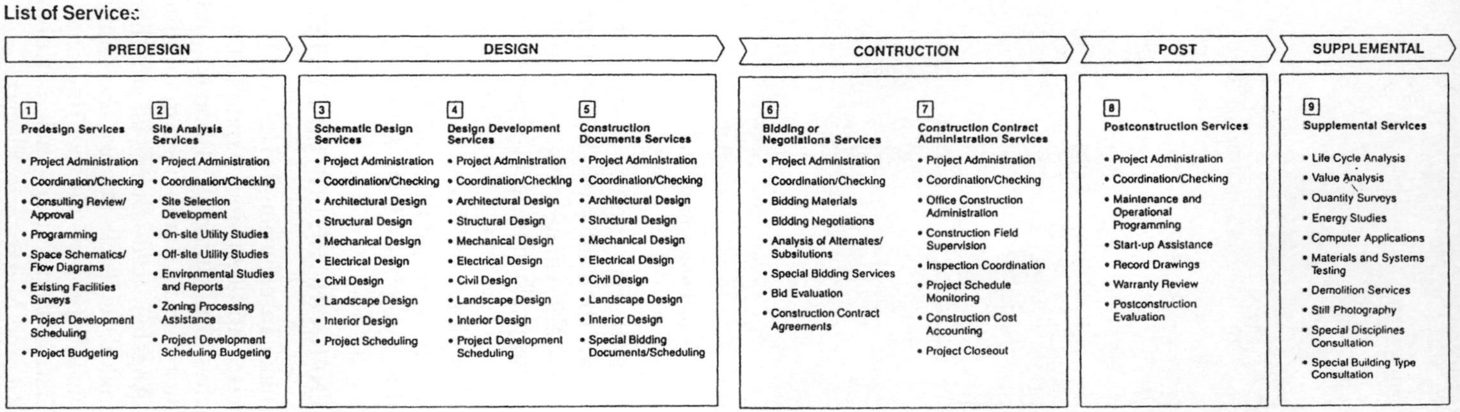

List of Service:

PREDESIGN

1 Predesign Services
- Project Administration
- Coordination/Checking
- Consulting Review/Approval
- Programming
- Space Schematics/Flow Diagrams
- Existing Facilities Surveys
- Project Development Scheduling
- Project Budgeting

2 Site Analysis Services
- Project Administration
- Coordination/Checking
- Site Selection Development
- On-site Utility Studies
- Off-site Utility Studies
- Environmental Studies and Reports
- Zoning Processing Assistance
- Project Development Scheduling Budgeting

DESIGN

3 Schematic Design Services
- Project Administration
- Coordination/Checking
- Architectural Design
- Structural Design
- Mechanical Design
- Electrical Design
- Civil Design
- Landscape Design
- Interior Design
- Project Scheduling

4 Design Development Services
- Project Administration
- Coordination/Checking
- Architectural Design
- Structural Design
- Mechanical Design
- Electrical Design
- Civil Design
- Landscape Design
- Interior Design
- Project Development Scheduling

5 Construction Documents Services
- Project Administration
- Coordination/Checking
- Architectural Design
- Structural Design
- Mechanical Design
- Electrical Design
- Civil Design
- Landscape Design
- Interior Design
- Special Bidding Documents/Scheduling

CONSTRUCTION

6 Bidding or Negotiations Services
- Project Administration
- Coordination/Checking
- Bidding Materials
- Bidding Negotiations
- Analysis of Alternates/Subsitutions
- Special Bidding Services
- Bid Evaluation
- Construction Contract Agreements

7 Construction Contract Administration Services
- Project Administration
- Coordination/Checking
- Office Construction Administration
- Construction Field Supervision
- Inspection Coordination
- Project Schedule Monitoring
- Construction Cost Accounting
- Project Closeout

POST

8 Postconstruction Services
- Project Administration
- Coordination/Checking
- Maintenance and Operational Programming
- Start-up Assistance
- Record Drawings
- Warranty Review
- Postconstruction Evaluation

SUPPLEMENTAL

9 Supplemental Services
- Life Cycle Analysis
- Value Analysis
- Quantity Surveys
- Energy Studies
- Computer Applications
- Materials and Systems Testing
- Demolition Services
- Still Photography
- Special Disciplines Consultation
- Special Building Type Consultation

Figure 3.16 Takenaka's Total Package System.

Takenaka recently constructed a 284,000-square-foot plant and office for Toyota Industrial Equipment Manufacturing Company in Columbus, Indiana; a 290,000-square-foot plant for I.I. Stanley; and a 180,000-square-foot warehouse for Tokai Rika, both the latter projects being in Battle Creek, Michigan. Takenaka's hotel construction activities include the 529-room, 570,000-square-foot Hotel Nikko in San Francisco, and the 780,000-square-foot resort hotel complex for the Hyatt Regency on Kauai Island in Hawaii. In 1991, Takenaka entered the tough Manhattan market as a general contractor and built the 22-story, 76,000-square-foot Nippon Club Tower.

The company offers its American clients the Takenaka *Total Package System* (TPS), as outlined in Figure 3.16, which includes services that range from predesign consultation, to design development, and construction-document services. TPS affords the client a single-source responsibility for design and construction that extends into postconstruction services and supplemental services such as life-cycle analysis, energy studies, and materials and systems testing, and even provides photographs for corporate brochures.

DESIGN-BUILD AND ITS RELIANCE ON QUALITY CONTROL

The design-build concept appears to be having a resurgence as more and more clients recognize the value of dealing with a single source for both design and construction activities. This single-point responsibility can bring a project from conception to completion in considerably less time than the more conventional owner-provided design process. Since the builder is also responsible for design completeness and accuracy, many of the disputes and claims arising from incomplete plans and specifications, or design documents inconsistent with the owner's requirements, are substantially reduced or eliminated. Once relegated primarily to a relatively narrow band of projects in the private sector, the design-build concept is spreading rapidly to the manufacturing sector, and is even being embraced by the public sector.

The United States Postal Service embarked on a major campaign in 1991 and 1992 to award contracts for new facilities via the design-build solicitations. And at a meeting of the National Society of Professional Engineers in early 1992, federal interest in design-build projects was a source of considerable interest, and it was noted that 200 projects within the General Services Administration's $4-billion-a-year budget were being awarded on a design-build basis.

The advantages of design-build as espoused by Takenaka are rather straightforward:

- The process can offer the highest quality with no apparent increase in construction costs.

- The potential for savings is great, inasmuch as the construction department can provide the design department with background information on what works and what doesn't work.

To enhance the company's position in design capability in the United States, and possibly other parts of the world, in 1989 Takenaka joined with The Architects Collaborative, an architectural firm in Cambridge, Massachusetts, to form a new corporation called TAC International. The Architects Collaborative (TAC) would own 51 percent of this new venture and Takenaka Design, Inc., the New York-based subsidiary of Takenaka, would be a minority owner with a 49 percent interest. TAC achieved international fame by virtue of the reputation of its founder Walter Gropius, the pioneer of the Bauhaus school of design, who in 1945 was a professor of architecture at Harvard. At the time of this partnership with Takenaka, TAC was listed by ENR as the tenth largest design firm in the country.

TAC International provided complete architectural and interior design, landscape architecture, and urban-planning services to clients in Japan and the United States. One of TAC International's first projects was a 24-story high-tech office building in Los Angeles where Takenaka was to provide a portion of the project financing and project-management services.

TOTAL QUALITY CONTROL

Renichi Takenaka, chairman of the board of the Takenaka Corporation, was fond of telling prospective clients, "If you want to meet me, please go see one of my buildings," so proud was he of the company's end-product.

During the late 1950s, construction activity reached a high pitch in Japan, fueled by the country's industrial expansion and by funds pumped into the economy by the U.S. government during the Korean War. Quality control was not a top priority among builders anxious to get back on their feet, but grumblings from long-term clients, and a drastic increase in job-site injuries and fatalities made some contractors stop and look at the dangerous waters they were entering. In 1955 Renichi Takenaka gave serious thought to the implementation of a company-wide quality-control program to improve the company's construction process.

Five years earlier, in 1950, Dr. Edward Deming had come to Japan at the invitation of the Science and Technology Federation of Japan, and although his teachings in America had fallen on deaf ears,

Japanese industrialists listened, learned, and began to implement Deming's lessons on quality control.

Dr. Tetsuichi Asaka, now 78-years old and a retired university professor, listened intently to what Deming had to say, and after meeting with Deming became one of his leading disciples in the country. Dr. Asaka began to discuss quality control with Renichi Takenaka, who immediately saw the value of this basic manufacturing concept but labored over how to adapt Deming's principles to the construction industry, and to his firm in particular.

First of all, "production runs" (future volume), contrary to workings within the manufacturing industry, were very difficult to predict in the building business. Secondly, construction sites, being outdoors, are subjected to the vagaries of the weather, unlike the controlled environment of the factory. Thirdly, most factories turn out mass-produced items, while each construction project is virtually a one-of design. And fourthly, whereas the production factory utilizes its own capital and its own hourly work force to create a product, the contractor relies on periodic payments from the client, and on labor furnished by outside specialty contractors, over which he does not appear to have complete control.

Although these differences were striking, Renichi Takenaka and Dr. Asaka felt that the Deming principles could somehow apply to the construction industry, and the corporation was introduced to TQC—*Total Quality Control*—in 1976.

The formulation of the plan revolved around three basic tenets:

1. All corporate managers and executives would be required to actively participate in the program.

2. The program was to be instituted throughout the company, in every department.

3. Efforts were to be concentrated on the quality of the design in the planning stage of a project, since upstream work during the design and planning stages was essential to the elimination of quality problems in the construction phase of the work.

The quality management concept would tackle three basic concerns of Takenaka, or in fact, any other construction company: ensure long-term steady profits; deliver a quality building to enhance the company's reputation for future work with clients; ensure that delivery of the product is made during the time specified in the construction schedule. Quality concerns focused on the four elements of the design-build process: function, economy, aesthetics, and social acceptance.

The *Total Quality Control* (TQC) program as introduced was based upon instituting the following policies:

1. Progress meetings would originate with the company president and general managers at headquarters operations, and would be expanded to include all branch managers. Other members of the company were to be made aware of top management's commitment to TQC.

2. TQC education would flow from upper management, down to middle management, and then to each and every member of the company.

3. The program was to emphasize the importance of policy management and upstream management of the construction process, which meant scrutinizing the design as it progressed.

4. All employees would be required to participate in the program as part of their daily routine, and in time a trend of improving quality would become apparent to them.

A president's QC progress meeting would be held on a regular basis to review and analyze each problem as it occurred and to determine what action was required so as not to repeat its occurrence. Quality concerns would remain focused on the planning and design stage: quality of design; quality of conformance; and quality during the construction process.

Since most general contractors employ large numbers of specialty contractors (subcontractors) in the construction cycle, if the quality of these subcontractors is not monitored and controlled, the general contractor's TQC program will fail. Takenaka began to encourage its subcontractors to institute their own QC programs, and in 1982, as an added inducement, established the Takenaka QC Prize to be awarded for excellence exhibited by a subcontractor. QC circles were encouraged in such a way that workers in one QC unit would be directed to complete a partially finished work task before passing that portion of work on to the next QC unit.

In 1980, Takenaka sought and obtained the Holy Grail of Japanese Quality Control awards, the Deming Award; it was the first contractor in the country to receive this honor. Takenaka, in 1991, may be poised on the threshold of a new era of international construction because of the company's origins in, and emphasis on, the design-build concept and commitment to the quality control that becomes an integral part of that scheme.

Not content to rest on past laurels, Toichi Takenaka is looking to capture another TQC prize, the Japanese Quality Control Award, an industry-wide prize open to Japan's industrial elite such as Sony, Matsushita, Fujitsu, and the like. Takenaka wants to be the first Japanese contractor to win this award so that it can add this to its other "first" lists, including the one for the Deming Prize.

Does TQC pay off? Just ask Mr. Takashi Hara. "In 1987 our corporate sales volume was approximately $7 billion. Sales volume in 1991 is $14.47 billion, more than twice as great. Profits in 1990 were $256 million, about three-and-a-half times greater than 1987 profits. So one can see that sales volume increased nicely over the years, but even more important, profits increased at a greater rate. Does Takenaka's policy of TQC pay off? I'd say the results speak for themselves."

TAKENAKA PAYS HOMAGE TO ITS PAST

Japanese architecture, and the builders who carried out these designs well into the late nineteenth century, depended a great deal on the skill of carpenters. And the skilled craftsmen working on many of these intricately carved wooden structures required proper tools. The Japanese have always had an affinity for wood, and the beauty and grace created and preserved in many ancient Buddhist and Shinto shrines is a tribute to the artistry and excellent skills of their carpenters.

The Carpentry Tools Museum

Commemorating the eighty-fifth anniversary of Takenaka's incorporation, the company established the Takenaka Carpentry Tools Museum in 1984 in Kobe City, the home of the first company headquarters in 1899. The stated purpose of the museum is twofold: to collect and preserve the tools from the past; and, secondly, by exhibiting these tools, "to convey to future generations the spirit and attitudes of traditional Japanese carpenters and blacksmiths."

The museum has three floors and a basement. On the first floor tools are chronologically displayed: primitive (12,000 B.C. to 300 A.D.); ancient (300–1185 A.D.); the Middle Ages (1185–1573); modern (1573–1868); and contemporary (1868 to the present). The second floor displays examples of traditional Japanese carpentry techniques including joinery details. Samples of 24 types of wood used in framing and for finish work are on the floor, and some full-size wooden frames and beams are erected. The third floor has a collection of cutting, trimming, processing, and finishing tools, paying respect to the skill of the blacksmith who forged many of these tools from raw blanks into what could qualify as works of art. A trip to the basement reveals row after row of metal shelving packed with more than 9,000 tools in the process of being cataloged or restored.

A video room allows the visitor to be transported back to the time when the master carpenter traveled to the forest to select the trees for his project, cut them by hand, and brought them back to his shop, where apprentices would strip the bark and begin the laborious task of turning round into square with razor-sharp axe and adze. The skilled carpenters would then take over, and with planes sharpened to surgical levels, remove tissue-thin strips of wood until the proper shape was achieved. Meanwhile, other craftsmen would be hammering and chiseling one of the many types of joints that would create the structural integrity of the framework when beam and column were fitted together.

The video permits one to view master blacksmith Tetsunosuke Miyano the 2d transform, as if by magic, an iron blank into a saw blade, using the most primitive methods to create an effective tool that looks like a piece of metal sculpture. After viewing the video and walking slowly around the museum, one can almost feel the presence of these wood artisans as they lovingly hone their chisels and shapers and begin the long slow process that will turn wood into art.

It is to Takenaka's credit that it has devoted so much time and money to preserve such an important part of its company's and country's heritage. Although Figs. 3.17 and 3.18 display some of the exhibit's collection, the intricacy and beauty of these tools can best be appreciated by

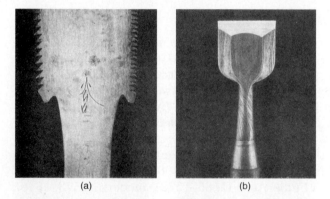

(a)   (b)

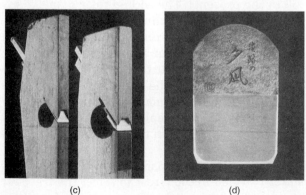

(c)   (d)

Figure 3.17 Some of the tools in Takenaka's Museum of Ancient Carpentry Tools .

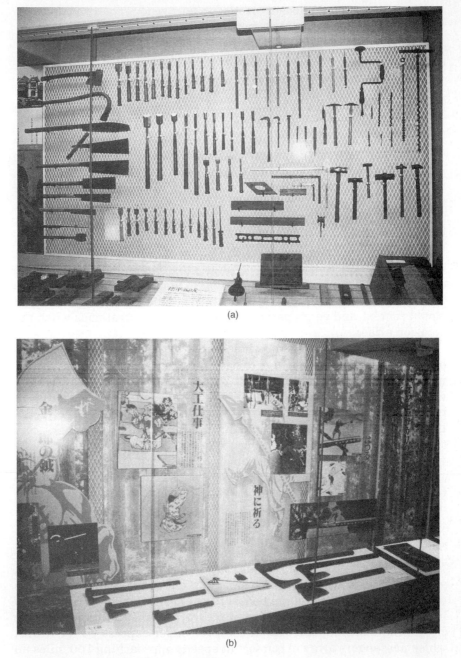

Figure 3.18 Some of the Museum exhibits.

visiting this unusual museum nestled in a tiny side street within walking distance of the railroad station in Shin-Kobe.

WITH REVERENCE FOR THE PAST, TAKENAKA LOOKS TO THE FUTURE

Mr. Toichi Takenaka is seated at a window table in the Crown Restaurant located on the 10th floor of the Palace Hotel in downtown Tokyo, a hotel the company built five years ago. The view across Hibiya Park, in full flower, is toward the Imperial Palace grounds. When asked to synopsize his company's future strategy, he smiles and says, "We must think globally and act locally." A rather simple statement but a profound one.

A construction company with Takenaka's considerable volume must be tuned in to global markets: where they are today, and where they are likely to be in the future. With the ever-shifting economic winds, today's source of construction revenue may slowly fade away, while other lucrative markets may be forming in another corner of the globe. So a progressive company must view the construction market in a global context and be prepared to shift marketing strategies when the occasion arises.

These shifting markets may, however, create protectionist attitudes by countries who may not wish to have foreign corporations drain business away from local industry. So Takenaka must learn to assimilate with and join local communities, local cultures, and local business enterprises when embarking on construction projects outside of Japan. By using the medium of joint venture and bringing local designers, contractors, and suppliers into the construction picture Takenaka will be viewed as a partner, not an interloper.

With just a few words, Mr. Toichi Takenaka has pragmatically plotted the future course of his corporation. But Takenaka is not without its dreams or concept schemes.

Super Cargo

Truck and car traffic in and around Japan's major cities is a nightmare, and traffic jams are almost ongoing. Once out of the city, traffic seems to flow rapidly, but hours can be lost before the almost open road comes into sight. Trains are the preferred means of transportation from one city to the next, and the *shinkanses,* for super-express bullet trains, whisk passengers away in comfort at speeds approaching 150 miles an hour.

Takenaka is looking to apply that same approach to the movement of freight, and it has proposed the "super-cargo" concept. Takenaka envisions a super-fast train operating on the principle of magnetic levitation, traveling through a fairly narrow tube-tunnel 8 to 10 feet in diameter. The proposed route of this first train would be between Osaka and Tokyo. Takenaka has put together a consortium that includes Sumitomo Metal, a company with considerable experience in constructing high-speed trains.

Sky City 1000

Not to be outdone by its competitors, Takenaka has developed a scheme for a super-high-rise building of Brobdingnagian proportions called Sky City 1000 (Fig. 3.19). This concept was created by a research group designated Group V1000, a committee comprised of Takenaka personnel and designers from ESCO Co., Ltd.

The structural design of Sky City uses 14 vertebrae, cup-like sections, each smaller than the next, until the entire 3280-foot height of the building has been realized. Where each section joins together, the space between the smaller upper section and the somewhat large-diameter lower section creates an atrium, permitting sunlight to enter into the lower pod.

(a)

Figure 3.19   Sky City 1000. (a) outside view.

(b)

(c)

Figure 3.19 (*Continued*) (*b*) base floor, with tennis courts, walks and greenery, and train station, (*c*) vertebralike structural sections of Sky City.

The lower diameter of Sky City at the top is 524 feet, while at its base it measures 1312 feet, and the entire floor area of the building amounts to 1797 acres (75 million square feet). The structure is designed to accommodate 35,000 residents and to provide office space for 100,000 people. According to Takenaka, the conical shell structure design not only permits sunlight to enter at each level, but by utilizing dynamic motion reduction systems, it can withstand an earthquake of magnitude eight, or the wind force of a typhoon.

Each of the 14 levels of Sky City is to have its own power-generating system and its own independent heating and cooling system, thereby permitting one section to be finished and occupied before the next one is totally complete. Monorails will provide transportation from the below-ground parking area to each section above, and three-storied elevators will connect each pod to the next one. The total cost of building Sky City 1000 is estimated at $35.4 billion.

In 1991 Takenaka took another look at the Sky City 1000 scheme created in 1989, and with a view toward earth-warming prevention, made some design changes incorporating various energy conservation measures; it built in more "green" areas to absorb carbon dioxide and reduce something known as heat-island phenomena. The result of this review created a new concept, renamed Eco-City, which is slightly taller, at 3756 feet, and has a total floor area of 62-million square feet.

In the summer of 1990, a research and development exercise was announced by the Engineering Advancement Association of Japan. The purpose of the research project was to develop various schemes to utilize urban space more effectively, and the idea of a vertical city was one approach. Contractors and representatives from heavy industry and the electronics field were all asked to participate in this research program, and Takenaka refined its previous designs to create the Tokyo Ecopolis: City 1000, a 3280-foot-tall building with a floor area of 72 million square feet. This is the scheme that was presented at the International Association of Architects, Ecopolis City of the Future exhibit, in Rio de Janeiro in 1992.

THE DEVELOPMENT OF UNDERGROUND SPACE

Takenaka is investigating another solution to urban overcrowding; that is, underground construction. Most Big Six contractors have had a great deal of experience in shield tunneling and slurry-diaphragm-wall construction. They are familiar with a variety of subsurface conditions, and if they put all of their knowledge and experience to use, vast underground structures are certainly within the feasibility realm. Takenaka envisions a subterranean plan incorporating a normal city infrastructure such as streets, transportation, energy sources, water supplies, and waste disposal systems, which would support various city activities above and thereby alleviate much of the current above-ground congestion.

Takenaka has developed the geoblock network concept that brings into play much of the technology already under way that must be in place to support this underground kingdom:

1. *Takenaka basement wall process (TBW).* A method of constructing temporary sheathing or used for cut-off walls

2. *Takenaka aqua-reactive chemical soil stabilization system (TACSS).* A system to consolidate soils by the reaction of water to specified chemicals

3. *Underground water recharge system.* Reinserting pumped-up water back into the ground through recharging wells

4. *Push-rod extruded concrete lining system (PRES).* A system using a reinforced concrete tunnel segment behind a shield-tunnel machine to build both large and small-diameter structures

5. *Extremely durable concrete and Seabetter concrete.* A mixture of high-density concrete, generally used under water

6. *Pressure-type smoke exhaust systems.* For underground structures

7. *Energy-conserving air conditioning systems.* For underground space, utilizing a heat pump and heating tower

8. *Botanical and greening technologies.* To allow trees and plants to thrive in underground spaces

9. *Light-collecting systems.* Where condensed sunlight is introduced to below-ground space

THE QUEST FOR ROBOTICS AND AUTOMATION

A company with such a long and successful corporate life as Takenaka has had may be expected to rest on its past accomplishments—its considerable construction experience and renowned design ability—but not this firm; it has forged ahead in such fields as construction robotics and automated building systems. Takenaka has been developing the following types of robots for use in its construction activities:

- Jet-Scraper, an automatic exterior wall coating removal robot with super-high-pressure water jets than can remove many types of exterior-wall coatings. It travels up and down the walls, eliminating expensive scaffolding and hazardous work conditions.

- Automatic exterior wall coating robots that can spray a wide variety of viscous paints on surfaces cleaned by other robots.

- A wall-climbing robot that can detect deteriorated or missing mortar joints in exterior-tile-clad wall sections.
- Screed Robo and Surf Robo (Fig. 3.20), highly mobile automated concrete-screeding and floor-slab-finishing robots.
- A horizontal and vertical concrete-distributing robot (Fig. 3.21).
- An automatic job-site reinforcing bar assembly robot to fabricate long sections of large-diameter steel-reinforcing bar, welding small channel irons at various points perpendicular to the bars to create a stable assembly that can be picked up and placed by crane.
- And, lastly, a series of automatic material-transporter robots: one that can unload, and others that can distribute materials horizontally and vertically.

These robots will prove invaluable as Takenaka continues to develop its building automation system.

THE ROOF PUSH-UP CONSTRUCTION METHOD

Takenaka was faced with what seemed like a considerable challenge when its client Mitsui Real Estate told Takenaka of its plans to build a 12-story building in Nagoya. There was an existing microwave line running 5 feet above the roof level of the proposed new building, and the use of a tower crane would interfere with this line. In the close quarters surrounding the site, it would be impossible to use a mobile crane on wheels or tracks. Furthermore, Mitsui said that the project would not be viable if they couldn't build the full structure of 85,443 square feet, so the height of the building could not be changed.

To solve this problem, Takenaka suggested using its newly developed roof push-up construction method—one of the first steps in an evolutionary process that would yield a fully automatic construction cycle. (See Fig. 3.22 for schematic cut-away of the system.) The roof push-up construction method involves building the top floor of a structure at grade level and pushing it upward as other lower floors are subsequently constructed. The sequence of operations for this newly developed process is as follows and is illustrated in Fig. 3.22*b*.

1. Pour the foundations for the high rise and install the first level of columns from below grade to grade.
2. Extend the next level of columns above grade, construct the roof deck, and prepare to lift it upward on the first row of columns extending above grade.

(a)

(b)

Figure 3.20 (*a*) Screed Robo and (*b*) Surf Robo.

Figure 3.21 Horizontal and vertical concrete-distribution robot.

3. Push up the next level of columns, attach them to the ones below, install beams, and assemble the circle cranes that will be used to pull subsequent columns up into place and install the temporary exterior wall supports. Weld columns and beams in place.

4. Push up the roof floor, install the temporary supports, and begin to construct the next floor-level below.

5. Push up the movable posts, install columns and beams, and continue until the entire structure has been raised.

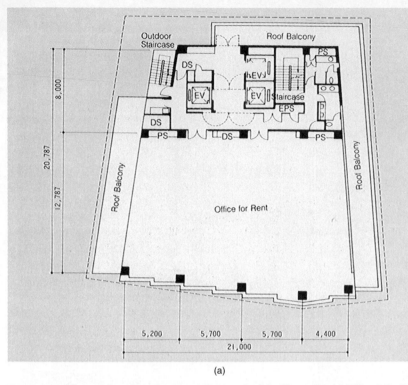

(a)

Figure 3.22 The roof push-up construction method in Yanagibashi Mitsui Building. (*a*) plan of the ninth floor.

6. Disassemble the lifting jacks and circle cranes.

The entire sequence is a complex, tightly controlled process and certainly more complicated than these line drawings suggest, but Takenaka sees much merit in the further development of this system. Buildings can be erected in restricted areas that would preclude the economical use of a crane; adverse weather conditions can be overcome by total enclosing each floor before it is lifted in place; and working at grade levels is much more efficient and much safer than working on elevated floors. As with its other Big Six competitors, the race to introduce a cost-effective fully automated construction cycle puts this roof push-up construction method in the company's priority column.

Takenaka intends to bring all of its design and construction and research experience to bear on these new concepts. This "design firm with construction capability," with its deep roots in the past and a strong vision of what the future holds, will provide this world with some interesting sights in the next century.

(b)

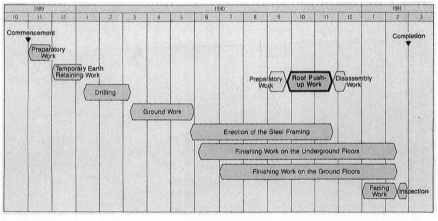

(c)

Figure 3.22 (*Continued*) (*b*) a schematic of the roof push-up system; (*c*) overall work process chart.

4

Obayashi Corporation

Renaissance for the
Twenty-First Century

Yoshigoro Obayashi founded his company in Osaka on January 25, 1882, and the modernization fever that was sweeping the country at that time provided a great deal of work for this young man who displayed superb management qualities along with his knowledge and expertise in construction matters.

With the advent of the Meiji era, Osaka, already an established center of commerce, looked forward to an increase in its industrial base as Japan began to think in international terms. Anxious to gain the respect of the Western world, Japan needed a system of currency, and Osaka was chosen as the location for the country's first mint. In 1870 the Osaka Mint, designed by the Western architect Thomas Waters, opened its doors and, to reinforce its status as a Western-type institution, forbade employees to wear the traditional topknots of the samurai class, and made the wearing of Western-style clothes a condition of employment. The Mint also gained notoriety by being the first establishment in Japan to employ the double-entry system of bookkeeping.

The founding of the Osaka Mint, the formation of the Osaka Spinning Company, and the construction of three government-operated factories a few years later helped the city regain much of its industrial base that had previously gravitated to the capital city of Tokyo.

The shallow water surrounding the port of Osaka severely limited the number and types of ships that could enter the harbor, and deephulled foreign vessels, in particular, had to anchor off Tempozan Hill where barges would shuttle their cargoes to the Osaka wharves. This inconvenience led to many ships being rerouted to Kobe, a fully accessible, deep-water port. In 1892 the city of Osaka, recognizing the need to provide deep-water harbor facilities, accumulated enough funds to engage the Dutch engineer Johannes de Reike to begin work on a com-

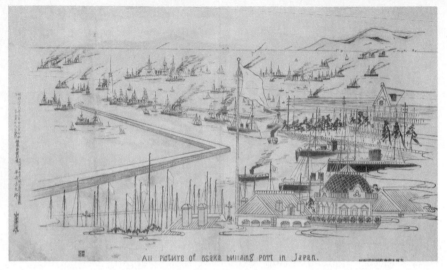

Figure 4.1   Artist's rendering of Osaka Harbor in the late nineteenth century.

prehensive port-reconstruction plan. With the outbreak of the Sino-Japanese War in 1894, the port city of Osaka took on added importance. Figure 4.1 is a nineteenth-century drawing depicting the scene around the harbor, and Fig. 4.2 is an early photograph of the harbor after it had been dredged to allow deep-draft vessels to dock.

Figure 4.2   An early photograph of Osaka Harbor opened to steamship traffic.

By 1889 Mr. Obayashi was able to obtain several major contracts for dredging Osaka Harbor and related construction work. The complete harbor project lasted eight years and became one of the largest construction projects during the Meiji era and, literally and figuratively, put Obayashi on the map. A few years later in 1903, the Japanese government announced a plan to hold the Fifth National Industrial Exposition in Osaka, and 13 countries were invited to Japan to participate in the event. The exposition would require a significant number of buildings to house the 276,000 exhibits, and Obayashi, having gained a reputation for rapid and high-quality work on the many harbor projects, was awarded most of the work.

Obayashi worked on the site for 15 months, and the 5.3-million visitors to the exposition gawked at steam cars, cameras, typewriters, and refrigerators, and sampled an entirely new food—ice cream. The Russo-Japanese War of 1904 provided more construction opportunities for Obayashi, and the company opened a branch office in Tokyo and changed the company name to Obayashi Gumi.

Just seven years later, in 1911, Obayashi secured two more contracts that would dramatically increase the company's visibility. First, it was selected to construct a major portion of the Tokyo Station building. This project was a Renaissance-style red brick structure (Fig. 4.3), designed by the then-distinguished architect Dr. Kingo Tatsumo. With four floor-levels encompassing a total floor area of 112,915 square feet, the Tokyo Station was the largest steel-frame building in the country at that time. With the rapid increase in railway construction in Japan during this time, Obayashi, like several other budding construction

Figure 4.3   The Renaissance-style Tokyo Railway Station as it looked in 1914.

firms, gained tunnel and bridge work, and the second major contract awarded the company was for the Ikoma Tunnel project for the Osaka Electric Railway Company.

Tragedy struck in 1914 while the company was working on the Osaka-Nara tunnel project, and a cave-in trapped men inside, resulting in the loss of 20 lives. The company's fortunes, however, took a turn for the better when, upon the death of the Emperor Meiji, Obayashi was selected to build the Momoyama mausoleum for the emperor in Fushimi on the island of Kyoto.

A NEW GENERATION ENTERS THE BUSINESS

In January 1916, Yoshigoro died, and his son Yoshio, just 22 at the time, was thrust into the leadership of the company, only to find that he would have to sell off substantial portions of the family assets to cover the existing loans his father had received from the Kitahama Bank. The company was on the verge of bankruptcy, but senior managers within the company, with the help of a few influential local business leaders, kept Obayashi afloat just in time to benefit from the fortunes of World War I, when the country's industrial and military institutions expanded to meet the demands of this conflict.

Obayashi was incorporated in 1918, and as Japan became more and more exposed to foreign trade, its economy blossomed, as did the company's construction business.

The Great Kanto Earthquake on September 1, 1923, in its wake left 140,000 dead, and mass destruction, particularly in the Tokyo-Yokohama area where it was estimated that at least one-third of Tokyo had been decimated and the entire city of Yokohama almost destroyed (see Fig. 4.4). Rebuilding these two cities provided much-needed work for the company, and the fact that the Tokyo Station building, along with three other of the company's buildings in the Tokyo-Yokohama area, survived this devastating earthquake added to Obayashi's growing reputation as a quality builder.

THE TAISHO PERIOD

The ensuing Taisho period that extended from 1912 to 1926, when Hirohito's father reigned, was a time when economic prosperity spurred the construction of Western-style office buildings in many cities throughout Japan. The U.S. firm, Fluor Brothers Construction Company of Oshkosh, Wisconsin, had been invited to Japan in 1918 to build three high-rise buildings, one of which was the seven-story Marunouchi Building in Tokyo. Obayashi was impressed by Fluor's

Figure 4.4 Aftermath of the great Kanto earthquake in Tokyo in 1923.

American-style construction and mechanization techniques, and prevailed upon that contractor to allow Obayashi to send two Japanese engineers to the United States for an 18-month training program. This may well have been the first instance of U.S. construction technology transferred to a Japanese contractor.

The present-day Fluor Corporation of Irvine, California, had its genesis in the Fluor Brothers Construction Company of Oshkosh. John Simon Fluor emigrated to the United States in 1888, and when his brothers Ralph and Casper joined him in Wisconsin two years later in 1890, they founded the company that bore their name. But Si, as he was known, left for California in 1912 to set up shop in Orange County, California, and create what was to become one of the largest construction companies in the Unites States—the Fluor Corporation.

It is strangely coincidental that the two fledgling builders—Fluor Brothers and Obayashi Gumi—should pick up their business relationship 70 years later when on January 12, 1988, Fluor Daniel, a division of the Fluor Corporation, announced a cooperative agreement with the Obayashi Corporation. Daniel Tappan, Jr., the CEO of Fluor Corporation, said, "Although we have had a major procurement office in Japan for 20 years, this agreement is an important first step in establishing an engineering and construction presence. Fluor Daniel has worked successfully with Obayashi in the United States, and we have been very impressed with its integrity, reliability, and qualifications. Our firms are highly complementary."

The Japanese divide periods of time in accordance with the reign of their emperors. The Meiji era extended from 1868 to the Emperor's death in 1912 and was followed by the Taisho era. Hirohito's ascendance to the throne, which occurred in 1926, made him the most visible Japanese ruler, and ushered in the Showa era. Since Hirohito's death on January 7, 1989, his son Akihito presides over what is now known as the Heisei era.

THE SHOWA ERA

Emperor Hirohito came to the throne at the time of the Great Depression and a time of financial panic in Japan, but because of Obayashi's work on the Meiji mausoleum, the company received a series of contracts from the Imperial household that helped to keep the company afloat in those perilous times.

Obayashi, like other major construction companies in the country during Japan's expansionist era in the 1930s, participated in the construction of war factories in Korea, Northern China, and Taiwan, along with similar projects within Japan itself. By the early 1940s Obayashi led all other Japanese construction companies in annual sales volume.

In October 1943, Yoshio Obayashi died and the company found itself without a president, because his son had become a member of the armed forces during this time of war. The end of World War II found Obayashi in precarious financial shape, and even though it received several contracts from the Occupation Government, the company did not begin to prosper again until the outbreak of the Korean War, when the entire Japanese construction industry was being primed by U.S.-funded military-related construction projects.

The huge amount of electric power required to run the plants and equipment demanded by the Korean War caused the government to create the Electric Power Development Company, empowered to spend 850 billion yen ($6.5 billion in terms of today's yen-dollar conversion rate, but difficult to equate to real dollars in the 1950s due to the fluctuation in exchange rates over the years), and Obayashi won an award for the construction of the Nukabira Dam, along with several other commissions as the Korean War escalated.

The company's first postwar overseas project was the construction of the Japanese Pavilion at the 1950 International Industrial Exposition in Pakistan.

The Japanese government War Reparations Program also provided work for several Big Six contractors in Southeast Asia. Obayashi was awarded a contract for the Musi Bridge project in Palembang, Indonesia, in 1962 and one year later found work building a department store in Jakarta and an agricultural center, stock farm, and rural medical center in Cambodia as part of this government program.

Toward the end of the 1950s, when the Japanese economy began to pick up steam on its own, Obayashi went public and listed its stock on the Osaka exchange. At the announcement of the 1964 Olympic Games and the Japanese government's commitment to spend one trillion yen on the facilities needed for this event, including infrastructure and the extension of bullet train routes, Obayashi's fortunes took another turn upward.

OBAYASHI TODAY

In 1990, Yoshiro Obayashi clearly stated his company's goals and responsibilities as it entered the twenty-first century:

> A company should be sociologically and philosophically in tune. But only a strong vital company can afford to be ideological. This we hope to accomplish with our new corporate program, which is aimed at creating a new Obayashi identity. We hope it will be a guidepost to our more than 11,000 company employees.
>
> Our objectives are to be an earth-friendly company, to be one that puts people first, and to be one that is able to create new senses of value. If we can achieve these goals, Obayashi Corporation will know no bounds.
>
> The twentieth century has seen amazing scientific progress. On the other hand, world ecology has been assaulted as never before.
>
> Our responsibility, as we move into the twenty-first century, is to find the proper balance with nature and to protect the ecology of earth. That is mandatory if we are to live peacefully and prosperously on this planet.
>
> We intend to fulfill our responsibilities by becoming a multinational company in every sense of the word. We will put our best people to work finding ecologically balanced solutions to environmental problems. And we will do our best to prepare a firm foundation for our second century.

As the company prepared for its 100th anniversary in 1992, a corporate restructuring took place to better position this $14 billion giant for the challenges it will face in the next 100 years.

RENAISSANCE 111

The company has launched Renaissance 111 and embarked on a program to project a new image. It officially dropped the "H" from the company name and "Ohbayashi" is no longer in vogue even though it is the correct spelling of the founder's name. Without the "H" corporate executives felt that the name rolled off the tongue better and faster (no stopping along the way with the "oh" sound).

A new corporate logo was developed to protect Obayashi's hope to "achieve harmony between human and earth"; the bright-green corporate color is meant to convey the lush vegetation of the earth, and the morning blue in the logo is to represent the dawn's blue sky, freshness, vigor, and stability. Even the company's uniforms have changed. They have been redesigned by Kensho Abe, a respected Japanese fashion designer, and their orange and mustard colors will be coordinated with the company's hard hats, safety belts, and safety shoes.

Renaissance 111 pledges that Obayashi will:

- Refine its creativity and perceptions, then call on the accumulated technology and wisdom of the company to add new value to the concept of space
- Expand its individuality, yet respect human frailties
- Stay in harmony with nature, blend in with local societies, and put its heart into creating a more vibrant, richer culture

Major emphasis is being placed upon increasing the company's marketing activities and striving to become one of the Big Three constructors in Japan. At present, Obayashi maintains its headquarters in the Chiyoda Ward of Tokyo and has a main office in Osaka where the company had its beginnings. As of 1991, the company counted 11,899 employees on its payroll in the following categories:

Architects	1311
Construction engineers	2899
Civil engineers	2110
Researchers/technicians	161
Computer systems engineers	140
Technicians in all other categories	1330
Administrative support staff	3948

It is well to note that fully 54 percent of all Obayashi employees are engineers, and that there is a ratio of one support member to every two engineers.

Within Japan, Obayashi maintains 12 branch offices and owns 24 subsidiary companies engaged in such diverse fields as the manufacture of furniture and golf-club resort management, and includes businesses involved in the following activities:

- Regional, urban, oceanic, and environmental development
- Engineering management and consulting services and services related to the above ventures
- Residential construction

- Sale, purchase, exchange, lease brokerage, ownership, real estate maintenance
- Manufacture and supply, sale and lease of construction machinery and equipment
- Manufacture and sale of concrete products, fireproof and non-flammable building materials
- Sale of construction materials for both interior and exterior use
- Furniture manufacture
- Maintenance and care of buildings, including security and guard services
- Acquisition, development, and licensing of software for industrial properties
- Information-processing services; sale, lease, and maintenance of office machinery and equipment, including computers
- Management of health, medical, athletic, and leisure-time facilities, hotels, restaurants, and travel agencies
- Operation of insurance agencies relating to automobile and non-life-insurance policies
- Landscaping, gardening, and horticultural services
- Loans, guarantees, and other financial services

OBAYASHI'S CORPORATE STRUCTURE

The company's headquarters are in Tokyo and it has a main office in Osaka. There are 16 branch offices throughout Japan, and Obayashi and its overseas branches span the globe with offices in Bangkok, Singapore, Jakarta, Beijing, Amsterdam, Sydney, Berlin, and the United States. The company's subsidiaries provide it with access to even greater market areas:

Thai Obayashi Corporation, Limited. Established in 1960, this local subsidiary now ranks among the top three general contractors in Thailand.

P.T. Jaya Obayashi. Founded in 1970 in Jakarta, Indonesia, this subsidiary has been instrumental in the development of several industrial parks in that country.

Obayashi America. Commencing its third decade in the United States, OAC has been very active in U.S. construction.

James E. Roberts–Obayashi Corporation. A West Coast joint-venture company now in its second decade.

Citadel Corporation. An American-staffed-and-managed subsidiary engaged in commercial and industrial construction, located near Atlanta, Georgia.

Obayashi Hawaii Corporation. Active in Hawaii since 1967, this real estate, residential, and resort development firm was formed in 1972.

Obayashi Europe B.V. Projects include the landmark Bracken House in London and the Urban Cely Golf Club in France.

Obayashi Properties (U.K.), Ltd. A development company founded in July 1987 and based in London.

E.W. Howell Co., Inc., Port Washington, New York. A recent (1989) purchase from the Norwegian conglomerate Selmer-Sande A/S (for a reported $7 million).

Obayashi Finance International (Netherlands) B.V. A corporation engaged in funding, financing, and bonding, along with development, real estate rental, and property maintenance.

Obayashi Taiwan Corporation. A building and civil engineering construction company formed in 1990.

Obayashi Philippines Corporation. A joint venture with a local Philippine company, D.M. Consunji, Inc., formed to serve the construction needs of Japanese companies locating in the Philippines.

Obayashi Singapore PTE, Inc. Recognizing the potential of this dynamic island nation, Obayashi set up a construction company subsidiary in Singapore in January 1991.

OBAYASHI FINANCIAL STATISTICS

During the period from 1987 through fiscal 1991, the Corporation achieved some rather impressive gains in orders received and profits attending this increased sales volume. The numbers below, except those converted to $U.S., represent billion yen.

	1987	1988	1989	1990	1991
Orders received	841.0	994.0	1194.0	1544.0	1990.0 ($14.22 billion)
Revenues	849.0	830.0	949.0	1159.0	1349.0 ($9.6 billion)
Gross profit	84.0	87.0	100.0	127.0	160.0 ($1.5 billion)
Net income	6.1	9.1	10.8	22.4	27.7 ($198.0 million)
Shareholder equity	157.0	166.0	187.0	227.0	251.0

These figures become more impressive when expressed as percent of growth over this five-year period:

	Percent of increase
Orders received	136%
Revenues	59%
Gross profit	90%
Net income	354%
Shareholder equity	60%

THE OBAYASHI CORPORATE ENVIRONMENT

The concept of lifetime employment is practiced at Obayashi, where newly recruited engineers join the company with the desire to remain there for the rest of their professional career. The company, in turn, assumes the responsibility for training these new recruits over the years to broaden their knowledge of the company, of business matters in general, and specifically in construction expertise. Each year, usually in April, applications for employment are reviewed and candidates chosen to join the company. This yearly hiring cycle is known throughout Japan as the "Spring Offensive."

The New Recruits

These new employees will form the same kind of "class" distinction as college freshmen and will come to refer to themselves in future years as the "Class of 1994," or whatever the year of their recruitment. Unmarried males will be required to live together in a company dormitory during their orientation period, and the sense of belonging to a specific group within the company will be enhanced by this period of time in which they get to know each other in the close quarters of their dormitory. They may even be taught the company song:

Let's make a rainbow bridge in the sky

If we build full of hope, songs of construction will echo

They will echo to tomorrow's sky

Obayashi Gumi is constructing the world

Let's sculpt dreams on Earth

New things will be created

The road starts from here and leads to a sparkling dawn

Obayashi Gumi is developing for the world

Training and Education at Obayashi

New employees are often placed on construction sites for a period of one to two years, where they will function as clerks, assistant field engineers, or assistants to the on-site project manager. After being with the company for three or four years, all employees, including the professional and administrative staff, will be given a short course lasting three or four days in which they will be taught to sharpen their communication skills. This will be the first of many in-house training sessions to increase the employees' general business education. At other points during the new recruits' career, more specialized programs will be made available to them. Small groups of 12 or less will be formed to discuss problems relating to inter-peer relationships and working with the older workers in the company. Employees may be shifted from one department to another so that they gain some knowledge of the workings of these various departments and develop a more global view of the Corporation.

Promotions-Salaries-Bonuses

As in the case in most large Japanese corporations, with few exceptions, promotions in Obayashi are based upon years of service—seniority. Although this concept is slowly changing, and many employees see the advantage of merit promotions, there is no general discontent with the seniority system. As one Obayashi engineer in mid-career stated, "We don't really mind waiting 10 years or so to become a section head, or waiting 20 years to become a manager. That's the way things are in Japan. The strength of our company lies within the cooperation that exists between all our people."

Salaries for most construction professionals at Obayashi are not too different from those in large American construction companies. However, this parity comes not so much from the amount of monthly salary as from the twice-yearly bonuses distributed in July and December. Salaries and bonuses will range from $40,000 for entry-level engineers to $90,000 for experienced project managers, but the much higher living costs in and around Japan's major cities sharply reduces spendable income.

The Company's Fringe-Benefit Package

The average cost of a condominium in the metropolitan Tokyo market in mid-1992 was $459,300, down 3.2% from the previous year; and with residential land selling for as much as $6 million for a quarter-acre lot, owning a home in the city is out of the question for anyone other than a millionaire. In addition, rentals in and around Tokyo are not at all reasonably priced for the average worker. A glance through the real estate section of the Japan *Times* in May 1992 revealed the following listings:

SENDAGAYA—cozy 3-bedrooms, stylish living room, and dining room—$6150 per month

SHIBUYA—BARGAIN—140 square meters (1506 square feet), 3 bedrooms, good sized living room—$4600 per month

OMOTESANDO—Super deluxe—4 bedrooms, maid's room, sauna, gym, swimming pool—$11,538 per month

Obayashi provides a housing allowance for its employees who must travel far outside the city limits to find affordable housing. The company's allowance takes the form of a 50 to 60 percent reimbursement of the cost of a rental apartment, with a cap on that amount which increases with the employees' seniority. A recent recruit may receive an allowance of $200 a month, permitting him to rent a $400 per month apartment, while a senior employee may be given $400 a month. The cap varies as the cost of apartment rentals vary around the country. In Tokyo, for instance, Obayashi places a limit of 65,000 yen on the amount it will pay. This is roughly equivalent to $500.

The company also reimburses employees for their train commuting fare, including the fare for *shinkansen*—bullet-train commutation expenses. When an employee is posted to a job beyond commuting distance from his home, the company reimburses his expenses on traveling home twice a month.

In Japan a national law dictates that the company is to pay a certain portion of the employee's health insurance premium and contribute to the national unemployment insurance program and the national pension plan. Obayashi has instituted a system which provides "a close examination of the stomach" and a complete medical checkup at low cost to any employee desiring such a service. The employees can also avail themselves, at low cost, of the company's health resorts spread out throughout the country.

Loans and savings inducements.   Just about everyone has heard of the Japanese penchant for savings. The national savings rate in Japan is approximately 28.2 percent of the country's gross domestic product, in sharp contrast to the 13.8-percent rate in the United States. Although these figures are somewhat misleading because they don't account for the forced savings aspect of home mortgage payments in the United States, an opportunity denied most working Japanese because of the exorbitant cost of home ownership, the Japanese do tend to bank a significant portion of their weekly salary. At Obayashi, to further encourage employee savings, the company offers slightly higher interest rates on savings and, conversely, offers employees lower-than-standard interest rates on loans. There is a stock purchase plan available, to which Obayashi contributes a portion of the purchase price.

Vacations.   Until last year Obayashi, like most Japanese construction companies, considered Saturday a normal work day, but now that policy has been changed and offices remain closed on Saturdays; this affords most employees, in effect, extra vacation days. But no matter what the vacation policy is, whether two or four weeks, company employees are reluctant to take that much time away from work. One Obayashi engineer said he would feel guilty taking a one-week vacation because it would place a burden on the other members in his department. He also said that from a higher management point of view, a long vacation might signal lack of interest in the company and create a black mark in his personnel file that would affect future promotion possibilities. Another engineer with eight years seniority said that he had taken a two-week vacation this year, but only because he got married and went on his honeymoon. He said he had been working very hard and was glad that the next day was a holiday. He was referring to Saturday.

The company owns several vacation resorts and will subsidize an employee's stay there. A family of four has to pay only for its meals; the company pays for the accommodations. The company also maintains arrangements with other hotels and resorts that offer Obayashi employees discounts.

OBAYASHI'S PRESENCE IN THE UNITED STATES

In 1966 Obayashi opened an office in Honolulu, Hawaii, and began construction on the Surfrider Hotel in Waikiki. Three years later the project was completed, and in 1970 the company finished construction on the Princess Kaiulani Hotel on the Big Island. Obayashi had been invited to Hawaii by its long-term Japanese clients to build these hotels, and being unfamiliar with U.S. practices, assumed the role of construction manager, utilizing American general contractors for the actual construction. A wholly owned Obayashi subsidiary, Obayashi Hawaii Corporation, with offices in the Pacific Tower in Honolulu, handles that company's real estate development company and has been actively involved in development throughout the Islands since 1972.

In 1972 Obayashi established its first continental U.S. office when the Obayashi America Corporation (OAC) went into business in Los Angeles. At that time the company formed the 2975 Wilshire Company, an office-rental management organization, and purchased James E. Robert, Inc., a condominium and apartment development company operating in northern California. In the years that followed, Obayashi worked mainly for Japanese clients, but in 1974 it set up a joint-venture agreement with the Tokyu Corporation to build a housing development in the Pacific Northwest. The ensuing Mill Creek complex near Seattle, Washington, became an award-winning project for the company, which took great pains to preserve the natural environment over substantial portions of this 11,000-acre site. Ultimately 3200 residential units were built in Mill Creek, along with a golf course and a shopping center.

The year 1979 saw Obayashi involved with its first public works project when it joint-ventured with a local company on the West Coast to successfully bid on a sewage-tunnel job, using its considerable experience in soft-earth tunneling to underbid the other contractors. Subsequently, Obayashi set up a heavy construction division in San Francisco and went on to win a federally funded tunnel project in Utah.

When the U.S. Army Corp of Engineers awarded the Elk Creek dam project to Obayashi, it brought the company notoriety in two ways. Using its expertise in roller-compacted concrete, an engineer from the Obayashi home office in Japan designed a conveyorized concrete plant to place more than 1.1 million yards of concrete, and in the process set a new record for concrete placement; it placed 12,392 cubic yards of ready-mix in two 10-hour shifts. Obayashi's involvement in this federally funded project came to the attention of Senator Frank Murkowski of Alaska and Representative Jack Brooks of Texas. The Brooks-Murkowski Amendment was just being passed in Congress, and one of its effects was to virtually stop Japanese contractors from bidding on federally funded projects, inasmuch as the bill gave the U.S. trade representative in 1987 the power to deny the Japanese access to U.S. public works projects until such time as Japan opened its market to American businesses.

Obayashi, in the meantime, opened offices in New York and had formed the Citadel Corporation in Atlanta, an open-shop general construction company established from the ground up, owned by a Japanese firm but staffed and run by Americans. Citadel completed its first factory project in 1987, a 110,000-square-foot plant for Enshu Light Alloy of Columbus, Indiana.

The largest project attempted by Obayashi in the United States at that time was the huge $1 billion Toyota automobile manufacturing plant in Kentucky. Acting as a construction manager, Obayashi hired five general contractors to perform most of the work. Imagine the surprise of one of these good ole boys, when executives from Obayashi reviewed their bid proposal and commented that their profit percentages were too low and should be increased!

Obayashi's U.S. operations have been growing ever since. In 1989,

Obayashi bought E. W. Howell Co., Inc., a Long Island-based contractor, from its Norwegian owner. E. W. Howell, whose marketing area extends to the northern and midwestern states, gives Obayashi a union contractor presence in those areas and one with experience in health care and institutional-facilities-type projects.

Mr. Seiichi Yabe, general manager of the U.S. Eastern Region of Obayashi Corporation, headquartered in New York, when interviewed in January 1992 said he is looking forward to growth in the United States, particularly at a time when many American construction companies are having trouble obtaining bonds. Mr. Yabe sees his company's $700 million bonding limit as an asset that will create many opportunities to joint-venture with American firms.

With only 12 Japanese nationals working in his company, Mr. Yabe views the Eastern Region under his control as basically an "American" builder. He recognizes the fact that the long-term relationship the company has with many of its clients and subcontractors in Japan is clearly different from relationships in the U.S., where "one-shot" business dealings are the norm, and his division is prepared to accommodate itself to the American market requirements. Obayashi must be prepared to solicit work based upon the premise of "low" bidder being a prime requisite for obtaining a contract award and, according to Mr. Yabe, his company will continue to seek work either as a general contractor or as a construction manager. Obayashi will pursue design-build commissions as well.

Due to the myriad variations in building-code requirements in the geographic area in which the Eastern Region operates, Obayashi prefers to use outside design consultants when assembling a design-build proposal, and the company does not employ an in-house architectural/engineering design group for that purpose.

Mr. Yabe said that his company must operate like an American contractor not only when bidding, but also in staffing the project when construction begins. Projects in Japan tend to be staffed in more depth than those in the United States, where very low profit margins prevail and there is little hope of repeat business with a client so that a contractor could count on profits from continuing work from that client. Obayashi has a strong commitment to delivering a high-quality building no matter how slim the profit margins and, according to Mr. Yabe, he constantly has to guard against losing this "Japanesism" when working with clients whose sole criterion appears to be "low bid." He does feel that there is a definite trend away from that kind of thinking in this country and, looking over the 20 years he has spent in America, he is beginning to see more clients interested in initial quality and life-cycle costs, rather than low bid.

A FEW OBAYASHI PROJECTS

In Osaka

Obayashi, with its origins in Osaka, naturally has a great many friends in that area, and today Obayashi is involved in several major developments there. The 31-story Hyatt Regency Osaka Hotel is the keystone building in the Osaka World Trade Center Complex, which will include a convention center, the World Trade Center Building OSAKA, and the Asia and Pacific Trade Center. At this time Obayashi has a contract to build the 520-room in-city resort hotel with a total floor area of 822,689 square feet. Obayashi holds a 20 percent share in the Hyatt Regency Osaka, Inc.

This part of Osaka undergoing revitalization is called the Nanko District, and Obayashi recently completed the Mizuna Osaka headquarters building there. This 31-story, 491-000-square-foot structure is headquarters for this Japanese sportswear and sporting goods manufacturer. In 1986 the Osaka government decided to build high-rise apartments on an 11-acre plus site that once served as the Yodogawa freight yard. Obayashi teamed up with the Matsushita Real Estate Company and long-time client Kintetsu Real Estate Company, and formed the MKO Group. MKO entered the design competition, came up with the winning design, and was assigned the development of A Block, a five-city-block area where it was to build 1100 apartments in a project subsequently called Sakuranomiya River City (Fig. 4.5). The MKO Group broke ground in mid-1989, and the project reached completion in March 1992, turning a dilapidated railroad yard into a showplace. The centerpiece of A Block, or Sakuranomiya River City, is the Water Tower Plaza building, at 41-stories high and 446-feet tall; it is the highest reinforced concrete building in Japan. During the construction of this building, Obayashi used its extensive in-house CAD/CAM capability to detail and fabricate all of the reinforcing bars in this high-strength concrete structure. In the Hyogo Prefecture, Japanese architect Arata Endo, a disciple of Frank Lloyd Wright, had designed the Koshien Hotel in 1929, with Obayashi as the builder. When a total restoration of this historic building was being planned, Obayashi was called in once more, this time to perform a complete renovation job. This 4-story, 66,890-square-foot building (Fig. 4.6) now stands as resplendent as it was when it was first built.

Renowned British architect Sir Norman Foster, working with Obayashi designers, created Century Tower, a 21-story office building situated on a hill above the Imperial Palace in Tokyo (Fig. 4.7). The unusual, trapezoidal, exterior bracing at the curtain wall exposes two floors at a time (Fig. 4.8), a most interesting view for passersby. Sir

Figure 4.5 The Sakuranomiya River City project in Osaka.

Norman has also been commissioned by Obayashi to design the Millennium Tower (Fig. 4.9) as its contribution to Japan's current super-high-rise competition. In the northern Hokkaido Prefecture, Obayashi recently completed the Alpha Resort Tomanu—an eight-story, 183,000-square-foot mountain resort hotel. Obayashi collaborated on the design of one of the largest indoor-water-sports centers in the world, centered around a 262-foot by 98-foot artificial-wave pool (Fig. 4.10), various saunas and spas are included within the structure.

(a)

(b)

Figure 4.6 Completed restoration of the Koshien Hotel.

Figure 4.7 Sir Norman Foster's Century Tower in Tokyo.

Figure 4.8 Century Tower's trapezoidal wall bracing with unusual two-floor view between bracings.

The Tokyo Broadcasting System Building Project

Obayashi has recently begun the construction of the Tokyo Broadcasting System Housou Center in the Akasaka section of Tokyo. Work on the foundations began on May 21, 1991, and the entire project is scheduled for completion in April 1994. This is a joint-venture pro-

Figure 4.9 Sir Norman's Millenium Tower—a 150-story concept.

Figure 4.10 The VIZ-Spahouse Tomanu in the Hokkaido Prefecture. (top) swimming pool, (lower left) jet spa cottage, (lower right) sauna cottage.

ject, with Obayashi having the dominant position with a 65 percent share. Kajima has a 25 percent portion, and Taisei has the remaining 10 percent. Designed by Nihon Sekkei, Inc., the building has an eye-catching style. Figure 4.11 displays a cutaway view of the TBS project,

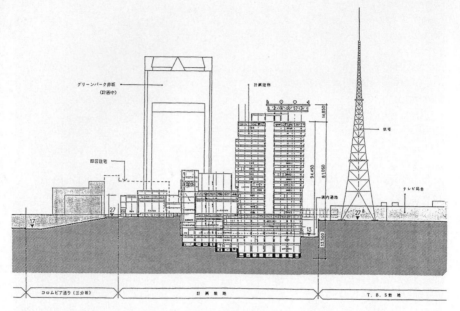

Figure 4.11   Cutaway section of the Tokyo Broadcasting System project.

with its underground structure and above-ground superstructure. The statistics surrounding the building are impressive:

Height: 20 stories, 1 penthouse, 2 underground levels, plus sub-basements, all add up to a height above grade of 313 feet and a total floor area of 1,131,220 square feet

Site area: 202,197 square feet

Structure: underground—steel and reinforced concrete; above ground—structural steel

Exterior walls: anodized aluminum curtain-wall and tile-clad precast-concrete panels

When completed, this building will have required 457,765 cubic yards of earth to have been moved, 1,397,500 square feet of concrete forms for the 111,172 cubic yards of poured concrete, and 7,000 tons of rebar. The structural steel framework weighs in at 33,000 tons.

THE FIELD STAFF

A walk through the Obayashi field office reveals the activity normally associated with Japanese contractors of this stature. Before entering the field office, one removes one's shoes and slips into a pair of sandals.

The interior of the field office is quiet, and the only sound that can be heard above the low-volume piped-in classical music is the click of a few computer keyboards and the soft padding sound of slippered feet on the carpeting. About six engineers in corporate coveralls can be seen working quietly at their desks, and off in the corner the general project manager can be observed talking to a few of his staff members.

This is but one level of a multi-tiered field-office complex for the general contractor and his joint-venture staff. Another similar three-story structure for the major on-site subcontractors adjoins these offices.

The staffing requirements for this project are quite extensive, as the organizational chart in Fig. 4.12 reveals. The general project manager has an assistant, designated as vice-general project manager, who oversees the activities of two construction managers: an as-built drawing manager and accounting manager, and a construction manager for mechanical and electrical work. There is another manager whose responsibilities encompass quantity surveying, subcontract agreements, and change orders. There are also second- and third-tier managers under the control and supervision of these first-line managers.

A walk through the subcontractor field-office complex begins with a visit to the mechanical contractor. There are two rows of drafting tables in the offices, manned by engineers who are creating piping, ductwork, and equipment-layout drawings. The scene in the electrical subcontractor's field office on the floor below is similar. The atmosphere is quiet; no radios blaring, not much conversation going on, and any that is at very low decibels. Everyone is working.

The next stop is to the ceiling subcontractor's field office, and here is where the relationship between Japanese designer and Japanese contractor hits home; the project designer establishes the design intent and depends upon the experienced general contractor to fill in the details and make the design work. One Big Six executive said that this practice can be traced back to a public law enacted during the Meiji Restoration, a law relating to the construction industry, which recognized only the contractor and client as parties to the construction process. During those days, the client furnished the contractor with all of the required equipment and materials for his project; the contractor was to supply only the labor to install this equipment and build the building. This public law stipulated that the contractor was to inspect all of the materials and equipment furnished by the client and, if they were defective, so notify the customer. But once accepted, the contractor would assume the responsibility for correcting any problems that might arise because the owner had supplied inadequate materials and/or equipment. Supposedly, this law provided the impetus for the contractors to develop their own in-house design capability in order to properly fulfill their client's requirements.

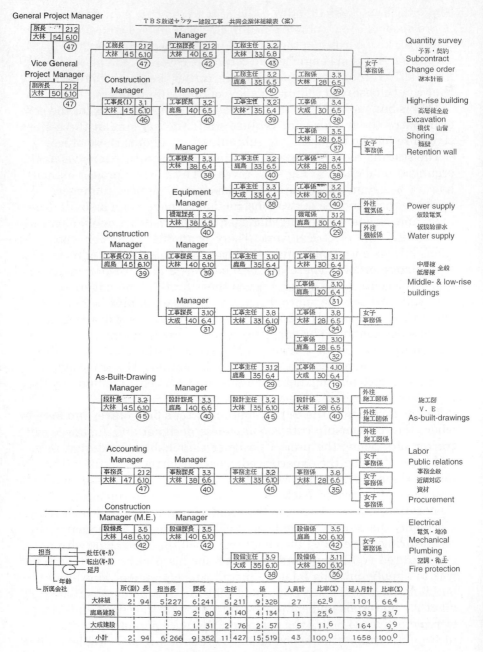

Figure 4.12 Staffing chart for the TBS project.

Looking over the shoulder of the ceiling contractor's draftsman, one can see the areas within the building to receive suspended ceilings. However, a reflected ceiling plan is not drawn; the architect leaves the grid pattern and the coordination of all lights and ceiling diffusers for the general contractor to handle. So the ceiling subcontractor is preparing shop drawings with the grid pattern, and indicating where cuts are to be made in the full ceiling tiles in order to make them fit the room's dimensional limitations.

THE PRESENTATION OFFICE

Mr. Shiraishi, the project manager, leads the way past the general contractor and subcontractor field-office area to another separate adjoining building. It is obvious that this office is used for designer and client meetings and for visiting firemen, because it is rather plush, with an expensive conference table around which a dozen or so comfortable upholstered chairs are placed. In one corner a model of the Tokyo Broadcasting System building sits on a presentation table bathed in the light of two overhead spots, and assorted project brochures are neatly stacked on another small table.

DIFFERENCES BETWEEN U.S. AND
JAPANESE CHANGE ORDERS

Mr. Toru Shiraishi, construction manager of the TBS Broadcast Center project joint venture office, is able to convey his thoughts and opinions very well, as he has an excellent command of English, acquired when he worked for several years with Citadel Construction, the U.S. Obayashi affiliate in Norcross, Georgia. When asked what differences he found between the American way of doing business and the Japanese way, he quickly points to the change-order process.

He zeroes in on subcontractors, stating that those in the United States are very quick to submit change-order requests as soon as a scope change is detected, and that in his opinion the cost of this extra work is rather high-priced. In Japan, agreements between general contractor and subcontractor generally include unit prices for most of the items in their scope of work, and these unit prices have been established by negotiation beforehand by the general contractor and subcontractors. When extras occur, these unit prices generally apply, but if an item of work is required for which no unit price has been established, the subcontractor and general contractor will sit down and negotiate a mutually acceptable price. Mr. Shiraishi said that in Japan a general contractor is hesitant to approach his client with a request for

additional monies when scope increases occur, but rather will dili-
gently attempt to find "trade-offs" to counter these extra costs.

But no matter how compensation is achieved, the inclusion of extra
work, or changes in the work, will not be allowed to change the original
completion date of the project. For example, Mr. Shiraishi talks about
the change in the curtain-wall that occurred two months ago. Shop
drawings for the anodized aluminum panels and the tile-clad precast
panels had been prepared, reviewed, approved, and returned to each of
these fabricators for quite some time, and both suppliers were preparing for production. The owner recently decided to change a significant
number of aluminum panels to tile-clad precast concrete, which also
meant a substantial change in the type and location of the clips required to secure these panels to the structural frame. Obayashi did not
broach the subject of an extension of project completion time, but will
take this change in stride, pricing out the difference in cost, with no
added premium time to maintain schedule. And if a particular subcontractor or several subcontractors find that they may have to work overtime to compensate for these design changes, they will do so, but won't
consider asking for compensation for that premium time.

QUALITY CONTROL AT OBAYASHI

Nothing illustrates Obayashi's commitment to quality control better
than the story of the flagpole. Several years ago, architect Cesar Pelli
was commissioned by the U.S. State Department to design a new building in the U.S. Embassy complex in Tokyo. The site selected was directly across the road from the Okura Hotel in the Toronamon section
of the city.

This new building was to have a facade with a great many rose-col-
ored reflective panes of glass, some in fixed lights, and some in operable windows. Most builders are aware of the slight distortions that
occur in the reflective qualities as these pieces of glass are manufactured and coated. Obayashi, cognizant of this fact, wanted to ensure
that the American flag raised on the flagpole in front of this new building would be reflected perfectly. When their glazing subcontractor appeared on the site with crates of glass, a crew, and a crane, Obayashi
stationed one of its engineers on the rooftop of the Okura across the
way. Equipped with a pair of binoculars and a walkie-talkie, he directed the selection of glass during installation. "That one's O.K. No,
no—take that one down; put up another. No, that's no good either, put
up another one. That's O.K.," and so on. The end result can be seen in
Figure 4.13. For those with a discerning eye, that slight waiver in the
middle light at the first and third floors was not caused by Obayashi,
but by someone who opened an operable sash a bit.

Figure 4.13   The U.S. flag as reflected in the glass hand-picked by Obayashi.

Of course, continuing with the "Japanese way," both general contractor and subcontractor are assured of being adequately compensated for their work at some point in their continuing relationship.

WHAT NICHE WILL OBAYASHI FILL IN ITS SECOND CENTURY?

The potential growth in Japan's domestic construction market, and in particular infrastructure work, if and when the government begins to release the billions of dollars verbally committed, should benefit Obayashi. In years past this company made a commitment to acquire the technology required to remain a leader in its field and to possess the equipment with which to implement this technology. As of 1992, Obayashi has the following construction equipment in inventory:

Tunnel-construction equipment	759 units
Road-building equipment	11 units
Specialized dam-construction equipment	65 units
Trucks, vans, and locomotives	1006
Excavators, backhoes, foundation-work equipment	1357
Cranes/cargo-handling equipment	853 pieces
Pumps, generators, etc.	15,797

The total book-value of all of this equipment is $100,284,610.

OWS-SOLENTANCHE

Obayashi has been using a subterranean-wall-construction technique known as OWS-Solentanche for the past 10 years. In mid-1992 they reported that they had installed more than 32 million square feet of foundation walls using this system. This record exceeds, by far, any such work put in place by other Japanese contractors, and comes close to being a world record.

The original technology for this diaphragm wall construction was developed in Europe in the 1950s, and involved injecting a soil-stabilizing slurry into a slit-like trench to build temporary retaining walls. This slurry-wall construction gained a great deal of popularity at that time. Obayashi saw this technology as a way to create below-grade reinforced concrete foundation walls in area-restricted urban projects with zero-lot-line tolerances.

In Japan, in the 1960s and 1970s, a spate of anti-noise and anti-vibration laws were enacted, and Obayashi marketed its *Obayashi wet screen* (OWS) system of wall foundation construction whereby armatures of reinforcing bars could be lowered into slit-like trenches, stabilized with the slurry mix, and then filled with ready-mix concrete. Noisy pile-driving and sheet-piling operations would no longer be needed in many cases.

Not only Obayashi, but many of its competitors were also offering this new foundation-wall construction technique, so the company needed a competitive edge. They found it after contacting Solentanche, a French excavation-machine manufacturer, and jointly they developed the Hydrofraise excavator, a machine that not only could dig more rapidly, but was capable of digging straighter and deeper than Obayashi had been able to before. Obayashi has consistently expanded the development of the OWS-Solentanche system, so that today they are able to construct underground foundation walls ranging from 6½- to 9½-feet wide and up to 328-feet deep.

Like other Big Six contractors, they too have their super-high-rise building concept, the Millenium Tower, designed by that noted British architect Sir Norman Foster. Millenium Tower, with its conical shape, will thrust its 150 stories 1968 feet into the air. Obayashi's supercomputer has already performed enough seismic and dynamic air-flow analyses to convince them that this concept could easily make the transition from drawing board to reality.

Obayashi possesses superb technology in nuclear-power-plant construction; Obayashi has worked at home and abroad with some of the world's most outstanding designers and it has a proven record of finding creative solutions to difficult problems.

Not all of Obayashi's research and new construction technologies have such lofty goals. It seeks the practical, too. On a construction project at its research center, it is using a unique concrete form to encase steel beams (Fig. 4.14). A three-sided form is made of aramid fiber-reinforced precast concrete, 25 millimeters thick (about 1 inch). When concrete encasement of columns takes place in an area where upon stripping the columns exposes them to public view, they may either be enclosed with gypsum drywall, or rubbed with a cementitious paste to achieve a smooth surface.

Obayashi asks the question, Why not create a form that if left in place will have a smoother outer surface that can be painted, and why not make that form out of a durable, fire-resistive material? Obayashi solved several problems with its new autoclaved form. Wrapped around a steel beam with reinforcing bars placed within the four corners of the "form," concrete is poured, and these smooth-surfaced forms, left in place, became the finished surface of the beams. Obayashi is carrying this concept one step further: With full, longitudinal and stirrup reinforcement, a structural cast-in-place concrete beam can be built using these forms, which will eliminate the need for stripping, form maintenance and replacement, and resurfacing. Production runs of the autoclaved, aramid forms may produce a very cost-effective end-product.

Figure 4.14   Obayashi's unique ALC concrete form.

In the words of Mr. Yoshiro Obayashi, chairman of the board, "Our vision has set the direction. Our management is aware of the company's priorities and has begun the time-consuming process of aligning every employee and every subsidiary company toward our goals. The next decade should see a renewal of the Obayashi Corporation—a renaissance."

Kumagai Gumi Company, Ltd.

Creating the Buildings and Infrastructure Society Requires

In November 1991 a group of Japanese construction professionals, in the United States on a fact-finding mission sponsored by the Ministry of Construction, commented to the writer that until recent years the term *the Big Six* was a misnomer—it should have been the Big Five, because Kumagai Gumi was not a member of the group. In Tokyo, one of Obayashi's managers said, "The Big Five mountain is very tall, and only when one begins to approach it will one realize how high it is."

In 1991 Kumagai Gumi employed 9135 people, of whom 3217 were architects, 3230 were engineers in various disciplines, and 2688 were administrative and support personnel. The company's sales for that year were $8.5 billion, and with a backlog of $14.5 billion and corporate assets amounting to $12.9 billion, Kumagai Gumi by then was a firmly entrenched member of the Big Six.

Apparently, for several years Kumagai Gumi had chosen to venture heavily into the international marketplace and not rely on domestic construction projects alone to fill its substantial annual sales-volume requirements. But when various world construction markets began to dry up, Kumagai Gumi again sought and obtained sufficient work in Japan to warrant its inclusion in the ranks of the country's top contractors—the Big Six.

The volume and complexity of the projects that this company pursued away from home were impressive: a 10.6 kilometer series of highways at the Jakarta Interchange in Indonesia; a rack-and-pinion railway in Australia; the Rogers Pass Tunnel in Canada—the longest such tunnel in North America; cultural centers in Hong Kong and Taiwan; and dams and power plants in Hong Kong and Sri Lanka.

Corporate president Taichiro Kumagai, in his annual report to the stockholders in June of 1991, stated that architectural construction accounted for the company's 9.2-percent increase in sales over those of the previous year; much of this growth came from the increased demand in Japan for condominiums and office buildings. The public sector in Japan also remained strong, and the Japanese government announced that it plans to inject more public funds into the domestic market for infrastructure work. Mr. Kumagai said that because the overseas market reflects the global real estate recession, the company did not view the United States market, nor those of the United Kingdom and Australia, as sources for major construction contract work in 1992. In February 1991 Kumagai Gumi issued bonds worth 50 billion yen ($384 million, using the conversion rate of 130 yen to the dollar) in Europe to support its operations in both Great Britain and Australia, because of the depressed real estate markets in those countries.

In the past few years the company has completed some interesting projects:

- *Agon-shu Head temple for the Agon Sect of Buddhism.*   Kumagai incorporated 1200-year-old Taiwanese white cedar into a modern, structural-steel framework. The roof contained 127,000 tiles, each carved with the wish of a member of the sect. The four main columns in the sanctuary were treated with 50 coats of lacquer. With its unusual blending of modern and traditional design, this probably is the last major temple to be built in this century.

- *The Tokyo Metropolitan Government office in Shinjuku ward, Tokyo (Fig. 5.1).*   Each of the Big Six contractors shared in the construction of this project, which consists of two towers joined to a seven-story assembly building at the center. The north tower is 48-stories high, as is the south tower. Designed by Kenzo Tange, this structure is now the tallest building. At a cost of $1.6 billion, no expense was spared to make this building Japan's showpiece.

- *The Asahi Beer Azumabashi building.*   Designed for one of Japan's largest brewers, this 22-story building is located on the Shimda River in Tokyo. The design is unique, and is said to portray a foam-capped mug of beer (Fig. 5.2).

- *The Bank of China building in Hong Kong, designed by I. M. Pei (Fig. 5.3).*   At the time of completion, this 70-story, $159 million, 1.39-million-square-foot intelligent office building was the tallest building in town, but when the new 85-story Central Plaza Building was completed in early 1993, the title passed to that one.

- *The Castle Peak A and B Thermal Power Stations in Hong Kong.* These are the largest coal and oil-fueled electricity-generating

(a)

Figure 5.1   The Tokyo Metropolitan Government office building. (a) the twin towers.

(b)

Figure 5.1   (*Continued*) (*b*) view from the lobby.

Figure 5.2   The Asahi Beer Azumabashi building (low building at center of photograph).

plants in Southeast Asia, producing 4350 megawatts of electricity and built at a cost of $502 million (Fig. 5.4). Kumagai Gumi also constructed units 3 and 4 of the Ohi nuclear power plant for the Kansai Electric Power Co. in Japan (Fig. 5.5).

- *New City Higashi-Totsuka in Japan (Fig. 5.6).* This residential project is built on a 43-acre site containing 3300 housing units. A stunning housing project for the elderly, Life-In-Kyoto (Fig. 5.7), is nestled in the mountain-side and contains 228 units, including an infirmary and recreational areas.

THE UNIQUENESS OF KUMAGAI GUMI

Unique in the way it was founded, this company is also unique in its approach to marketing its construction expertise, and even in the way it created its corporate logo, or *monshu*. This is a company that bears watching.

Founder Santoro Kumagai began his business career as a minor civil servant who worked for the police department in Tsuraga, a city in the Fukui Prefecture, in the northcentral section of Honshu Island, bordering on the Sea of Japan. Restless to learn more of the world, Santoro

Figure 5.3 I. M. Pei's Bank of China building in Hong Kong.

wanted very much to move to Yokohama, but was discouraged by his uncle who wisely told him, "That city will be much too sophisticated for a small-town boy like you. Stay here and make the best of things." And so he did.

Santoro turned to working with stone and became skilled in making religious monuments. When he was 29-years old, he ventured into construction work as a stonemason. The year was 1891. The expansion of the railway system in Japan, which had begun some 19 years before,

Figure 5.4 Hong Kong's Castle Peak thermal power station.

Figure 5.5 Japan's Ohi nuclear power plant complex.

Figure 5.6 New City Higashi-Totsuka 3300-unit housing development.

Figure 5.7 Life-In-Kyoto, an unusual housing project for the elderly.

was still proceeding at a rapid pace, and there was a fair amount of stone roadbed work to be done. Young Kumagai began to capture some of this railway roadbed work while continuing with his stonemasonry, and he obtained a contract to built a large stone wall for the Eihei Temple in the Fukui Prefecture.

Late in the Meiji Era, around 1905, the need for electric power grew in Japan, and with the abundance of fast-flowing rivers and streams, building hydroelectric power plants became a major construction activity. At about this time Santoro Kumagai met Bunkichi Tobishima, head of a growing construction company in Fukui, and Mr. Tobishima hired Kumagai to do some of the stonework for the new Kyoto Electric hydroelectric plant in Nakao. Kumagai continued to work for Tobishima, alternately as an employee and as a subcontractor for the next 10 years.

While he was employed by Tobishima, Kumagai had the good fortune to meet Mr. M. Makita, a young graduate engineer from the Iwakura School for Railway Construction. This relationship was to continue for decades. Their friendship grew from their first meeting at Tobishima and reached its zenith when Makita, who joined with Kumagai in the formation of Kumagai Gumi, became the company president and later, after Santoro Kumagai died, chairman of the board.

Santoro had established a reputation early on as a dedicated contractor with integrity, and one who was willing to take the risks inherent in the business. In 1934 in the Nagano Prefecture, positioned halfway between Tokyo and Fukui, the Sanshin Railway Line was planning to build a 27-mile-long extension along the Tenry U River. Construction work would entail building some 54 short-span bridges and 116 tunnels, most of them rather short, but all involving drilling through rock. Because of the shaky financial position of the Sanshin Railroad Company, other construction companies declined to even bid the project, but Kumagai did. Three years later he completed the work, received payment in full, and gained a reputation as a highly qualified contractor who was not afraid to tackle complex, risky projects.

Kunagai Gumi was formally incorporated on January 6, 1938, with Santoro Kumagai as president, his son Tasaboro as vice-president, and long-time friend and associate Makita as general manager. The next year, in 1939, Santoro entered the political arena and won a seat as congressman from his local area. At that time he assumed the post of chairman of his company, and his son became president. Mr. Makita became president of Kumagai Gumi in 1967, and in 1979 on the occasion of the company's fortieth anniversary, was elected chairman of the board. Makita remained active in the company until his death at age 92. In fact, that very year, when construction sites were closed all over Japan for a national holiday, he went abroad so he could check on the progress of several major overseas projects. Subsequently, in 1979 Taichiro Kumagai, grandson of the founder, was installed as president of the company, where he remains today guiding the company through some of the most intriguing projects in its history.

KUMAGAI'S UNIQUE MARKETING STRATEGY

Many Japanese construction firms ventured into overseas construction after 1945 when the Japanese government became involved in reparations work, but Kumagai Gumi looked beyond that approach to contract awards and, early on, began to seek out commercial ventures and establish commercial contacts. The firm saw an opportunity to create its own market via a vehicle known as BOT, *build-own-transfer*. Simply put, a BOT scheme involves identifying a need for a project, assembling a team with the ability to design, construct, finance, maintain, and operate the facility, and after a certain pay-back period, turn the project over to a local concern or government agency at no cost to the new owner. Kumagai Gumi was able to create several construction projects for itself by utilizing this approach, and continues to do so even today as its latest tender proposal, one for the Western Harbor Crossing in Hong Kong, is in the process of being prepared.

Kumagai Gumi has already completed two such projects: The Ski Tube, a rack-rail train system and accompanying infrastructure in New South Wales, Australia; and the Eastern Harbor Crossing in Hong Kong. Kumagai currently is under contract and in construction on two other BOT projects: The Second Stage Expressway in Bangkok, Thailand, and the Sydney Harbor Tunnel in Sydney, Australia. Due to its successful completion of the Eastern Harbor Tunnel BOT project in Hong Kong in 1989, Kumagai Gumi is one of just two groups being requested to submit tenders on the Western Harbor Tunnel proposal, valued at $5 billion. More about both of these projects later in this chapter.

KUMAGAI'S GLOBAL APPROACH

A brief look at Kumagai Gumi's global directory of branches, offices, and subsidiaries attests to this company's stature in the field of international construction. The following are Kumagai Gumi's overseas offices and branches:

Hong Kong Branch, Causeway Bay,   Canada Office, Toronto, Canada
Hong Kong

Far East Branch, Anson Road,
Singapore

New York Office, New York, N.Y.

Amsterdam Branch, Amsterdam,
Netherlands

Los Angeles Office, Los Angeles, Calif.

Australia Branch, North Sydney,
N.S.W., Australia

Caribbean Office, Puerto Rico

Beijing Branch, District Beijing,
China

Hawaii Office, Honolulu, Hawaii.

Pan American Branch, Redwood City,
Calif.

Saipan Office, Garapan Saipan, MP

Philippines Branch, Metro Manila,
Philippines

Sri Lanka Office, Colombo, Sri Lanka

London Branch, London
SW1Y 4JU, England

Guam Office, Agana, Guam

Indonesia Branch, Jakarta,
Indonesia

South Pacific Office, Papua,
New Guinea

Singapore Office, International
Plaza, Singapore

Bangkok Office, Bangkok, Thailand

Malaysia Office, Kuala Lumpur,
Malaysia

Istanbul Office, Istanbul, Turkey

Taiwan Office, Taipei, Taiwan

The company has various principal subsidiaries and affiliates, as follows:

Kumagai Doro Company, Ltd., Tokyo, Japan. Pavement, road builder, civil-engineering projects

Sampo Special Construction Co., Ltd., Toyokawa, Japan. Diaphragm-wall contractor and pile-driver

Nippon Dome Structures Co., Ltd., Tokyo, Japan. Plan, design, research, develop all-weather retractable roof domes

Nippon Prestressed Concrete Co., Ltd., Tokyo, Japan. Manufacture and sale of pre-stressed concrete

Nichiyu Koki Co., Ltd., Nagoya, Japan. Manufacture and sale of construction materials

Kumagai International, Ltd., Hong Kong. Real estate, financial services for the Kumagai group

New Hong Kong Tunnel Co., Ltd., Hong Kong. Eastern Harbor Crossing Co., Ltd., Hong Kong

The last two companies listed above are both involved in the management of the rail and vehicle tunnels.

Shenzhen Kumagai Engineering and Design Co., Ltd., Shenzhen, China. Construction in China

P.T. KADI International, Jakarta, Indonesia. Construction in Indonesia

Taiwan Kumagai Co., Ltd., Taipei, Taiwan. Construction in Taiwan

Summa Kumagai, Inc., Manila, Philippines. Construction in the Philippines

Kumagai-Zenecon Construction Pte., Ltd., Singapore. Real estate, construction in Singapore

Zenecon-Kumagai Sdn., Bhd., Kuala Lumpur, Malaysia. Real estate, construction in Malaysia

Bangkok Expressway Co., Ltd., Bangkok, Thailand. Management of Bangkok Expressway

Kumagai (N.S.W.) Pty., Ltd., New South Wales, Australia. Real estate, construction in Australia

Kumagai Australia Finance Ltd., New South Wales, Australia. Financial services

Kumagai Gumi Properties, Ltd.; Kumagai Gumi U.K., Ltd.; KBS U.K., Ltd. Three firms involved in real estate and construction in the United Kingdom

Kumam Corporation, KG Land California, Kumagai Gumi International U.S.A., KG Land New York, KG (Hawaii Corporation), Kumagai Properties, U.S. and Hawaii. Kumagai Gumi's construction and real estate firms in the United States

Kumagai Gumi (Hong Kong), Ltd.

One of Kumagai Gumi's most successful affiliates is Kumagai Gumi (Hong Kong), Ltd., established in October 1973 with an initial capitalization of HK\$292,000,000 (equivalent to US\$37,387,007). When it was first organized, Kumagai Gumi owned 100 percent of this company, but after selling a major portion of its equity now retains a 35-percent share.

Mr. C. P. Yu is a Chinese national who now heads the company as deputy chairman and managing director. Mr. Yu's previous association with the company dates back to the 1970s when he was one of its transportation and excavation subcontractors. He has been credited with much of the company's success in obtaining a large portion of the burgeoning Hong Kong construction market. The forthcoming transfer of the government of Hong Kong to the People's Republic of China in 1997 appears to have had a stimulating effect on that country's economy.

According to one source, employment has grown by 10 percent a year for the past five years. Fifty-nine corporate regional headquarters were established in Hong Kong between 1985 and 1990, and the financial community can count on 165 licensed banks to serve its needs. The new airport to be constructed at Chek Lap Kok will be able to handle 80 million passengers a year, three times the capacity of the present one.

A representative of one of the other Big Six firms told the writer that Kumagai Gumi is the strongest of all the Big Six contractors in Hong Kong, thanks to the presence of its Hong Kong affiliate and the capable Mr. Yu. A glance through the Hong Kong Yellow Pages seems to back up this statement. Kajima Overseas Asia PTE, Ltd., has a telephone listing under "Building Contractors," as does Takenaka Hong Kong., Ltd., and Taisei Corp., HK. Shimizu Corporation is listed under "Contractors, Engineering—General." Kumagai Gumi, Hong Kong, with its Chinese managing director, is heavily involved in the construction of the new billion-dollar airport project and has obtained contracts for a bridge, a viaduct, and the North Lantau Expressway.

The company sold one of its development projects, the New Ocean Centre, and a substantial profit will be realized in fiscal year 1992. A 26,000-square foot luxury condominium project is under way in Kowloon and another 10,000-high-end project is in design development. The company is also developing property in Southern China. A 500,000-square-foot residential building is under way in Dongmen, and a 1.1-million-square-foot housing development is in progress on Hainan Island, in cooperation with the Bank of China. All of this work contributes to the financial growth of the company. Although turnover and profits took a slight dip in 1990, 1991 appears to have been a banner year, as witness the figures below, all expressed in Hong Kong dollars, which at the time of writing were valued at HK $7.4 to one U.S.A $1.

	1987	1988	1989	1990	1991
Turnover (in $B)	1.754	3.74	3.1	2.99	2.6
Profit before taxes (in $M)	91.0	147.0	106.0	101.0	262.0
Retained profits (in $M)	16.0	37.0	13.0	27.0	145.0

Converted into U.S. dollars at the HK $7.4 valuation, 1991 represents total billings or a turnover of $353,108,000, profits before taxes of $35,405,000, and retained profits of $19,594,594, or 5.5 percent of sales.

THE INTERNATIONAL PRIVATIZATION MARKETPLACE

Private funded, owned, and operated infrastructure projects are rare in the United States, but they are becoming increasingly popular in other parts of the world. Governments around the globe are welcoming participation by the private sector in what heretofore were publicly owned and financed infrastructure projects. The governments of Great Britain, Greece, Mexico, and the United States recently have become very receptive to proposals from builder-designer-banker consortiums to build and operate infrastructure projects, and then transfer ownership back to the government entity at some future date when project payback has been reached, a concept called build-operate-transfer.

The criteria for a successful BOT project are rather straightforward. The proposed project must:

- Be in alignment with government policy and/or strategy
- Be of a practical nature and fulfill a defined public need
- Be financially viable and economically justifiable
- Be environmentally sound
- Not require government assistance in any way—no unsecured loans, guarantees, or tax concessions, and no assumption of risk
- Be turned over to the governing body at no cost at the end of the payback period.

BUILD-OPERATE-TRANSFER (BOT); BUILD-OWN-OPERATE (BOO)

There are a number of BOT projects in various stages of development and execution in both the Western and Eastern Hemispheres today, and Kumagai Gumi has become a major player in several of these ventures.

Trafalgar House, the British conglomerate that includes the construction giant Davy Corporation and John Brown Engineers and Constructors, Ltd., was designated to build England's first privately funded toll road, the 33-mile-long Midland Expressway. The $460-million project will be paid for by tolls to be collected over 53 years by Midland Expressway, Ltd., a company jointly owned by Trafalgar House and Italy's top-rated trading and industrial company, state-owned Italstat. In August 1991, Britain's Department of Transportation awarded Trafalgar House another BOT contract. This one was for a six-lane, 30-mile highway to be built in the northeast part of Birmingham, England.

Trafalgar House recently completed the construction of Tate's Cairn Tunnel in Hong Kong, a BOT project in which the British firm secured the tunnel franchise, and arranged for the financing, design, and construction of this HK$2.15-billion project. Payback will occur from the collection of tolls from the 50,000 vehicles using the tunnel daily. At the end of the 30-year franchise period, ownership will revert back to the government of Hong Kong. Trafalgar House also is involved in other BOT deals and *build-operate-own-transfer* (BOOT) projects in the United Kingdom and Indonesia.

In March 1992, Greece announced a plan to seek billions of dollars of highway construction work via the BOT contract format. A 30-mile-long highway from Elevsis to the new airport at Spata will be worth $1 billion, another BOT project for a harbor crossing at the Gulf of Corinth is valued at $428 million, and a tunnel linking Perema with Salamis Island has been estimated at $134 million. Mexico is now embarked on a campaign to complete the construction of some 4,000 miles of concessionary roads by 1994. Some of its BOT projects already under way have experienced serious cost overruns, which are being blamed on faulty bid documents and government-set toll charges that discourage drivers; some charges are as high as twenty-five cents per mile.

The European subsidiary of the Texas-based Enron Corporation, in conjunction with the Wing-Merrill Group of Houston, as of this writing, is far along in wrapping up an agreement with Turkey to begin construction of a $1 billion, 1,700 MW BOT co-generation plant in that country.

Utilizing GAMA, a Turkish general contractor, this Texas-based group plans to sell electricity to local utility companies and local industries, assuming the role of a typical United States regulated utility company, but with a different twist. At payback time, the Turkey Electric Authority will own this gas-fired, combined-cycle plant without having to pay a cent.

In Canada, Strait Crossing Inc., a consortium of SCI engineers and constructors, based in Calgary, and the Northern Construction Company, Ltd., along with GTMI (Canada), Ltd., was selected as the apparent low bidder by the Public Works of Canada on a BOT proposal to build a prestressed box-girder bridge across the Northumberland Straits. This 8.25 mile crossing will connect Prince Edward Island with New Brunswick, and will take five years to complete. The projected cost of $1.2 billion will be repaid by tolls collected by Strait Crossing Inc., and once the bridge is in place will be supplemented by an annual government subsidy derived from savings accrued from reduced operating expenses of existing ferry systems.

The Commonwealth of Puerto Rico has opted for the BOT approach to construct a bridge across the San Jose Lagoon to handle the traffic to the Luis Munoz Marin International Airport. Their Department of Transportation and Public Works negotiated a BOT contract for a $350-million highway from San Juan to Fajardo on Puerto Rico's east coast. A Spanish-backed consortium that includes a local construction company began work on the bridge in 1992 and the highway work will commence in mid-1993. Three other road projects in the United States are now considering BOT as an alternative financing medium: the 15-mile-long Dulles Toll Road extension in Virginia; a ten-mile toll road in San Diego; and a 30-mile beltway project in Denver. The planning for these three projects is progressing very slowly because the BOT concept goes against the grain of conventional public policy in this country. Perhaps a closer look at how build-operate-transfer projects originate and progress in other countries would be worthwhile for many of our money-starved public agencies.

To a lesser degree, *build-own-operate* (BOO) projects are also being considered in the marketplace. This type of project differs from BOT in that the initiating group designs, finances, constructs, and operates a project, but with an eye to syndicating all or a portion of its equity at some future date. The risks involved in this kind of venture can be significantly higher than those associated with BOT projects.

KUMAGAI GUMI AND BOT

Kumagai Gumi is no stranger to privatization and the BOT concept. Its first such project involved building a rack-railroad system, a railway tunnel, a small railroad station, and a 1452-bed hotel and restaurant complex in the ski resort area of Kosciusko National Park in New South Wales, Australia. Although this particular project, which was completed in 1988, did not prove to be financially successful, it allowed Kumagai Gumi to gain valuable experience in assembling a BOT project and to acquire more local-construction-market knowledge.

The government of Sydney, Australia, is desirous of building a tunnel under its harbor, and has solicited proposals from several consortiums. Kumagai Gumi has won the award. It will team up with Transfield, Australia's largest privately owned construction company. The entire project is budgeted at $554 million, but with interest, principal repayment, and other costs, the total amount to be financed will reach $750 million, making it the largest privately funded construction project in the country's history. The Transfield-Kumagai Joint Venture will put up a $40-million performance bond and will provide a $40-million loan. When the project is completed, paid for, and turned over to the New South Wales government in 2022, its value at that time is projected to be $2 billion.

Because of its financial strength and its expertise in undersea-tunnel construction, Kumagai Gumi formed the Sydney Harbour Tunnel Company, Limited, and has commenced to build the mile-and-a-half tunnel, the undersea portion of which is 3149 feet long. Kumagai Gumi will utilize the immersed-tube-assembly method for the tunnel portion of the project, and will receive a 30-year lease to operate the tunnel. Construction costs will be financed by a long-term bond issue which will be repaid from the tolls being levied on the existing Sydney Harbour Bridge beginning in 1987, and with the tolls levied on both the bridge and the new tunnel that were completed in 1992. Ownership of the tunnel will remain with the Sydney Harbor Tunnel company, Limited, until the 30-year payback period has been reached.

Kumagai Gumi has also entered into a BOT agreement with the government of Thailand, and is in the process of constructing the Second Stage Expressway System in Greater Bangkok.

THE EASTERN HARBOR—BOT AND KUMAGAI GUMI

In 1984, Kumagai Gumi, after making significant studies of the transportation system in Hong Kong, approached the government with a proposal to construct a combined rail and vehicle crossing under the eastern harbor from Kowloon from the mainland to the island of Hong Kong. Kumagai Gumi suggested that this project be approached from a BOT standpoint, and it planned to team up with the Marubeni Corporation, one of Japan's huge trading companies. After much deliberation, the government of Hong Kong decided it would be in its best interest to solicit open tenders, and on April 1, 1985, received bids from nine international consortiums. Kumagai Gumi was short-listed with two other groups, and at that time expanded its consortium to include the *China International Trust and Investment Corporation* (CITIC), a business corporation with the status of a ministry in the People's Republic of China, and Lilley Construction, Ltd., a Scottish civil engineering concern with previous experience in mass-transit construction in Hong Kong. Paul Y. Construction Company, Ltd., one of Hong Kong's leading civil engineering companies, was also asked to join the group, and the *New Hong Kong Tunnel Company, Ltd.,* (NHKTC) was formed.

The final proposal was to include a franchise for a combined road and rail tunnel which was to extend from Kwun Tong on Kowloon Peninsula to Quarry Bay on Hong Kong Island (see Fig. 5.8). The road-tunnel franchise was to remain in effect until the year 2016 and the rail tunnel until 2008. Although NHKTC was planning to maintain and operate the vehicular tunnels, it planned to lease the rail portion to the Mass Transit Railway Corporation, which would operate and maintain this line along with the others under its existing system.

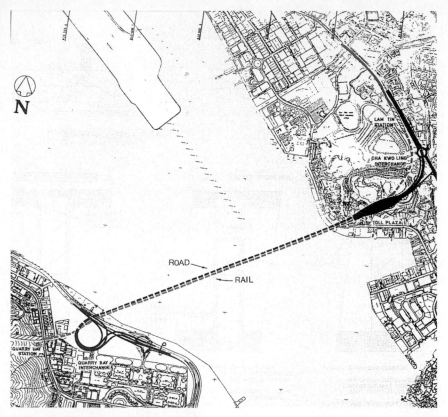

Figure 5.8 The route of the Eastern Harbor Tunnel project in Hong Kong. Quarry Bay in Hong Kong is on the left (west); Kowloon is to the east.

Kumagai Gumi would be able to establish a toll schedule that could be increased over the years to allow for inflation. The tolls collected and the money received from the rail lease would provide the payback for the entire project.

In December 1985, Kumagai Gumi was notified that it was the successful tenderer, and the necessary legislation was enacted on July 17, 1986, allowing the project to proceed. Upon receiving notification that it was the successful tenderer, Kumagai Gumi brought on board Freeman Fox, Ltd., and Oakervee Perrett and Partners as part of the design team. Both of these firms had considerable geotechnical and road, rail, and bridge experience in the area.

Next, the financial package had to be assembled. (For ease of reference, Hong Kong dollars will be used. The conversion rate to U.S. currency in early 1993 was HK\$7.12 to US\$1.)

FINANCIAL PACKAGING

NHKTC required a HK$4.4-billion financing package, which was arranged exclusively by Shearson Lehman Brothers, Inc. Fifty banks around the world participated in the debt financing of HK$3.3 billion, including the Bank of China, Barclays Bank, Hang Seng Bank, the Bank of Tokyo, the Mitsubishi Bank, the Long-Term Credit Bank of Japan, Ltd., Banque Indosuez, and CITIC. An additional HK$1.1 billion in equity financing was provided by NHKTC's shareholders.

CONSTRUCTION OF THE PROJECT

Kumagai Gumi used its immersed-tunnel-technique process for the under-harbor portion of the project. A total of 15 precast, reinforced-concrete tunnel sections were produced on land at a specially prepared site, and were towed out to sea, and sunk and positioned on the seabed that had been prepared to receive them.

To create an area in which to produce these concrete tunnel sections, it was necessary to blast and excavate an area of approximately 13.6 acres at the base of a mountain on the Kowloon Peninsula side, immediately adjacent to the harbor. In this area, sections of the prestressed-concrete tunnels were produced, with steel bulkheads cast into the form at each end of the tunnel section; these effectively sealed each unit. The "drydock" production area, which was excavated to below sea-level, was flooded until each tunnel section floated. The gate separating the drydock from the harbor was raised, and a tug towed each section out to sea, where it was precisely lowered by one of Kumagai Gumi's floating rigs (Fig. 5.9).

The seabed already had been prepared with a leveling course of aggregate obtained from the drydock blasting operations, and at each of the four corners where the section of the tunnel was placed, specially constructed inflatable-rubber leveling cushions had been placed by Kumagai divers. After being lowered to the seabed, starting with the first section at the Hong Kong side, the final height adjustments were made before the next section was joined to the preceding one. The joining sequence, as shown in Fig. 5.10, was achieved by jacking sections together after inserting a water-tight gasket. Water was pumped out of the tunnel section after this seal was in place and the steel bulkheads removed by using a cutting torch.

This completed this part of the operation, which was repeated until the entire tunnel has been set in place. Aggregate was pumped under the jacking spuds to completely fill the voids, and additional aggregate was placed entirely around and over each tunnel section for protection.

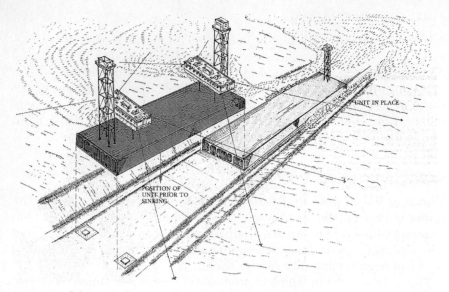

Figure 5.9 Schematic diagram of a tunnel section being secured prior to being flooded and submerged.

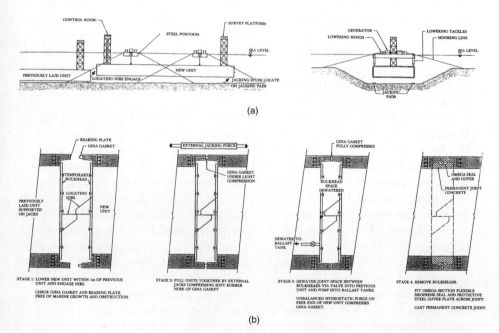

(a)

(b)

Figure 5.10 Diagrams of the sinking and joining of prestressed-concrete tunnel sections.

The placement of aggregate was carried out by specially designed marine equipment consisting of a floating barge and two telescoping placement arms that lower themselves to the sea bottom and pump the crushed stone uniformly under each tunnel section, coming up slowly along the sides of each section to complete its work.

The statistics involved in the construction and placement of the fifteen immersed tube tunnel sections are impressive:

Length of immersed tunnel.   6100 ft (about 1.5 mi)

Size of tunnel sections.   All units are 116-ft wide and 31.9 ft high

- Five units are 419.84-ft long and 10 units are 400-ft long.
- The longer units weigh 4716 tons, and the shorter units weigh in at 4496 tons.

Materials used.   73,000 tons of reinforcing steel, 523,000-cu yd of concrete, 2,616,000-cu yd of aggregate as fill under and around the tunnel sections

Work force.   1,750 men at peak time

In addition to the immersed tunnel sections, Kumagai Gumi had to construct 3.17 miles of highways as approach roads and an additional 2300 feet of overhead rail lines, plus an additional 1.2 miles of undergound approach sections.

The term of the vehicular-traffic tunnel contract is 30 years, and the rail-tunnel contract runs for 18 years. NHKTC's responsibilities include "policing" the tunnel for speeders and toll "beaters," notifying the local Hong Kong police of violators, and notifying them of all accidents within the tunnel or on the approach roads to it. NHKTC maintains private guards who act as policemen but who can only report, not arrest. They have a Hong Kong–trained fire department and own several vehicle-towing rigs. All of these operations are controlled and monitored by the closed-circuit television sets in the modern administration building (Fig. 5.11a, b, and c). The area where the drydock was created is now being developed as a parking lot with ancillary structures planned for the future (see Fig. 5.12).

The Eastern Harbor Tunnel went into operation in September 1990, four months ahead of schedule, and vehicular traffic tolls of HK$20 (US$2.70) are being collected daily. Although it is too early to determine its profitability, Mr. K. Torigai of Kumagai Gumi's Hong Kong regional main branch office said that the break-even point was reached in mid-1992.

(a)

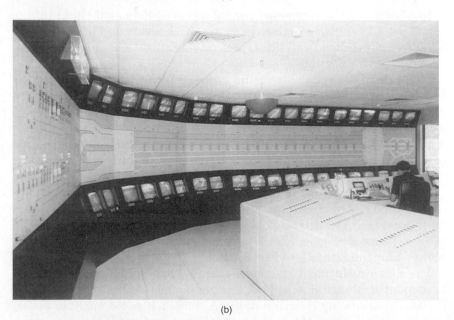

(b)

Figure 5.11   New Hong Kong Tunnel Company project. (*a*) view from the Administration Building to the toll gates. (*b*) array of TV monitors in the Control Center.

(c)

Figure 5.11 *(Continued)* *(c)* the tunnel approach from the Kowloon side.

Figure 5.12 The Harbor Tunnel drydock area that now serves as a parking lot.

BOT IN THAILAND

Traffic flow in and around Bangkok, Thailand, is rather heavy, and the First Stage Expressway System, also known as the Chalerm Mahanakorn Expressway, which was completed several years ago, carries an average of 230,000 vehicles per day. To alleviate more traffic congestion in the central Bangkok metropolitan area, another expressway system was needed and the *Expressway and Rapid Transit Authority of Thailand* (ETA) began to consider construction of the *Second Stage Expressway,* termed "SES." Through the cooperation of the Japan International Cooperation Agency, an economic and social feasibility study was conducted in mid-1982 and a final report was submitted to the ETA in January 1984. Based upon the favorable results of the survey, the government passed a resolution in 1987 allowing it to consider a BOT-type project.

Kumagai Gumi formed the Bangkok Expressway Company, Limited, a consortium of local companies and banks, and with one other bidder, the Thai Expressway Development Joint Venture, responded to the Thai government's tender. Kumagai Gumi's group won the award, and construction began in 1990. When it was completed and opened to the public, a ring-road around central Bangkok was created that reduces travel time from one section of the city to the other by at least 20 percent—and at no cost to the taxpayers. This is just another instance of an innovative company like Kumagai Gumi, with some assistance from its government arm, the Japan International Cooperation Agency, being able to capture a valued contract in the overseas construction market.

KUMAGAI GUMI'S TOYOKAWA WORKS—
ANOTHER COMPETITIVE EDGE

Following the end of World War II, Kumagai Gumi recognized the need to mechanize its operations. Mr. Makita, looking out over the devastated land of his country, had the foresight to see that hundreds of unskilled workers would no longer be available to excavate building sites mostly by hand, or to jack-hammer their way through tunnels. Machines would do the job more quickly and economically.

In December 1945, just six months after the war was over, Kumagai Gumi established a construction-equipment factory in Nagoya under the name of the Nagoya Works. In 1961, having outgrown its existing facilities, Nagoya Works moved to Toyohama City, where it remains today, spread out over nine acres and employing 400 workers. The Toyokawa Works not only repairs the company's construction equipment, but it has the capability to design, fabricate, and assemble new machinery and equipment. Designing and constructing belt conveyors is a specialty of the Works. One such system installed at a land-reclamation site in Suma has already loaded 400 million tons of soil onto barges. A 17-mile-long conveyor-belt system in Indonesia has been used by the Bukit Asam Coal Mining Development and Transportation Project to off-load coal from an open-pit mine to waiting transports.

In 1952 Kumagai Gumi developed and employed the first shield-tunneling assembly ever designed and constructed by a Japanese contractor. Since that time the Toyokawa Works has constructed approximately 25 percent of the nation's shield-tunneling machines and is currently working on a monstrous, 41-foot-diameter machine to be used on a tunnel under Tokyo Bay.

The Works also develops new construction products such as KSP, a spirally ribbed steel pipe that provides extra strength and durability in domestic-water-line installations, irrigation systems, and some types of fuel-delivery lines. Jacking devices for lift slabs are designed and built at this facility, and a hydraulically powered concrete-demolition machine known as the KBB Building Breaker has been created by the Works. It employs a blade-shaped edge and a receiving device mounted in a "U"-shaped frame to rapidly shear off sections of concrete walls that are placed between the edge and the receiver.

KUMAGAI GUMI'S CONSTRUCTION VESSELS

Because of its limited buildable space, Japan has seen industry gravitate to its coastal areas and utilize reclaimed land for expansion. Kumagai Gumi, recognizing the need to service these kinds of clients, has acquired a fleet of specialized marine equipment with outstanding performance capabilities. The Toyokawa Works provided much of the engineering and fabrication expertise to help assemble this fleet.

Kurojishi No. 1.   The first large pile-driving vessel in Japan, capable of driving steel pipe piles up to 8ft in diameter and 230ft long. Kurojishi can lift piles weighing as much as 80 tons and can also be used as a floating crane.

Shirokuma No. 11.   A floating concrete-ready-mix factory with cement and aggregate storage capacities of 654 cu yd. Its long-arm concrete pump is used to deliver ready mix to the many off-shore projects it services.

Tsukudo No. 1.   A self-elevating platform (SEP) equipped with DeLong hydraulic jacks. After setting its legs on the sea floor, the vessel elevates itself above the surface of the water to create a stable working platform for constructing marine abutments, caissons, and quays. Tsukudo can operate in depths of 131 ft and where there are 21-ft seas or where tidal-stream velocity reaches 37mi/hr. The special air-actuated jacks required by Tsukudo No. 1 were also fabricated at the Works.

Tsukudo No. 2.   A second-generation, catamaran-type SEP, with DeLong Jacks, capable of reaching a depth of 82 ft, has a jacking capacity of 2160 tons and the ability to lower its jacks at a rate of 3 ft/min. Tsukudo No. 2 is 200 ft long and 102 ft wide.

Kumagaimaru No. 1.   A powerful tugboat pusher that can move rock- and sand-laden barges loaded with as much as 3270 cu yd of material.

WHAT THE FUTURE HOLDS FOR KUMAGAI GUMI

Mr. M. Makita, grandson of the ex-president and chairman, who is now the assistant manager of the Public Relations Division says that the depressed real estate market worldwide has taken its toll on Kumagai Gumi's profits for 1992. Corporate profits will be lower because of the carrying charges on many of the company's substantial real estate holdings in Sydney, Australia; London, England; and the United States. As an example, America's Tower, a 50-story, million-square-foot building on the Avenue of the Americas in Manhattan, began as a Kumagai development venture, but construction stopped for more than a year while financial and legal difficulties with its U.S. joint-venture partner were being resolved. Kumagai Gumi initially had a 50-percent stake in the project, but its New York subsidiary, KG Land, headquartered at Columbus Circle, had to buy out the remaining 50 percent to prevent the loss of the entire project. America's Tower was finally completed in May 1992, not the most opportune time to begin to rent upscale office space in a depressed real estate market.

But the future looks bright for this company. Another harbor crossing in Hong Kong is in the works—the Western Harbor Crossing—and Kumagai Gumi is a strong candidate to win the award. Kumagai's proposed consortium is quite substantial in its own right. It consists of CIDIC, its Chinese government partner on the Eastern Harbor Tunnel Crossing; the Nishimatsu Construction Company, a Japanese contractor with a significant number of construction projects under way in Hong Kong; and Kerry Properties of Malaysia, a developer that owns, among other properties, the Shangri-La Hotel chain in Asia. Kumagai Gumi has selected three design firms for the project: Maunsel, a British-owned Hong Kong-based firm; Acer, also British-owned, and one of the designers on the Eastern Harbor Crossing job; and the renowned U.S. engineering firm Parsons, Brinkerhoff.

Kumagai's competition is formidable and consists of the Wharf Company, a Hong Kong holding company; Costain, a United Kingdom construction company; Tarmac, another United Kingdom builder; and the Japanese contractor Aoki Construction. A main consideration for award selection will be the schedule of the tolls to be levied. However, technical expertise, developer experience, and design considerations also will play a major role in the selection process.

In the meantime, Kumagai Gumi is involved in other work in the Hong Kong area. The Western Harbor Crossing, valued at $500 million, is merely one part of a gigantic new international airport program being undertaken. This involves the creation of a man-made island off the coast of nearby Lantau Island, west of Hong Kong. A new airport will be built on this island, and a series of roads, bridges, and tunnels will be required to carry traffic from the airport through a portion of the New Territories onto Kowloon, and through the Western Harbor Tunnel onto Hong Kong Island. Kumagai Gumi has been awarded a contract to perform rock-tunneling on Tsing Island as part of the overall project, and Kumagai Gumi Hong Kong, Ltd., was awarded a land-reclamation contract in western Kowloon in connection with the master plan. This *Port and Airport Development Scheme,* (PAADS) has been conservatively valued at US$16 billion, and the scheduled completion date for the entire system is 1997,—incidentally, the year Great Britain formally turns Hong Kong over to the Chinese government.

In Australia, Kumagai Gumi is awaiting word on a proposal to construct a *very fast train* (VFT) from Sydney to Melbourne. In a joint-venture proposal with partner Broken Hill Properties, an Australian steel and mining company, this privatization project would provide passengers with a three-hour trip over the 600-mile distance between these two cities.

Kumagai Gumi prides itself on its tunneling and civil engineering expertise. From the early to the late 1960s, the company's annual construction volume consisted of 70 percent civil work and 30 percent architectural work such as offices and other commercial buildings. During the early 1970s, civil work and architectural construction was split fifty-fifty, but at present civil engineering accounts for only about 20 percent.

SHIELD TUNNELING—ANOTHER KUMAGAI GUMI ADVANTAGE

The three most common methods of constructing tunnels are the open-cut method; the *new Austrian tunnel method,* known as NATM; and shield tunneling. The open-cut method needs little explanation and is used in urban and suburban areas for subway and underground utilities installations where areas can be closed off or traffic diverted while excavation takes place. NATM involves excavation, support setting, shotcreting, and rock-bolt setting, a construction sequence that generally allows work to proceed at 100 meters (328 feet) per month.

Shield tunneling requires what has come to be a very sophisticated piece of equipment, capable of boring through rock and soft soils at a rapid pace, stabilizing the surrounding soils as it travels and piggybacking the tunnel segments either with metal or reinforced concrete. It is an indispensable method of constructing tunnels in congested urban areas, where any disruption to the flow of traffic on the surface cannot be tolerated. Shield tunnels allow work to proceed underground with little or no apparent change in the traffic patterns. It is the preferred method of tunnel construction in Japan.

Shield tunneling is not really a new form of construction; it was used for the first time in 1825 in London, England, when a cross-river tunnel under the Thames was built to connect the northern and southern parts of that city.

In 1952 Kumagai Gumi became the first Japanese contractor to construct its own shield machine, and since then it has completed more than 217 miles of tunneling using this method. The company is also at the forefront of new shield-tunneling technology. Shield tunneling is particularly effective in soft and weak soils. As the shield machine advances through these kinds of soils, a bentonite-type of high-density slurry frequently is used to stabilize the soils surrounding the machine's cutting head. The resulting mixture of mud, muck, and slurry is removed from the excavated area by pump or conveyor.

This slurry system requires large-scale equipment to produce the slurry, deliver it to the shield machine, and dispose of the muck contaminated with the bentonite slurry, which has environmental problems and is expensive. Kumagai Gumi now has developed a foam-shield method using a patented shaving-cream-like foam that is injected at the front of the shield face. The foam improves the workability and lowers the permeability of the excavated muck, preventing the formation of liquefied sand and "blowing out" at the end of the screw conveyor, which removes it to the surface. The foam in the excavated muck disappears in a relatively short time, so disposal is not a problem. The manufacture of the foam on the site is much easier, and the foam not only gives the soil excellent stability, but actually helps to improve the tunneling machine's performance.

Kumagai Gumi's latest development in this field is the *multicircular face* (MF) shield machine, which cuts a cross section like a pair of glasses. The machine consists of two shield machines joined together in such a way that one face overlaps the other. One machine face extends out beyond the other, which enables the MF shield to bore a double-track tunnel in only one pass.

Kumagai Gumi plans to use this new machine on the 2050-foot-long Kyobashi Tunnel which will connect the Tokyo Underground Station with the Shin-Hatchobori Underground Station on the Keiyo Midtown Line. The MF shield being used for this tunnel is 24-feet high, 40-feet wide, 29-feet long, and weighs about 1000 tons. By using combinations of two or three MF shields, many different tunnel configurations can be created in less time and at less cost.

What is being touted as one of the world's largest shield machines, a 1430-ton monster with a face diameter of 41½ feet, is now being used by Kumagai Gumi to extend the Shinkansen bullet train on the new Tohoku line to Tokyo Station. This tunnel, called the Okachimachi Shield Drive Tunnel, will extend for 1623 feet at a depth of 91.8 feet, and run from Ueno Station to Tokyo Station. A segment-erection robot originally developed by Kumagai Gumi will ride behind the shield machine, performing its work with an accuracy of ±0.3 millimeter.

The Japanese government's announced program to inject trillions of dollars into its domestic construction market over the next decade undoubtedly will produce some huge infrastructure projects to raise the standard of living of its citizens. If these commitments come to fruition, Kumagai Gumi, with its proven track record in completing major civil engineering projects, will have a very bright future.

6

Taisei Corporation

Building for a Lively World

The Taisei Corporation (pronounced Tie-Say) is a member of the Fuyo Group, a loosely knit association of 29 of Japan's leading industrial and commercial concerns. The Fuyo Kai is a steering committee (*sha-chokai*) within the Group that is composed of presidents of the 29 member companies. This steering committee meets regularly to exchange information on new business ventures, joint-venture possibilities, and views on serving the public and the local environment in which member companies conduct their business.

The Fuyo Group sponsors a series of conferences each year to address topics with a bearing on the growth and well-being of each company in the group. For instance, the Fuyo New Kansai Airport Conference has conducted joint surveys and research on matters dealing with the economic enhancement of the airport region; the Fuyo Research and Development Conference undertook studies on issues relating to industrial research and development and its effect on Japan's industrial revolution; and the Study Group Promoting the Use of Space Stations is a think tank devoted to studying new technologies and materials for their commercial application in space.

Members of the Fuyo Group span the country's entire industrial spectrum:

Canon Inc. Makers of cameras, business machines, optical products

The Fuji Bank Ltd. One of the world's largest banks

Hitachi, Ltd. Electrical and electronics products manufacturer

Keihin Electric Express Railway Co., Ltd. A railway moving 1.16-million passengers each day

Kubota, Ltd. Farm, construction, and industrial equipment manufacturer

Kureha Chemical Industry Co., Ltd.   Industrial chemical manufacturer; chemical engineering services

Marubeni Corporation.   Japan's leading *sogo shosha* (trading houses)

Nichirei Corporation.   Japan's largest refrigeration warehouse operator, the third-largest worldwide

Nihon Cement Co., Ltd.   Cement, construction, and building materials

Nippon Oil and Fats Co., Ltd.   Chemicals, food products, industrial coatings, and medical products

Nippon Seiko K.K.   Ball- and roller-bearings manufacturer, automotive parts

Nissan Motor Co., Ltd.   Automaker

Nisshin Flour Milling Co., Ltd.   Food and fine chemicals

Nisshinbo Industries, Inc.   Textile manufacturer; automobile brakes, papers, and foam products

NKK Corporation.   Steelmaking, advanced materials, and electronics

OKI Electric Industry Co., Ltd.   Maker of information-processing equipment, electronic devices

Sanyo-Kokusaka Pulp Co., Ltd.   Paper, pulp, forest products

Sapporo Breweries, Limited   Beer, soft drinks, wines, and spirits

Showa Denko K.K.   Chemicals, gases, carbons, ceramics, aluminum

Showa Line, Ltd.   Marine transport

Taisei Corporation.   General constructor

Tobu Railway Co., Ltd.   Private railway operating the longest lines in Eastern Japan

Toho Rayon Co., Ltd.   Textile/industrial-fiber manufacturers

Tokyo Tatemono Co., Ltd.   Real estate brokerage; sales/leasing of apartments, offices

Tonen Corporation.   Petroleum refining

The Yasuda Fire and Marine Insurance Company, Ltd.   Non-life insurance

The Yasuda Mutual Life Insurance Company.   Life insurance and reinsurance.

The Yasuda Trust and Banking Co., Ltd.   General banking, trust business

Yokogawa Electric Corporation. Industrial measuring and control equipment

The economic power of the Fuyo Group is impressive, and in 1988 its total yearly sales were equal to 8 percent of Japan's Gross National Product.

TAISEI'S ORIGINS

As a member of the Fuyo Group, modern-day Taisei Corporation reflects its origins, begun in 1873 when Kibachiro Okura (Fig. 6.1) formed a construction company named Okuragumi Shokai. This was just another enterprise in his expanding business empire. Okura, who ran the Okura Trading Company (see Fig. 6.2), was a businessman, not a builder; he viewed the construction industry as another source of income, unlike the founders of the other Big Six companies, who began as carpenters or stonemasons and then started their own construction businesses.

Okura, who was awarded the title of baron by the Japanese government in 1915 for his outstanding contribution to the country's industrial and cultural climate, had many contacts in the commercial field, and he used them to obtain construction contracts for his newly formed building company. In 1874 Okura established the Okura Trading Company in London, and a short while after that, in 1879, started a leather and shoe manufacturing business in Japan.

Japan was emerging from its long period of isolation, and Western technology was being eagerly sought. Mr. Okura's young construction company had an auspicious start in that process when in 1882, in Tokyo, it completed the installation of the first electric-arc-lighting system in the country. The construction of the country's railway system accelerated at that time, and Okuragumi Shokai was given contracts to furnish various types of machinery that was required by that industry. Okuragumi Shokai's first major construction project was the Shinbashi Railroad Station, the end of the line for Japan's fledgling railroad system. This project was the country's first station. By 1887, the Okura construction division had grown to the point where it was split off from the parent company and became known as Nippon Doboku Co., Ltd.

At about that time the Japanese government asked Okura to build a brewery in Sapporo, the first in Japan. When this brewery, named the Dai Nippon Brewery, was completed, it was operated by Okura at the request of the government. Although Kirin Beer claims the honor of being the first brewery in Japan, the records of the Okuragumi Shokai prove otherwise. And like so many other builder-client relationships in

Figure 6.1 Founder, Baron Kibachiro Okura.

Japan, Dai Nippon, whose name was later changed to the Sapporo Brewery, remains Taisei's client to this day.

In 1992 Sapporo Breweries approached Taisei with the request that it be the lead contractor in a major development the brewery was planning in Ebisu, 3-chome, Meguro ward in Tokyo. The old Nippon Breweries, Ltd., property was to be redeveloped, and this 21-acre site would be known as Yebisu Garden Place, where a 450-room hotel, a

Figure 6.2   The Okura Trading Company building in 1880.

shopping promenade, an office complex, 1020 residential condominiums, the Tokyo Metropolitan Museum of Photography, and a cinema complex would be built.

To back up its commitment to build a top-quality project, Sapporo will move its headquarters from Ginza to Yebisu Garden Place. This project, destined to start in 1994, is valued at $869 million, and the Taisei Corporation will have an 80 percent portion of the joint-venture construction contract.

Kihachiro Okura formed a joint stock company and built the first Imperial Hotel in 1888. Okura, who by that time had become a collector of oriental ceramics and painting, displayed many of these articles in this hotel, of which he became president. The Imperial Household held stock in the building, which was situated between Hibiya Park and the Imperial Garden in Tokyo, and this added substantial prestige to the hotel. In 1911 this site was selected for the construction of another Imperial Hotel (Fig. 6.3). It was designed by Frank Lloyd Wright and was destined to become a world-renowned structure.

Okura's business empire continued to grow during the early part of the twentieth century as he became involved in the fire and marine insurance business, textile manufacturing, ocean transportation, real estate, the expansion of his hotel ownership, agricultural business, and

Figure 6.3   Frank Lloyd Wright's Imperial Hotel in Tokyo.

the automotive and battery businesses. Okura Civil Engineering (Fig. 6.4) opened an office in Manchuria and benefited from the Japanese military build-up in that country in the 1930s. In Japan, the company constructed the Kobe Railroad Station, the Okura tunnel project, and the Tokyo Subway Ginza Station (Fig. 6.5). Baron Okura contributed to the public welfare by building Okura Park and establishing the Tokyo Economic University.

Okura joined the ranks of the *zaibatsu* (large trading company) cliques just as events were developing that would bring Japan into the vortex of World War II.

POSTWAR CHANGES WITHIN THE CORPORATION

After the end of World War II, when General MacArthur's staff instituted its Americanization process, the zaibatsu trusts were dismembered, and Okura's and its Nippon Doboku construction company's existence were challenged. This nearly led to its demise until shares of stock in the company were distributed to its employees. The previous board members were dismissed, and new executives were brought into the company to complete the purge. In 1946 the company took its pre-

Figure 6.4 Okura Civil Engineering office in 1915.

sent name, Taisei, formally known as Taisei Kensetsu Kabushiki Kaisha. And today Taisei is the only Big Six construction company that can trace its roots back to those prewar zaibatsus, giant trading companies like Mitsubishi, Sumitomo and Mitsui that consisted of 20 to 30 large industrial firms clustered around a powerful bank.

Figure 6.5   Tokyo Subway Ginza Station in the mid-1930s.

After Japan's surrender in 1945, the U.S. military establishment began to construct several large-scale projects on Okinawa, and Taisei initially was awarded a $250,000 contract. Shortly thereafter, the company formed a joint venture with another Japanese contractor, and participated in what was then an extremely large project, $6.1 million, to build several barracks and support buildings for U.S. military forces on the island.

Later, the Korean War and the 1964 Olympics held in Japan gave a boost to the country's economy and the fortunes of the Taisei Corporation.

TAISEI TODAY

The Taisei Corporation, with headquarters in the skyscraper section of the Shinjuku ward, Tokyo (Fig. 6.6), employs 12,383 architects, engineers, and administrative staff. It consists of 76 subsidiary and affiliate companies involved in real estate, construction-equipment manufacture; transportation; mechanical-equipment manufacture; hotel, golf course, and resort management; financial services; and insurance.

In 1991 Taisei reported sales of $13,254,000,000, starting the year with a backlog of $14,861,000,000 and ending it with a backlog of $19,778,000,000. The company realized a net income of $233,674,000 at year's end, and its asset base increased to $18.9 billion during the

Figure 6.6   Taisei corporate headquarters in the Shinjuku section of Tokyo.

same period. Slightly less than 70 percent of the company's sales came from building construction, 22.9 percent were generated by civil engineering work, and 7.8 percent came from real estate sales. The balance of the yearly revenue was derived from other business dealings.

The company maintains 10 office branches in Japan, and overseas offices in the United States, Great Britain, Hong Kong, China, Malaysia, Indonesia, Singapore, Thailand, Taiwan, France,

Luxembourg, Spain, Germany, and Holland. This is in addition to 23 affiliated companies, which include the following U.S. subsidiaries:

Taisei America Corporation, New York, New York

NAT Capital Corporation, New York, New York

Taisei Construction Corporation, New York, New York

Taivan Corporation, Dallas, Texas

Taisei Hawaii Corporation, Honolulu, Hawaii

GCH Acquisition Corporation, Monroeville, Pennsylvania

In January 1990, Taisei purchased Hawaii's largest mechanical contracting firm, Au's Plumbing and Metal Works, on the island of Oahu.

Currently, Taisei is involved in several huge construction projects throughout the world. Close to home in nearby Yokohama, Taisei is building the Landmark Tower, the centerpiece and gateway to the $15-billion Minato Mirai 21 project. When complete, at a total height of 970 feet, it will eclipse the new 797-foot-high Tokyo Metropolitan Government buildings and become the tallest building in Japan. During the construction of this building Taisei has been using four of the world's largest climbing-jib-type tower cranes, each of which weighs 35 tons, has an operating radius of 115 feet, and can lift 70 tons; this surpasses the previous record of an 82-foot-operating-radius crane capable of lifting 35 tons.

Minato Mirai is located in District 25 of Yokohama, and two years ago the local government decided to develop adjacent District 24. Taisei will become the lead company in the consortium charged with constructing another billion-dollar urban-renewal effort known as "Core City."

Tokyo International Airport, also known as Haneda Airport, is undergoing a major expansion program, and Taisei has a dominant position in a joint-venture contract to construct the 2755-foot-long West Passenger Terminal building.

Taisei's civil engineering expertise is brought to bear in its role in the construction of Kawasaki Artificial Island, located 3 miles off shore in Tokyo Bay. When it is complete, the east section of this island, a circular concrete structure with a circumference of 656 feet and a diameter of 328 feet, will act as a base for the shield-tunneling operation that will take place directly under it. Taisei currently is constructing Metropolitan Subway system No. 12 in three phases: Phase 1 is three-miles long, Phase 2 is 5.6 miles, and Phase 3, begun in 1992, will comprise a 17.9-mile circular section.

Taisei's work load, however, is not restricted to the Japanese domestic construction market. The company has just completed the 11-story

Guam Palace Hotel, with 403 guest rooms and amenity areas that bring the hotel's total floor area to 373,300 square feet. Taisei was commissioned to build a 3800-foot-long breakwater in Male, the largest marine project ever attempted in the Maldives; and in Nepal, the company joint-ventured with a Chinese concern to build a power plant to supply most of the electricity to Katmandu, the country's capital.

CREATING A "LIVELY WORLD"

In 1990, recognizing that the construction industry in Japan needed improvement in order to attract employees in a rapidly changing demographic market, Taisei's top management began a concerted effort to attack the industry's "Three D's"—dirty, dangerous, and demanding. A new corporate logo was adopted, and its three colors—green, turquoise, and blue, were meant to coincide with the firm's new slogan, "For a Lively World." At the job site, Taisei began to wrap its buildings in huge nylon sheets that imparted a cocoon-like appearance and acted as safety nets for both workers and passersby. Otherwise drab pedestrian fencing was adorned with works of art, and on one job site in Tokyo's exclusive Ginza section, a historical map of the area was painted on the building's ground-floor enclosure.

Mr. Kenji Shimakawa, the manager in charge of corporate planning, says that Taisei wants to be "a company of dreams and hopes, implementing work with perspiration." They want to be number 1 in the construction industry while fulfilling the following commitments:

- Provide for a happy and active life for everyone involved in the corporation.
- Produce high-quality work and maintain customer satisfaction.
- Work in harmony with nature.
- Be a prolific product producer—in planning, construction, and recycling.
- Be an environment-conscious contractor.
- Continue to produce the Taisei brand of construction with high value added.

The corporation's main thrust in the next century will be in planning and design work, construction maintenance of existing buildings, and recycling of older structures. Taisei wants to expand its business overseas, and is looking to its R&D facilities to develop products that will be based upon the value-added concept.

Taisei's concern for the environment manifests itself in many ways. In 1988, the company opened its Bio-Engineering Research Institute in

Narashino City, Chiba Prefecture. This four-story structure with at-tached greenhouses focuses its research activities on plant biology and water treatment. The laboratories in this building contain sophisti-cated equipment to investigate cell cultures, gene exchange, and the separation of microorganisms, an essential element in water-treat-ment studies.

With the use of electron microscopy, specialized chemical analysis equipment and experimental plants that will be propagated in the greenhouses, the company plans to develop new products for the agri-culture industry. During a recent visit, a new strain of tomato plant was seen growing. One of the researchers said they had grafted a tomato plant onto a sweet potato stem, and the tomatoes produced by this hybrid appear to have less acidity. Taisei is experimenting with various strains of grass in an attempt to develop the perfect mix of har-diness, drought resistance, and shade-loving qualities in one plant. If called upon by a client to suggest a low-maintenance, hardy ground-cover for an atrium, or another less-than-optimum growing environ-ment, they will be ready with a practical solution.

Extensive research is ongoing in the field of waste and water treat-ment and recovery, and intensive research in one laboratory is concen-trating on the production of a plastic material produced by bacteria that would also be biodegradable. For this product the Institute has been using bacteria found in raw sewage; if a breakthrough occurs, the potential is considerable, since it would result in recycling certain types of sewage into a reusable, biodegradable product.

Taisei's Bio-Engineering Research Institute could be a powerful tool in attracting new clients in the future.

CONTRIBUTIONS TO THE PUBLIC DOMAIN

Taisei's contribution to a "lively world" does not end at the construction site or in the research center. The company has been sponsoring sev-eral sporting events such as the Yokohama Boating Heaven yachting tournament, and it also endorsed the "Treasure of the Golden Pharaohs" exhibition at the Tokyo Art Museum. Taisei published a se-ries of illustrated books for children, to create an awareness of the im-portance of construction work in everyday life, and acquired 190 examples of Le Corbusier's artwork, a lesser-known product of this world-renowned architect who died in 1965. This collection, purchased from a Swedish businessman several years ago, will soon find a home in Japan, and Le Corbusier's Picasso-like images will be able to be viewed by art lover and architect alike.

Taisei sponsors an annual performance of Beethoven's Ninth

Symphony by the Japan Philharmonic Symphony, and it also is a sponsor of the Fuyo Musical Theatre. The company's philanthropic endeavors are not limited to Japan. Shortly after the 1989 earthquake in San Francisco, both the parent company and its U.S. affiliate made a substantial donation to the San Francisco branch of the American Red Cross. Taisei America Corporation regularly contributes to the United Way, and in 1990 made a $50,000 donation to the Scripp's Clinic and Foundation in San Diego, California. And, like several other Japanese subsidiaries in the United States, Taisei has actively sought to establish a relationship with academia.

INVOLVEMENT WITH HIGHER EDUCATION
IN THE U.S.

Taisei has chosen to establish links with the University of California at Berkeley, with whom it has had a relationship since the 1970s. In 1989 Berkeley Chancellor Heyman paid a visit to Taisei President Satomi to discuss the corporation's continuing financial support for the university's Center for East Asian Studies. Taisei annually enrolls several of its employees in Berkeley's School of Architecture, Business and Engineering, and in its Lawrence Research Institute and Center for Real Estate Program. Taisei sponsors an intern program whereby 15 to 20 American undergraduate and graduate students each year work for Taisei for three months to promote an international awareness for both teacher and pupil and create an atmosphere conducive to an exchange of ideas and cultures.

THE PERSONNEL POLICIES OF THE
CORPORATION

The lifetime-employment concept is a part of the corporate policy of each Big Six construction company. At the heart of this concept is the establishment of a special relationship between employer and employee that mirrors the social compact that has existed in Japan for thousands of years. New recruits are hired with the understanding that they will devote their entire working career to the company, who in turn will train them and look after them until retirement. Most employee wage scales and company benefits are based on longevity rather than merit. The hiring and promotion practices of Taisei are much the same as those of the other Big Six contractors; salaries and other fringe benefits may vary somewhat, but remain basically similar.

Each year between August and October the annual recruiting drive begins, and anywhere from 380 to 500 people are invited to join the company, depending upon the corporation's backlog and future personnel requirements. About 50 percent of the new applicants will be architects, 25 percent will have degrees in civil engineering, 20 percent will hold degrees in economics and the law, and the remaining 5 percent will have completed other courses of study. These new recruits identify themselves by the year in which they joined the company, so that in years to come they will be known as the Class of 1994, or whichever year they were hired. It is expected that these new recruits will remain with the company until mandatory retirement at age 60.

Salaries and Bonuses

A new recruit at Taisei who joins the architecture or engineering department can expect a starting salary of about $18,000 a year. The new recruit will spend a year or two at a construction job site, and possibly spend several years in various departments within the company while gaining a generalist's education before being assigned to a more or less permanent department. Both salary and responsibility are based on seniority, and by age 40, the position of *kacho,* or manager, may be achieved, carrying with it a salary of about $41,500 per year. At age 50, if the employee follows the career path designated by the company, he or possibly she may expect to be appointed *bucho,* or general manager, of a department or section. At that time, the bucho's salary will have increased to between $64,500 and $69,000 a year.

Even if an employee does not achieve the position of kocho or bucho, he will probably receive the same salary at that point of tenure with the company.

This system of salary increases based upon longevity, and not so much ability, does not seem to bother employees. Those workers with proven ability and the corresponding title and salary do not appear to resent other "classmates" who do not contribute as much to the corporation but still receive the same salaries as the high performers. This is dismissed as the "Japanese way."

Bonuses are awarded each December and June, and although they are based upon corporate profits, each of these semiannual checks can amount to the equivalent of several months' salary. Taisei, like its other Big Six associates, believes in promoting the further education and professional advancement of its employees. Take the case of Mr. Toshihiko Omoto, first-class civil engineer, a graduate of Kyoto University with bachelors and masters degrees in civil engineering, who has been working for Taisei since 1974. Reading from his resume:

> For the first three years, I worked for domestic construction projects and then I was transferred to the International Division in 1977. Since then I have been working for overseas projects, including refinery construction

in Nigeria, wharves construction in Korea, site-preparation work in Borneo Island, Malaysia, refinery construction in Kuwait, and a hydro-electric power plant project in Indonesia. I have worked as either a site engineer, a deputy manager, a chief engineer or a chief negotiator for disputes resolution.

During the time between assignments for overseas projects, I am in charge of the section to take care of issues arising in overseas projects, especially issues concerning contracts. Between 1989 and 1991, I studied Construction Law and Arbitration in London University. While staying in London, I became an Associate Member of the Chartered Institute of Arbitrators. Now, I am stationed in the head office in Tokyo, in charge of the contract section of the Civil Engineering Department, International Division of Taisei Corporation.

Normal Work Week and Vacation Time

Most Big Six Japanese construction companies have abandoned Saturday as a work day in the last few years, and now the normal week consists of Monday through Friday, with work starting at 8:30 in the morning and ending at 5:00 P.M. However the work day does not usually end at that time. If one's work is not finished at the end of the normal work day, the company generally will authorize overtime so that the employee can complete his or her daily assignment. Many people are reluctant to apply for overtime pay since these requests may be looked upon by their supervisors as an inability to complete a task in the allotted time; so they can be seen working at their desks long after 5:00 P.M. completing their assignments without requesting additional compensation.

It is also usual for members of a work group to spend time together after work, having a few beers and getting to know each other a little better.

There are many traditional holidays in Japan that provide additional time off for the corporate employee. Between December 30 and January 3, most companies close for the New Year's holiday season, and in August most large corporations celebrate a five-day holiday called Obon, a time when it is the custom to return to one's ancestral home and pay respects to the family—both living and deceased. Founders Day is another corporate holiday at Taisei.

Vacation plans do vary somewhat from company to company, but at Taisei the following vacation schedule is in effect:

After 10 years' employment.   One week's vacation plus a 100,000-yen gift (about $77 at 130 yen to the dollar)

After 20 years' employment.   One week's vacation plus a 100,000-yen gift

After 25 years' employment.   Two weeks' vacation plus a 300,000-yen gift ($231)

This vacation schedule is somewhat deceiving, given the summer and winter corporate closings for New Year's and Obon.

If no vacation time is taken, the company allows an employee to accrue up to 45 days unused time in case it is needed for an emergency. In actuality, male employees annually take an average of 6 to 7 days vacation time, while female employees tend to take more time off each year.

Retirement Benefits

As mentioned earlier, at Taisei, as at most other major corporations, mandatory retirement, except in unusual cases, is reached at age 60. At the time of retirement employees are given the option of receiving a monthly check for the rest of their life or a lump-sum payment, half of which is presented at retirement and the balance paid out over the ensuing months until the entire amount has been disbursed. Under the normal monthly pension check-disbursement arrangement, retirees receive approximately $1923 a month, or $23,077 a year.

Other Company-Provided Benefits

Both housing and apartment rental units in and around Japan's major cities are very expensive. A cozy three-bedroom, stylish living room and dining room apartment in a desirable section of Tokyo can be had for $6100 a month; a "bargain" two-bedroom apartment in Roppongi, a modish part of Tokyo, costs about $4100 a month, and a one-bedroom in Ikebukuro, a fair distance from center city, can be rented for about $1300 a month. Most employees must live an hour or two by JR (Japan Railway) from their offices in Tokyo in order to find reasonably priced accommodations.

Many construction companies own large apartment buildings solely to provide moderately priced living quarters for their employees. Taisei maintains 1000 units for family housing and about 600 units for single workers, and the company will contribute about $331 toward an employee's monthly rental costs. If someone wishes to purchase a home, the company will provide a low-interest loan at about 3.8 percent for as much as $230,000, to enable an employee to become a home owner. Taisei also reimburses employees for commuting expenses to and from work.

Another unusual benefit offered by the company is in the form of an educational scholarship for the children of employees who may have died during their employment with the company. The corporation provides a monthly payment of $308 to those children while they pursue their education, through age 22, a time when university studies generally are completed.

A CLOSE LOOK AT A TAISEI CONSTRUCTION PROJECT

The West Passenger Terminal building project at the Tokyo International Airport, also known as Haneda, is located about a one-hour drive southwest of Tokyo. This airport handles a large volume of passenger traffic from China and other Asian countries, and is inadequate to assimilate the rapidly increasing landing and take-off activity.

In all respects, this is a huge construction project (see Fig. 6.7), and like most major construction projects in Japan, includes a number of general contractors in the joint venture (see Fig. 6.8). The entire airport-expansion program includes the completion of three new runways, new East and West Passenger Terminal buildings, and various support facilities, including five new aircraft hangers. When completed, the new runways will be able to handle 630 landings and take-offs each day. The site encompasses 1968 acres, all of it reclaimed land.

The West Terminal building has a footprint of 913,210 square feet, with a total gross floor area of 3,106,600 square feet. The contract amount for this building is $769 million.

The entire expansion program will take place in three stages (see Fig. 6.9):

Stage 1.   New A runway (completed in March 1988)

Stage 2.   The West Terminal building (completed in March 1993)

Stage 3.   B and C runways and East Terminal building (to be complete in 1995)

Taisei's involvement at this time includes the construction of the West Terminal building. A second, smaller contract was received to build five aircraft hangers. The basement structure work (Fig. 6.10) has already been put in place; the above-ground structural framework has been completed, and the building envelope is scheduled for completion in 1993. There appears to be a great deal of work remaining and not more than nine months remaining in which to do it, but Taisei remains confident that the completion schedule will be met.

The joint-venture project is divided as follows:

Taisei Corporation	50%
Kajima Corporation	13%
Overseas Bechtel	10%

(a)

(b)

Figure 6.7   Views of the West Terminal building project at Haneda Airport; (a) from the runway side, (b) with the control tower at left.

TOKYO INTERNATIONAL AIRPORT WEST PASSENGER TERMINAL BUILDING CONSTRUCTION PROJECT

EXECUTION PLAN

TOKYO INTERNATIONAL AIRPORT WEST PASSENGER TERMINAL BLDG.
CONSTRUCTION PROJECT JOINT VENTURE

TAISEI CORPORATION	KAJIMA CORPORATION
OVERSEAS BECHTEL INC.	SHIMIZU CORPORATION
TAKENAKA CORPORATION	OBAYASHI CORPORATION
TOKYU CONSTRUCTION CO., LTD.	TODA CORPORATION
SATO KOGYO CO., LTD.	JAL CONSTRUCTION

Figure 6.8 The cover of the *Tokyo International Airport Terminal Building Execution Plan.* Joint-venture participants are listed.

Takenaka, Shimizu, Obayashi, Toda Construction,   less than 5% each
Tokyu Construction, and Sato Kogyo

Mr. Katsuhiko Ogura, a Taisei veteran of 24 years, is the general project manager for this project, and he also wears the hat of general manager of the company's Tokyo Office No. 10. He has an assistant general project manager working under him, and also has a project manager in charge of mechanical/electrical/plumbing, one in charge of general construction work, a third in charge of engineering, and a fourth manager directing administrative functions. Under each of these project managers are several "section heads," referred to in Japanese as *koji kocho*. (*Koji* means section, *kocho* is head or leader.) The construction project manager has five koji kochos reporting to him. All together, Taisei has 50 staff members on site; 47 are engineers and 3 are administrative staff. There is a total of 146 construction staff members housed in the project's 14,000 square feet of field-office space.

IMPLEMENTATION PROGRAM

In implementing the Offshore Development Project, it is necessary not only to take into consideration the trend of demand for air service but the progress of the waste material dumping project and the road expansion project, including the plan to construct a road through the middle of the airport. In other words, the three projects of airport development, reclamation works and road development must be coordinated. Thus, the implementation of this project will be carried out in three stages as shown in the diagram below.

FIRST STAGE: COMPLETION OF THE NEW A-RUNWAY

The paving works on the New A-Runway started in January 1984 and completed on February 29, 1988. Total construction was finished in late March, 1988.   On July 2, the New A-Runway was placed in service.   This will increase the aircraft operations (takeoffs and landings) by 20,000 operations per year or 50 times (25 round trip flights) per day.   The first stage construction is intended to meet the rapidly increasing transportation demand for the present time.

SECOND STAGE: COMPLETION OF THE WEST TERMINAL

Major airport functions such as the passenger terminal and control tower will move to the offshore developed area.   As operations begin in the West Terminal the Wangan (Along the Bay Expressway), Arterial Ring Road 8, Tokyo Monorail extension to the West Terminal and the Keihin Kyoko Electric Railway connection with the monorail will also commence operations.   The second stage will improve passenger service with the new terminal building and ground transportation facilities.

THIRD STAGE: COMPLETION OF NEW B-RUNWAY, NEW C-RUNWAY AND THE EAST TERMINAL

In the third stage the expansion plan will be nearing completion. The New B and C Runways will be completed with the finish of the expanded area of reclaimed land. As the passenger facilities are expanded into the East Terminal the airport access road linking the terminal with Arterial ring Road 8 will be opened.   Further study of the reclamation works and coordination of the construction schedule must be made prior to the full operation of the third stage. Present forecast is around 1995.

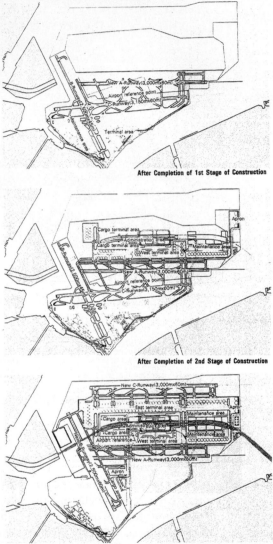

Plan of Haneda Airport Offshore Development Project

After Completion of 1st Stage of Construction

After Completion of 2nd Stage of Construction

After Completion of 3rd Stage of Construction

Figure 6.9   Three stages of the Tokyo International Airport expansion plan.

It is interesting to note that Taisei, with a 50 percent interest in the joint venture, has 50 people on staff, while Overseas Bechtel, with a 10 percent interest has only a staff of five, who are involved solely in the preparation of critical path method (CPM) scheduling.

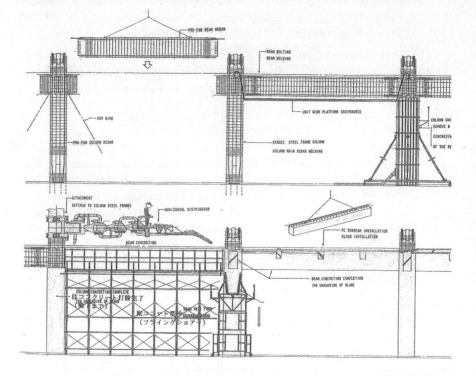

Figure 6.10 Schematic of the Tokyo Airport Terminal basement structural-framing plan.

According to Mr. Ogura, all of the 146 field office personnel are answerable to him, even though they are employed by another construction company. All of the joint venture personnel assume one identity, that of the joint venture, and the only difference between them is the source of their monthly paychecks. Mr. Ogura sets forth some of the data concerning this project:

- There are six floors in the West Terminal building, plus one basement level. The maximum height of the building is 118 ft. The gross floor area is 3,107,118 sq ft.

- The building is set on 2985 three-ft-diameter steel pipe piles, driven to depths of between 141 and 259 ft.

- The foundations consist of cast-in-place and precast-concrete slabs and sub-beams.

- There are two incoming 66-kv power lines, eight 6-kv substations and 95 secondary transformers.

- There will be two gas turbines installed, to generate 3000 kv each.

- Potable water storage tanks with a capacity of 401,000 gal will be set in place; 528,000 gal of treated water will also be stored; and 37,000 gal of hot water storage is provided.

- A central plant will provide steam heat; air-conditioning will be distributed by 313 air-handling units, 727 fan-coil units, and 94 package units. A total of 442 fans will provide local ventilation.

As of May 1992 there were 1500 construction workers on site and that number increased to approximately 2000 by late summer of that year.

As the West Terminal building nears completion, some of Mr. Ogura's staff will merge into the other joint-venture project to begin the construction of the five aircraft hangers. Tokyu Construction is the major JV partner in this project, and Taisei has only 10 percent participation. Other members of this joint venture are Obayashi and Sato Kogyo. Mr. Ogura says that two of his more important functions at the job-site involve quality control and safety, and Taisei has implemented strong programs in that regard.

QUALITY-ASSURANCE SYSTEM

At Taisei, quality control begins at the inception of the construction program when the branch general manager, construction control, and engineering department review the client's construction program. As the project progresses through the conceptual design stage, the company's design department enters the picture to convert the client's program into a preliminary design for construction analysis. The estimating and construction-control departments scrutinize the designer's work with an eye to developing construction methods and details that can be built to the company's quality standards. The branch office construction-control department is the office that will become involved in the actual construction work on site when the design has been completed and a contract is executed between the client and Taisei.

In most Japanese construction projects, the client does not provide a complete set of design documents, preferring to have the builder establish the construction details as the contract negotiations progress. The builder's staff of architects and engineers provide the final details, and that is where the ability to draw upon the company's experience in quality design, and hence quality control, come into play.

The design and functionality of the building are reviewed by several departments during the design completion stage, creating, in effect, a peer review. When a complete design has been effected by another firm, Taisei holds a drawing examination meeting prior to construction, and thoroughly reviews all aspects of the design, to anticipate potential construction problems and propose alternate solutions prior to the start of the project rather than waiting until construction is under way.

Detailed shop drawings are prepared at the job site by Taisei and by their key subcontractors. Taisei maintains a *Building Construction Control Standards* manual which contains the necessary points to be checked during construction as well as the sequential control items for each phase of construction. The company's Quality Control Section makes periodic inspections between construction phases to ensure that work is proceeding in accordance with Taisei's building quality, efficiency, and workmanship standards.

At the time of delivery, both client and contractor inspect the building to ensure that all tasks have been satisfactorily performed, and at that point Taisei transfers the relevant documents to the owner, explaining all of the various functions of the structure and recommending certain maintenance procedures.

Taisei's Maintenance Service Section assumes certain responsibilities once the building is turned over to the client, and inspections are made 6, 12, and 24 months after delivery. At the client's request, the Maintenance Service Section will make further inspections to determine if correct preventative maintenance programs are being properly carried out in the new building.

The key to success in construction quality control begins with a careful inspection of the design documents and ends with several postconstruction inspections. During these postconstruction inspections, any defects or problem areas are corrected and notes are made that will be transmitted back to the Design Review Section for future design considerations.

TAISEI'S COMMITMENT TO SAFETY, AND ITS IMPLEMENTATION

Japan, like the United States, has federal regulations governing jobsite safety. The Law on Occupational Safety and Hygiene covers inspections of machinery, boiler and pressure vessels, working conditions in various industries, and regulations pertaining to the temporary housing provided for workers near the job site.

Taisei has its own extensive safety program, and the priority target for 1992 was the virtual elimination of all fatal accidents. The frequency of accidents in the company decreased in the period between 1985 and 1990, and although the severity of each accident was also reduced, it reached a very low point in 1985 that could not be sustained. The total hours worked between 1985 and 1990 did not vary a great deal, but fatalities grew from four in 1985 to ten in 1990, a disturbing fact for Taisei; thus their present emphasis is the total elimination of job-site deaths due to accidents.

Headquarters has set up a Safety Administration Department charged with the following responsibilities:

1. Establish safety goals by creating a five-year safety plan.
2. Target certain areas for concentrated effort during a one-year period.
3. Gather data on the current safety statistics and the general health levels of all employees.
4. Initiate the procedure of conducting daily safety patrols on all job sites.
5. Analyze and evaluate the safety data transmitted back from the sites.
6. Direct and guide branch offices in implementing the program.
7. Assist subcontractors in establishing and implementing their own safety programs.
8. Issue reports and findings to managers and supervisors relating to the safety in their areas.

Like most general contractors in Japan, Taisei subcontracts almost 100 percent of its construction work to specialty contractors; therefore, the thrust of its safety program must be focused toward these groups. Taisei requires all subcontractors to sign onto a safety program.

Subcontractor Oath of Safety and Sanitation

Each subcontractor must sign a four-page "Written Oath of Safety and Sanitation," agreeing to appoint an on-site safety representative and abide by the following comprehensive list of safety rules and regulations:

- Instruct all full- and part-time employees in the company safety program.
- Liaise with the general contractor and all other subcontractors on the site with respect to safety rules, regulations, meetings, and inspections.
- Conduct periodic safety meetings on site.
- Participate in the general contractor's daily foreman meetings.
- Prohibit sick workers from coming to work.
- Eliminate unsound construction practices.
- Ensure that all workers have had their medical exam before commencing work.

- Inspect and approve the use of all equipment, tools, and vehicles brought onto the site by the company who owns them.

- Follow daily maintenance and inspection procedures prescribed by the general contractor when using its equipment.

- When an accident occurs, investigate it promptly and take measures to prevent its happening again.

KY Working Manual

Not so much a manual as a daily report, the "KY Working Manual" (see Fig 6.11) is a form that is completed as the Taisei Safety Patrol supervisor makes his rounds. This form lists the dangerous operations being performed, notes potential safety hazards that could cause accidents while performing those operations, and states countermeasures that need to be instituted to prevent accidents. The daily "KY Working Manual" is posted in a highly visible area on the site until it is replaced by an updated report the following day. Each work-crew supervisor is required to review the contents of this posted KY manual the following morning with his assembled workers before they begin their day's work.

At that morning meeting, the day's activities are reviewed, and if they include any operations from the previous day, the KY manual will be used to call attention to possible problems and the countermeasures that need to be taken to prevent an accident. Everyone present at the meeting is then made aware of the recommended changes in the working procedures for the day.

Daily Safety Routine

The daily job-site safety program conducted by Taisei at the job site is as follows:

1. Post the "KY Working Manual" for the day and review its contents.

2. Start the morning group exercise to limber up the workers' muscles.

3. Check out personal and construction equipment before the start of the work day.

4. Conduct safety patrols periodically during the work day.

5. Conduct a safety meeting daily, usually at mid-afternoon.

6. Clean up the day's debris—a clean site is a safe site.

There are daily safety programs, weekly safety meetings, and monthly accident prevention conferences known as the Safety Cycle (see Fig. 6.12).

Month: Date:	KY Working Procedure	Job:
Procedure	Do you find any probable danger? (Indicate the most probable.)	Countermeasures
1. Loading materials	Fall of hoisted loads	1. Arrange an off-limits area. 2. Hoist wire to be checked by Mr. _____ 3. A signal to be given by Mr. _____ after he has left load-lifting area.
2. Setting a main rope	Step onto the ground	1. Work with a safety belt hung from the frame materials.
3. Allocating bracing timber	Stumble onto the ground	1. Walk with a safety belt hung from the main rope.
4. Fitting of frames	Falling off due to a loss of balance	1. Walk with a safety belt hung from the main rope. 2. Framing and bracing to be executed from both sides.
5. Fitting of handrails around the end part of frames	Stumble onto the ground	1. Work with a safety belt hung from the frames.
6. Installation of working floor	Fingers pinched due to fitting being carried out while materials in hand	1. Alternate hands when receiving successive spans
7. Fitting of stairs and handrails	Feet injured due to materials being dropped on them	1. Work in cooperation with the partner, confirming his signal
Company's name:	Foreman's name:	No. of workmen

Figure 6.11   Typical entry form from Taisei's "KY Working Manual."

Over the years Taisei's safety program has paid off. The frequency of job-site accidents has been lowered from 1.39 in 1982 to .97 in 1990, and the severity of the accidents has been reduced from .75 in 1982 to .60 in 1990.

NEW PRODUCT AND CONSTRUCTION TECHNOLOGY

Each member of the Big Six endeavors to create a product or process that makes it unique, one that it can point to with pride and say, "Look

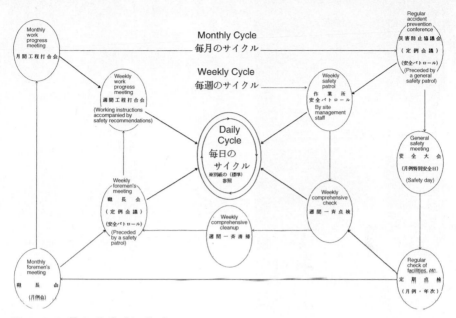

Figure 6.12 Taisei's Safety Cycle.

what we've done that no other construction company in Japan has been able to do." There is also a great deal of one-upmanship among Big Six contractors. If one builder develops a super-high-rise building concept of 1000 meters, another builder will race to publish a concept for a 1001-meter-tall building. So it is with Taisei in the development of Taisei 100—a one-hundred-story, 1574-foot-tall building that will incorporate many innovative engineering developments that are required for building such a tall building in as active a seismic zone as Japan.

The structure of Taisei 100 consists of four vertically defined blocks or building sections. The bottom section is octagonal in shape, and the second block, intended to be stacked on the lower one, is circular. The third block is square, and the uppermost block takes on the shape of a cross (Fig. 6.13). The octagonal-base structure has a footprint of 91,460 square feet, and each section placed upon this base is configured for aesthetics as well as to provide some stability from wind loading and seismic disturbances. But the full measure of resistance to swaying in the wind and protection against earthquake damage are provided by Taisei-developed passive and semiactive damping devices.

Foremost among these damping devices is DREAMY (*damping resisting amplification by means of a yoke*), which utilizes the lever principle to create resistance to forces imposed upon the building by wind loading or earthquakes: A combination lever and damper device is incorporated into the structural framework of a building (Fig. 6.14). The

Figure 6.13 Taisei 100 concept with different sectional configurations.

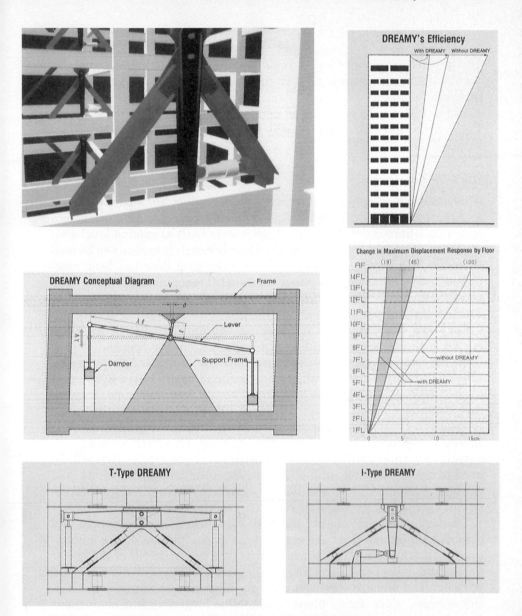

Figure 6.14 DREAMY—Damping device for high-rise buildings.

lateral movement of the building's frame activates the lever portion of DREAMY, which in turn transforms the frame motion into large movements of the damper's piston. The damper exerts a force that resists the motion of the lever, and the faster the piston motion, the more effective the damping.

The installation of DREAMY is rather straightforward, maintenance is relatively easy, and associated costs are low. That DREAMY is effective can be confirmed by the results of dynamic earthquake analysis performed by the company's 3-D shaking-table tests conducted at its research facility.

Taisei 100 may be constructed using the company's newly developed T-UP method, a step along the way to a fully automated construction-erection cycle.

The T-UP Approach

In an attempt to create a safer workplace, reduce construction costs, and increase quality, Taisei has developed a concept of building construction where the top floor of a high-rise is built at ground level and, via hydraulic jacks, raised when the floor beneath it is ready to be constructed. This sequence is followed until the first floor has been completed and remains in place, since all upper floors previously have been jacked into place. Figure 6.15 represents the schematic approach to this T-UP construction sequence.

Each Big Six contractor is pursuing the development of an automated building scheme, and each company's modus operandi varies from its competitors'—some to more noticeable degrees than others. The T-UP method involves the construction of a core tower in the center of the proposed high-rise building. The top floor, encompassing the roof structure, is constructed with truss-like roof members, and wraps around the center core. The outer perimeter of this top floor extends somewhat beyond the footprint of the building. This "hat" section, as it is called by Taisei, will be fitted out with overhead cranes that will be used to raise, assemble, and place beams, columns, floor systems, and exterior wall sections as the floors below are constructed and subsequently jacked up as the "hat" rises around the center core.

The hat section covers the floors being worked on underneath and provides protection from the elements. The completion of the foundation work takes place concurrently with the construction of the upper floors, and Taisei envisions using robot-controlled excavators for that purpose. The Japanese penchant for prefabrication manifests itself in this scheme, since Taisei plans to assemble large building-component modules off-site, where they can be built under strict quality-controlled conditions. These preassembled components, such as exterior wall sections with windows, then would be installed quickly and accurately by robots at the job-site.

Taisei sees this T-UP method as one that allows the site project manager to concentrate on a degree of quality control not possible with piecemeal construction sequences using conventional building technology. The ability to prefabricate large parts and modules off-site under

2. A *'hat'* is built around the core. Overhead cranes lift beams, floors, walls and other large sections. As work finishes on each floor, the hat lifts hydraulically to the next level. Once all floors are finished, the hat becomes the building's top floor.

1. A *core* is gradually built up, supporting the structure, providing earthquake resistance, and serving as a frame supporting the entire T-UP system. As the core rises, the rest of the building follows closely.

3. While the hat is raised along the core step by step, *robots* prepare lower floors by finishing interiors and installing fixtures.

4. With T-UP, upper level work begins before foundation and excavation work has been fully completed. Robots work *above and below ground, simultaneously.*

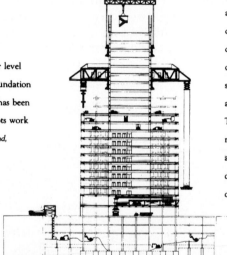

5. Large building *modules* are assembled away from the construction site, under conditions of strict quality control. Once at the site, these sections are installed quickly and accurately by robots. The confusion and danger of manual processes are eliminated, allowing the site manager to concentrate fully on quality control.

Figure 6.15 Taisei's T-UP approach.

controlled conditions by machines should ensure the contractor and his client a high-quality product. And, lastly, Taisei sees this method of construction as one that would also guarantee a safe and clean working environment.

Taisei's X-Seed 4000 Concept

Going the competition one better, Taisei announced its "X-Seed 4000" concept—a building that would rise 4000 meters in the air. That's 13,120 feet! When it made the announcement about X-Seed 4000, Taisei made it very clear that this structure was visionary and would serve to promote a new technological development that could result in better urban planning in the next century. But even as a futuristic concept, this scheme staggers the imagination.

This conical-shaped structure, with components in tension and compression, looks for all the world like a man-made Mount Fuji (Fig. 6.16). X-Seed 4000 will have a circular base approximately 3.7 miles in diameter, and this base will cover about 7413 acres, creating a total effective usable building area of 12,355 to 17,000 acres, enough room to house 500,000 to 700,000 residents.

Three concentric circular frames with a core frame in the center and an outer frame would organically link the overall structure into a "space net" structure. This behemoth would have a floating foundation, and is meant to be built on the sea or on a huge lake. The space from grade level to an elevation of 6500 feet in X-Seed 4000 would be devoted to residential, commercial, and administrative functions, while the areas above the 1.23-mile level would contain a nature and space observation center, energy plants, and an ultra-panoramic sky resort. In Japan, what is fantasy today could become reality tomorrow.

Figure 6.16   X-Seed 4000 ultra-high-rise, space-net structure concept.

Taisei's Robots

Automated building systems and computer-assisted construction work is made somewhat easier with robotics, and Taisei has many robots in its tool box:

- A large exterior-column-painting robot
- An exterior-wall-tile inspection robot
- An exterior-wall-painting robot
- A steel-reinforcing-bar-fabrication robot
- A concrete-spraying robot
- A shield-segment-transportation robot
- A wallboard-manipulating robot
- A ceiling-panel-manipulating robot

This "lively world" envisioned by Taisei will require the company to seek answers to the overcrowding of urban areas and maintain that difficult balance between development and the environment. Taisei's long history of meeting the challenges in civil engineering work will be put to the test in this new era of concept for the health of our planet. And it will take all of the creativity and imagination this corporation can muster to explore and master the expanding frontier of new construction in the coming century. The Okura Trading Company has certainly come a long way in the past 119 years, and the baron would be pleased with the results of his labor.

Chapter 7

Shimizu Corporation

Striving for Excellence

The Shimizu Corporation considered 1991 a pretty good year. It had begun the year with a $17,422,000,000 backlog and won new contracts worth $17,398,000,000. The corporation's net income for 1991 was $317,501,000 and its total asset value climbed to $16,403,000,000.

Among the Big Six there is an informal competition to determine which company leads in work completed for the year, based on dollar volume of new orders received and profits earned. This is called the "Triple Crown." Shimizu won the Triple Crown in 1988, 1989, and 1990. In 1991 it won only two legs; the third crown, for highest profit, went to the Kajima Corporation. But Shimizu Corporation looks to the future with great expectations, just as it has done since the company was founded 188 years ago.

THE BEGINNING

Kisuke Shimizu grew up during the latter part of the eighteenth century in the Toyama district of Japan, located on the Sea of Japan side of the island of Honshu.

This was the time of the Tokugawa Shogunate, which dated back to 1600 and was to continue until 1868 when the Meiji Era began. During this period in Japan's history, feudal lords ruled over castle towns, and the samurai played an important role in society, not so much as soldiers as for filling the ranks of the civil service. In the Tokugawa society, the samurai ranked first in a descending order of hierarchy that included farmer, artisan, and, lastly, merchant. Japan's economy began to grow during the latter days of the Tokugawa Shogunate, and while Osaka became the country's financial and economic center, Edo was the most heavily populated.

Kisuke Shimizu moved to Edo, the old name for Tokyo, to set up shop in 1804. At that time the population of Edo was about 1.3 million, making it the most heavily populated city in the world, and Shimizu began to find ample carpentry work in this bustling city. As he obtained more commissions, he honed his skills until he had graduated to the status of master carpenter. His first major construction project, a small hotel in Edo, had been authorized by the Tokugawa Shogunate; however, during construction, the client's source of funds dried up, and Shimizu completed the project with his own funds. He actually operated the hotel for many years thereafter.

Like many Japanese people at that time who lacked a male hier, Kisuke Shimizu, who had no son to inherit his growing business, adopted a young man who was subsequently known as Kisuke Shimizu II. Shimizu II, who was born in 1815, became a very talented designer and during his lifetime was considered one of Japan's greatest pseudo-Western-style architects.

As the Meiji Era approached and the age of Western-style buildings came into vogue, Shimizu II's talents were much in demand. In 1871 he designed and supervised the construction of the Tjukiji Hotel for Foreigners in Tokyo. His First Mitsui Bank Headquarters, designed in 1871, and three years later, his Second Mitsui Bank building won much acclaim throughout the architectural community in Japan. The company experienced continued growth during the mid and latter part of the nineteenth century as its reputation as a quality builder and Shimizu II's as an outstanding architect grew.

This fledging company prospered during the early twentieth century, adopted a corporate structure in 1915, and changed its name to Shimizu Gumi. The mid-1930s saw the company expanding its operations into Manchuria, North China, Taiwan, Korea, and Hong Kong, along with other Japanese construction companies who followed the country's overseas military and economic expansion programs.

Three years after the end of World War II, the company formally adopted the name Shimizu Construction Company, Ltd. Along with the other large construction companies in Japan, Shimizu prospered because of the large volume of construction work generated by the build-up of the U.S. armed forces during the Korean War, when Japan assumed a major role as a staging area for that conflict. Vast sums of money subsequently flowed into the economy to create and construct the facilities for the 1964 Olympic Games.

But 1973 brought with it a distinct and sharp downturn in construction activity in the country. Contractors refer to this period as the start of the construction "winter" in Japan, which lasted until 1986. The major construction companies in the country had to look to international markets to satisfy their appetite for big projects. In 1973

Shimizu opened a subsidiary in Brazil, Construtora Shimizu Do Brasil, Ltd., and the next year it opened offices in San Francisco and New York. That same year operations were started in Micronesia, and offices were opened in Dusseldorf, Germany; Sydney, Australia; and Singapore. A joint-venture company was formed in Indonesia, and in 1975 another joint-venture operation was established in Saipan. Shimizu began to acquire construction technology from Europe, forming an operational tie-up with Gadelius International AB from Sweden, and obtaining cooling-tower technology from a West German firm. As Japan's construction winter deepened, Shimizu increased the pace in which it established overseas offices—in Canada, additional offices in the United States, Guam, the United Kingdom, China, Malaysia, and Australia. Today, the company has a total of 22 offices in North America, 4 in South America, 23 in Europe, 4 in Africa, 2 in the Middle East, 13 in Oceania and the Pacific Rim, and 23 in Asia.

Although most winters are followed by spring, not so with construction. The year 1986 saw a construction boom begin in Japan—the construction "summer"; Shimizu's overseas market volume dropped from 16 to 6 percent as the company picked up more and more business in its home country. And although the economy has cooled in Japan, in 1992 the government's announcement of a trillion-dollar commitment to infrastructure construction appears to have set the stage for another 10-year boom.

SHIMIZU'S NEW CORPORATE HEADQUARTERS

In 1992 the corporation moved its headquarters (Fig. 7.1) into a new building named "Seavans" in the Shibaura section of Tokyo. Located on a waterfront canal that adjoins Tokyo Bay, Shimizu occupies one of the two 24-story glass-curtain-wall buildings on the site. The other building belongs to *Nippon Telephone and Telegraph* (NTT) and is joined to its twin by a barrel-vaulted atrium. As a condition to the issuance of a building permit, Tokyo's Department of Buildings stipulated that the atrium must be open to the public, and the completion of the interior landscaping, with its gently flowing fountains and retail space, now makes it a pleasant place in which to stroll.

The Shimizu Corporation recently opened the Zero In, a physical fitness club in the Atrium, complete with a medical check-up and counseling clinic, exercise equipment, swimming pool, sauna, and lounge. Although from all outward appearances these two 328-foot-tall glass and aluminum curtain-wall buildings reflect standard construction design and detailing, under its skin, the Shimizu building contains some rather unique features. While under construction, a spray fireproofing

Figure 7.1 Shimizu's new corporate headquarters complex.

robot could be observed on the upper floors applying fireproofing materials to the steel frame, not too successfully at times, but attempting to
make the difficult transition from an experimental to a production
model.

Housed on the fifth floor of the building is Seavans Eye, a live, in-
house TV broadcasting system staffed by professional announcers.
Every morning beginning at 10:00 A.M., Miss Aoyama and Miss Hatano
go on the air broadcasting Shimizu company news, construction-indus-
try news, and general news items that are displayed on TV monitors
placed strategically throughout the headquarters building. Many Big

Six contractors experiment with new products and systems in their own buildings as part of their ongoing "real time" research programs, and Shimizu is using parts of its new facility to investigate ways to improve productivity in an office environment.

Amenity Demonstration Room

Shimizu has built several office areas in Seavans where lighting, sound, smell, air flow, and visual factors can be controlled and modified, and the resultant effects on workers can be observed and monitored. On the fourteenth floor of its building, offering a sweeping view of Tokyo Bay, Shimizu has installed an olfactory-enhancing system called Aromanity. This system is designed to be attached to the building's central HVAC system, and can inject a small amount of a concentrated fragrance into the air stream at regulated intervals. The subtle aroma can be made to resemble a woody scent, jasmine, lemon, or a wide range of other pleasing odors.

Mr. Hideo Inamura, interviewed in his office in the Shimizu building, said that the company is convinced that worker satisfaction and productivity can be improved in an office environment if noise and odor can be controlled. Researchers working for the company have experimented with many masking agents and sounds to determine which ones produce the best working environment. Office noise is a real problem, but the absence of noise is also a problem, as Shimizu researchers discovered; they have experimented with piped-in synthesized ocean-wave and babbling-brook sounds in an effort to achieve the desired effect in employee satisfaction.

Working with University of Tokyo Professor Shizuo Torii, a defined correlation was found between olfactory nerves and the brain. Professor Torii said that heretofore it had been difficult to ascertain this link because the standard electroencephalogram equipment was not sensitive enough to pick up this brain activity. By focusing on a narrow band of EEG waves known as "party waves," he was able to discern that certain smells affect brain activity. Professor Torii discovered that the scent of jasmine excites the brain, while the odor of lavender has the opposite effect.

Shimizu, checking out Torii's laboratory findings, took a more pragmatic approach to the experimentation; over a period of one month it kept track of a computer operator's errors when jasmine, lavender, and lemon scents were introduced into the air stream. It found that lemon odors resulted in a 50-percent reduction in errors when compared to no scents having been released. Each of the other scents produced a reduction in errors, but not as dramatic as the one the lemon scent produced.

Picking up on Shimizu's research, Hitachi Credit performed a similar test on telephone operators in its building. When an apple or a lemon scent was released into the air, Hitachi found 80 to 90 percent fewer errors being made.

Shimizu's Aromanity system currently is available to Japanese subscribers on a lease-only basis. The company estimates that the cost to scent a 1000-square-meter area (about 10,760 square feet) is between $1154 and $1231 per month. These costs include leasing the machine, maintenance, and the cost of the essential oils used to create the scent. Since the system was introduced in 1989, Shimizu has leased fifty machines to 30 customers.

Shimizu is very much concerned with what it terms "technostress," an office environment that has become increasingly cramped and crowded with automated electronic machines. It took five years of experimentation before Shimizu felt its environmental amenity system was ready to be marketed, and it feels that with its introduction, significant strides are being made in reducing technostress.

Although several experts criticized some of Shimizu's methods, such as attaching electrodes to workers to determine their levels of sensory stimulation, the company deemed this research important enough to employ these means, which were by no means harmful, either physically or emotionally. With an impeding shortage of office workers, Shimizu wishes to present the most hospitable environment so that it can attract and keep the best employees.

HI-TECH AND THE SHIMIZU JOB SITE

Shimizu's presence in Japan's domestic construction market is much in evidence, from its participation in such giant development projects as Yokohama's $15 billion Minato Mirai, to restoration work at the sacred Meiji Shrine in Tokyo. In the Minato ward of Tokyo, Shimizu is constructing what for them may be a rather modest project—a 56,000-square-foot multistoried office building, and a 31,380-square-foot residential condominium (Fig. 7.2).

A glance at a normal work day on the job gives some insight into the thoroughness with which the company approaches the management of its projects.

A Day in the Life of a Shimizu Construction Project

The normal work day begins at 8:30 A.M. and ends at 5:00 P.M. There is a one-hour lunch period and 15-minute breaks at 10:00 in the morning

Figure 7.2 Model of the office-condominum project in Minato-ku.

and 3:00 in the afternoon. Alternate Saturdays are designated as workdays.

Shimizu, as the general contractor of this multiuse project, has subcontracted all of the work in a manner similar to that used by American contractors; but that is about where the similarities end. All workers on the site assemble at 8:30 A.M. in an area outside a Shimizu field office on a floor of one of the two buildings under construction. One of Shimizu's six project staff members starts the morning program by leading all workers in five minutes of warm-up exercises conducted to music.

After this brief period of muscle stretching, the Shimizu field engineer and his assistant move stanchions in place, each of which bears the name of a subcontractor currently working on the site that day. The subcontractor foreman and his workers line up behind their marker (see Fig. 7.3). A wall-mounted bulletin board is illuminated, a public address system is activated, and the Shimizu engineer begins to discuss the day's work schedule. The engineer points out those areas in the building where most of the activity will take place and cautions everyone about certain daily procedures that may be hazardous; i.e., load-

Figure 7.3 The morning line-up at the subcontractor meeting.

ing rooftop equipment at the office building with the crane that will be arriving soon (see Fig. 7.4.). This daily work-activity-update session lasts for about 10 or 15 minutes, and when it is over the results of the previous day's late-afternoon safety patrol are announced. Any violations or unsafe conditions noted during that walk-through are pointed out briefly once more. A new worker arriving on the job site that day will be requested to introduce himself at this morning meeting and identify the subcontractor with whom he is affiliated. Each new arrival is greeted by applause from all of the other workers, and after his introduction and when the morning meeting has been adjourned, this new worker is briefed on Shimizu's on-site safety program before being allowed to enter the work area.

The Shimizu field engineer conducting the morning meeting then asks each subcontractor foreman, one by one, to briefly describe that company's planned work schedule for the day and the areas in the building or on the site where its crews will be working. Each statement is met with acknowledgments from all workers as they respond with "*Hi*"—Yes.

The general meeting then breaks up, and all workers face each other and check each other's safety equipment. "Hard hat on and chin strap in place?—Hi!," Safety belt attached and buckled?—"Hi"! and so on, until each item of personal protection has been properly checked.

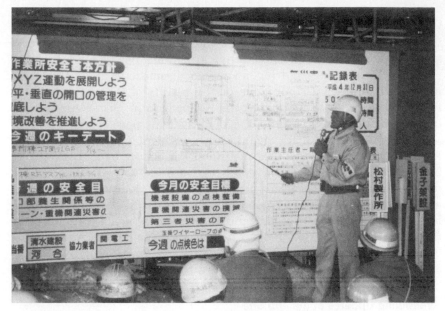

Figure 7.4 The Shimizu engineer points out the areas of concern for the day.

Figure 7.5 The subcontractor, meeting with his men after the general meeting.

Each subcontractor foreman then meets with his circle of workers (Fig. 7.5), and a brief run-through of their day's activities will be reviewed once more before all of them head off to their assigned workstations. A walk through the building after work has begun reveals no radios or boom-boxes blaring away, no discussions among workers about last night's baseball game or the results of the summer Sumo wrestling matches being held at the Kokogekan in Tokyo. All seem to quietly go about their assigned tasks at a steady pace.

The Japanese fetish for cleanliness is evident everywhere. In one area of the building, steel fireproofing materials are being troweled by a worker on a rolling scaffold. A laborer working with the mechanic is on his hands and knees with a brush and a scoop cleaning up droppings as they occur. Even when trash and debris is discarded temporarily it is done in an orderly fashion. Random pieces of gypsum wallboard are not strewn about the floor but are neatly stacked against a wall in plastic bags awaiting disposal. Cleaning is performed daily, but each Thursday a concentrated building cleaning program takes place.

Scheduling Updates at the Job Site

Shimizu staff members meet at 11:30 each morning to review the construction schedule and update it when necessary. This schedule update and current manning chart are rather hi-tech affairs. In their temporary field office, a lap-top computer rests under an overhead projector that projects the computer screen onto a white-faced wall-mounted bulletin board (Fig. 7.6). The Shimizu field engineer assembles his group, and with a light pencil touches the bulletin board (Fig. 7.7) that displays the day's projected manpower requirements. Alongside the line containing the tile worker's manpower, he removes the number "2" with his light-pencil and writes in the number "3" which then is instantaneously transferred back to the laptop. After updating the number of workers currently on the job with the light-pencil, the computer makes its memory adjustment, and the field engineer taps a button below the screen, and a hard copy of this day's manning chart is produced, as shown in Figure 7.8.

Anticipated deliveries are also reviewed, scheduled, and entered on a form (Fig. 7.9); not only is the material or equipment to be delivered indicated, but the anticipated time of arrival and the location on the site or within the building where it is to be delivered is noted also. A copy of this projected and updated delivery schedule is sent to the guardhouse.

At 1:00 P.M. each day, Shimizu's field staff meets with each subcontractor foreman to review the next day's work schedule. The updated manning chart is passed around, and agreement is reached on the

Figure 7.6 The lap-top computer casting its readout onto an electronic bulletin board.

Figure 7.7 A Shimizu engineer updating with a light-pencil.

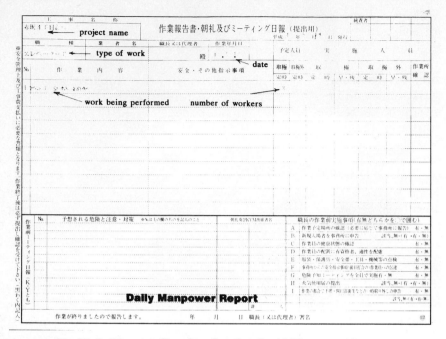

Figure 7.8 The "Daily Manning Chart" produced at the 11:30 A.M. meeting.

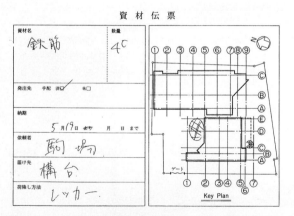

Figure 7.9 A shimizu material delivery ticket showing the locations of deliveries.

number of men required for each trade the following day. This is entered into the computer via the light-pencil and on the bulletin board. A hoisting schedule for elevator usage the next day is also developed at this meeting.

Shimizu had six in staff at this job-site, including a project manager, an assistant project manager, and various field engineers, including its first female engineer, hired by the corporation in April 1992.

Along with an impression of a well-organized, extremely clean job site, the construction materials and the methods of application and installation, would reveal no major differences between this project and one in the United States except for a product called ALC. Japanese contractors seem to use *autoclaved lightweight concrete* (ALC) panels in lieu of fire-rated gypsum drywall partitions in stairwells, around elevator shafts, and in other areas requiring a fire rating. These ALC panels are 100 mm thick (3.9 in.), about 30 in. wide, and 10 to 12 ft high. They have tongue and groove edges and can be set in place rather quickly. When faced with a layer of drywall or troweled on surfacing material, they create a tough, fire-resistive partition.

FROM INNER SPACE TO OUTER SPACE

Not satisfied with its expansion of branch offices around the world, in April 1987 Shimizu established its Space Project office to explore space-related construction and engineering research. These endeavors were to focus on the design and construction of ground-support facilities and the design and construction of space-based structures. The Ralph M. Parsons Company of California teamed up with Shimizu that year to provide technical assistance on some of these space-related projects, and CSP Associates, another U.S. firm working with Shimizu, formed the basis for the creation of CSP Japan, Inc., a space-industry consulting firm. Some of this research activity may have been generated by the Japanese government's renewed interest in space exploration.

Japan's national Space Development Agency is increasing its efforts to develop a housing module for the moon in anticipation of being able to house three astronauts there for durations of two to three weeks. NASDA's Tsukuba Space Center began to develop this concept in 1986, and plans are under way to develop and build a four-module space station that could circle the earth in low orbit in preparation for a moon trip. Both NASDA and the *Ministry of International Trade and Industry* (MITI) is exhibiting increased interest in establishing a moon base, and work is progressing on perfecting the LE-7 cryogenic rocket to power the first stage of its H-11 launch vehicle.

Shimizu has been actively involved in conceptually developing a series of spaceports (Fig. 7.10) to be located in Hokkaido, Japan, and in Australia, Hawaii, and Florida. These projects will serve not only as potential launch sites for space-traveling vehicles, but also will be international research complexes involved in a whole host of space-related

Figure 7.10 Schematic of Shimizu's spaceport.

scientific pursuits. Shimizu envisions the construction of these space-ports as multifunctional complexes that will have a positive economic impact on the surrounding areas and act as nuclei around which other construction projects will evolve. It feels that the company will then be in a good position to capture any of this related construction work.

Along with space planning, Shimizu has been working on products and systems that could be used in the construction of lunar colonies. The development of a lunar concrete is being pursued. This material would use minerals obtained from the Moon's crust. Initial research reveals that when subjected to a chemical reduction process and mixed with aggregates, a kind of lunar concrete could be produced, resulting in an ideal end-product for the radioactive atmosphere of the Moon. This lunar concrete would be used to build hexagonal building blocks in a honeycomb structure similar to the one depicted in Figure 7.11.

The Space Project office is conducting research on *closed ecological life-support systems* (CELSS) incorporating the regeneration of human wastes for biomass production and food processing, and converting carbon dioxide into oxygen.

Shimizu's 35-person space-research team is also working on refining its "Star-Bay 3" connectors (Fig. 7.12), which would form the basis of a lightweight truss system that could be incorporated into space-station construction. In conjunction with research being carried out with Carnegie Mellon in Pittsburgh, Pennsylvania, Shimizu is actively pursuing the development of robotics to assemble these trusses in space.

Figure 7.11 Honeycomb structure made of lunar concrete block.

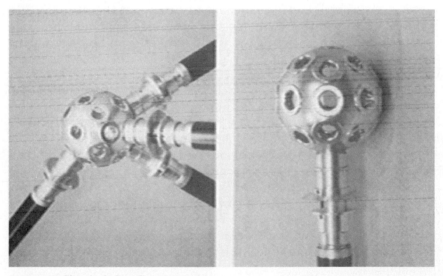

Figure 7.12 Shimizu's Star Bay 3 connectors.

In December 1990 Shimizu announced the proposed construction of an orbiting tourist resort, one that would be positioned 280 miles above Earth and be able to accommodate 100 guests and crew. Shimizu's Space Project office led by General Manager Seishi Suzuki will focus on the construction engineering associated with four categories:

- Space stations, space factories, and other types of platforms in orbit
- Bases on the moon and other planets
- Rocket-launching facilities and related support systems including those used for research, experiments, and production
- Space-related information services and associated services such as personnel training

In order to accomplish its goals, the Space Project office has affiliated itself with a worldwide network of advanced research and development partners: J.M. Beggs Associates; The Ralph M. Parsons Company; C.S.P. Associates; Bell and Trotti, Inc.; Carbotek, Inc.; Binistar Inc.; Carnegie Mellon; the University of Colorado at Boulder; the Institute of Space and Astronautical Science; the College of Agriculture at the University of Tokyo; and the School of Medicine at the University of Nihon.

SC RESEARCH CENTER, INC.

Like each of the other Big Six constructors, Shimizu maintains a sophisticated research and development institute, but the company also realizes that corporate growth depends upon a well-planned corporate strategy based on a knowledge of world markets and how these markets may shift. This is one of the reasons for the creation of SC Research, Inc.

Mr. Yo Hisatomi, a first-class architect-engineer with more than 30 years' experience at Shimizu, is the organization's research director. Mr. Hisatomi spent 10 years as a site engineer for Shimizu, and 10 more years in the company's R&D department, after which time he was appointed the manager of research for an additional 10 years. He then moved over to the company's international division, spending his last three years before mandatory retirement in corporate planning. Although the Corporation has its own corporate planning and strategy department, Shimizu felt that the creation of a "think tank" independent from the pulls and tugs of the corporate environment could provide an "outsider's" view of how the world's construction markets may be shaping up.

Mr. Hisatomi is of the opinion that Japan's domestic construction market will present more opportunities for the company in the near future than many international markets. Asian markets bear careful watching, according to Mr. Hisatomi, and there will be many opportunities for builders in Vietnam, Thailand, Singapore, and, when political changes occur, in North Korea. He is keeping an eye on Siberia and the Russian port area of Vladivostok as places where industrial activity could create considerable construction work. Soon he will be traveling to Great Britain to study the European Economic Community and its market potential. It is his opinion that Japanese contractors will have a tough time cracking that market, although it may be made somewhat easier if they are requested to build there by their long-term Japanese industrial clients expanding manufacturing and distribution facilities in the EC.

Vietnam, in his opinion, represents a potentially strong emerging market for construction. The country has considerable oil reserves and an abundance of other natural resources. With a population of 68 million, Vietnam has a large untapped labor force, albeit much of it unskilled. Tourism could be a major industry, but it has been hampered by a lack of infrastructure. Local electric power is so unreliable that hotels must have a 100-percent back-up emergency generator system. The government of Vietnam is now friendly toward foreign investment and investors, and may welcome investment seed-money offered by the Japanese government's Overseas Development Agency. Shimizu will keep a close watch on construction markets in that country, because a boom could take place within the next three to five years. This is the kind of information SC Research gathers and passes on to the Shimizu Corporation. SC Research has a branch office in Cambridge, Massachusetts, where Shimizu has maintained a relationship with the Massachusetts Institute of Technology for many years. Shimizu currently is sponsoring a five-year program at MIT to investigate possible future joint-research projects. It has elected, initially, to proceed with a joint study on facility management, a field in which Japanese contractors feel that U.S. firms have a distinct edge.

SHIMIZU'S U.S. OPERATIONS

Shimizu has branch offices and subsidiaries in New York, New Jersey, Massachusetts, Georgia, Illinois, Texas, Arizona, California, Kentucky, Washington, and Hawaii. The company opened its first United States offices in New York and San Francisco in 1974. Some of its major projects in the United States at this time are the America Plaza in San Diego, a 34-story, 569,000-square-foot office building with retail space on the lower levels; the 500-room San Antonio Hyatt Resort Hotel, complete with an 18-hole golf course; and on the island of Mauna Lani in Hawaii, the 542-room Ritz Carlton Mauna Lani Hotel.

In 1991 the U.S. market represented 26 percent of Shimizu's overseas-subsidiary construction-contract awards. Europe accounted for almost 48 percent, while the Asian market contributed 20.5 percent, and Oceania 5.46 percent. Development projects reflect a slightly different balance, wherein America represented 37.5 percent of all overseas development projects, with Europe contributing 33 percent, Oceania 20 percent, and Asia only 9.5 percent.

Over the past 18 years Shimizu has built many corporate headquarters buildings in New Jersey, office parks in Arizona, and hotels in California; but one of its more memorable projects may be the *Advanced Semiconductor Technology Center* (ASTC) that was planned for IBM in East Fishkill, New York. That project taught Shimizu the nuances of American construction.

In 1986 IBM was planning the construction of a new technology center at its East Fishkill, New York, facility, just five miles or so south of its huge complex in Poughkeepsie. IBM had two goals in mind as it planned for the ASTC:

1. This 300,000-square-foot facility must be designed and built within two years.

2. This facility must be world class, with levels of environmental purity and vibration-free structures of a degree never before achieved.

IBM's Real Estate and Construction Division began discussions with Shimizu to acquire its construction expertise necessary to achieve these goals. After visiting with company officials in Japan and learning that Shimizu had achieved a Class 1 clean-room capability, IBM was greatly impressed. It was also noted that Shimizu had extensive experience in clean-room filtering systems capable of trapping particles 0.5 to 0.3 microns in size. A tour of Shimizu's Institute of Technology, with its recently completed Vibration Testing Laboratory containing the largest triaxial vibration table in the construction industry, convinced IBM that it had found its contractors for the ASTC project.

Shimizu was authorized to proceed with design work. During the summer of 1986, Shimizu worked closely with IBM's engineering group. Language and cultural problems presented themselves and were quickly solved. Engineers in Japan worked almost 24 hours a day to resolve problems and compensate for the difference in time zones. When it was 7:00 A.M. Monday morning in East Fishkill, it was 7:00 P.M. Sunday night in Tokyo.

Shimizu hired the architectural-engineering firm, Giffel Associates, Inc., of Southfield, Michigan, to assist in preparing the design. Giffel previously had worked with IBM on the design of several of its other facilities over the years, and this U.S. firm would be able to assist Shimizu in complying with the local building codes and local construction practices.

In November 1986 Shimizu, acting in its capacity as construction manager, hired Indiana contractor Huber Hunt and Nichols (HHN), and the next month HHN began site work and started to pour foundations. HHN had worked with Shimizu on other projects around the country and was familiar with working conditions in East Fishkill.

As with most fast-track jobs, the need for rapid drawing production and budget preparation began to strain the relationship among client, designer, and contractor. When the contractor requested reasonably completed design documents in order to firm up the initial estimates, designers had a tough time in producing drawings because of the complexity of the project and user-driven changes; and the owners were nervous about rising costs. A great deal of work proceeds with all parties "at risk," and these pitfalls were especially evident in this project.

When the construction manager and the owner met in February 1987, Shimizu indicated that the budget had to be increased by 40 percent, due, in part, to its inability to obtain the best possible price from subcontractors who were somewhat nervous about working for a foreign construction manager. Shimizu had little experience working with local subcontractors and no experience with U.S. specialty-product manufacturers. The short bidding-cycle exacerbated the situation, and the very nature of this complex project caused bidders to consider including a contingency factor.

Now only were the HVAC systems designed for extremely close temperature and humidity-range tolerances, but specialty piping and high-purity gas-delivery systems would add substantial costs to the design. High-purity copper and stainless-steel piping systems would have to be installed and cleaned, pressurized, purged, and tested with *ultra-high purity* (UHP) nitrogen, argon and helium gases. These UHP gases were to be 99.9995% pure, with total impurities less than 1 ppm and total hydrocarbon content less than 0.2 ppm. Intricate client-furnished equipment-turnover procedures, including mechanical testing, piping qualification testing, purity testing, and numerous certifications would also add substantial costs to the project.

Shimizu, unfamiliar with many American specialty-product manufacturers, was going to specify products by Japanese manufacturers whose products they knew could meet its expectations. Shimizu expected IBM to react to budget increases like any of their long-term Japanese clients, who recognized that the best efforts were being made to control costs, with little or no avail, and therefore the initial budget would have to be increased. Not so with IBM, who became very upset, and requested that Shimizu complete the design as quickly as possible.

The relationship between IBM, Shimizu, and HHN deteriorated to the point where the Japanese firm was offered a contract by IBM to act solely as a consultant during the construction. IBM began to search the countryside for another builder, finally settling on Walsh Construction of Trumbull, Connecticut. Although the contract award was higher than the original budget and Shimizu's initial estimate, Walsh

Construction, a division of the Guy Atkinson Company of San Francisco, proceeded to engage the E & F Construction Company of Bridgeport, Connecticut, to continue with all of the concrete work. Other subcontractors were hired and brought onto the site, and the project shifted into high gear.

Each partner to the construction process learned a great deal. IBM knew that without Shimizu's experience and its role as consultant, the project would not have met all of its performance requirements. Walsh Construction benefited from the knowledge it gained working with Shimizu and its unique state-of-the-art technology placed under Walsh's control. Shimizu learned a great deal about relationships, or lack thereof, when working with American clients and subcontractors.

SHIMIZU'S COOPERATION WITH ACADEMIA IN NORTH AMERICA

Like many other Japanese corporations with a strong U.S. presence, Shimizu wishes to become involved in more than just construction work in America. It wishes to enter the academic world to learn from our scientists and researchers, and possibly increase the knowledge of the entire industry. Shimizu has also formed an affiliation with several Canadian universities. At Victoria University and Simon Frazer University in British Columbia, Shimizu has established a summer-intern program whereby selected students are offered a paid summer job working with the company in Japan. The interns are housed in Shimizu dormitories and need only pay for their airfare to and from Japan. Some doctoral candidates are also invited to spend time at Shimizu for periods of up to a year. For these advanced-degree candidates, Shimizu pays all living and transportation expenses.

In 1984 Shimizu donated $500,000 to Harvard University's Graduate School of Design. This money was to be used to establish a laboratory for construction technology research and to add courses to the school's building technology curriculum. The company also donated CAD equipment to the architecture department. An exchange program was to be created to further the studies of both Shimizu employees and Harvard faculty.

In 1988, the S. Technology Center America, Inc., was established in Cambridge by Shimizu. The mission of S. Technology Center America is to internationalize the company's R&D capabilities and develop R&D relationships with U.S. research organizations and construction engineering firms. S. Technology would be on the lookout for any promising U.S. construction-technology developments and pass them on to the company in Japan. The Center has sponsored several research projects at various American universities around the country and has begun to develop relationships with a number of U.S. engineering firms.

Shimizu is studying robotics jointly with the faculty and staff of Carnegie Mellon, and at Stanford University in California they are participating in an artificial-intelligence program. At the University of Texas at Austin, Shimizu is working with researchers on welding techniques and, to the north, the Corporation is cooperating with the Canadian government on nuclear-waste-disposal research. The company currently is spending about $3 million on studies overseas.

SHIMIZU LOOKS TO THE TWENTY-FIRST CENTURY

Each Big Six company has announced a new plan for the coming century, setting goals for increased involvement in cleaning up the physical environment and becoming better global neighbors. Shimizu is no exception, and in the spring of 1991 it launched its new corporate strategy "SHIM-21," which seeks to make the company "a comprehensive organization of human environments." Chairman Teruzo Yoshino and President Harusuke Imamura profess to improve project planning, accumulate more strength in high-technology areas, push forward in innovation and company renewal, and drive the organization forward into the twenty-first century. Chairman Yoshino looks to develop new businesses and strengthen existing facets of the company's construction, engineering, and development activities. Shimizu has always been strong in the private sector; only 18 percent of its orders received during 1991 came from civil engineering work, but the company has considerable experience in railway construction, industrial civil works, road building, and water and sewage-treatment plants. But while other construction companies may have had to assume substantial losses in recent years because of heavy investment in the development side of the business, Shimizu had only 3.8 percent of its 1991 orders originate from its own real estate development projects.

The ability to provide not only architectural and engineering design, but process engineering capability as well, is seen as a growing field for large construction companies. Shimizu recently entered into a contract with a Swiss pharmaceutical company for constructing a new plant, to include equipment layout and installation. It has expanded its Process Engineering Department so that it now has 15 engineers who can assist clients in "marrying" their manufacturing process to the building under design. Although some clients may prefer to purchase their own process equipment, Shimizu will develop the most efficient production layout and assist in the installation of the equipment as it arrives at the new plant.

The corporation performed this task successfully for Konica when that company hired Shimizu to design its new photo-sensitive paper-manufacturing plant and assist in designing the manufacturing process. Shimizu credits Taisei Corporation with establishing the first process engineering department of any Big Six contractor. Taisei engineers developed expertise in the metal-plating industry and were able to obtain several lucrative contracts because they had this in-house process-engineering capability. Other Big Six builders gravitated to other areas of the process-engineering spectrum; for example, Kajima and its automobile-manufacturing process-engineering expertise, which worked so successfully in the United States.

IS THE FUTURE HERE TODAY?

Many construction companies in Japan have been developing and are continuing to develop robots, and Shimizu has its share. Major construction company R&D institutes in Japan have embarked on these projects for two basic reasons—to be ready with a machine when the shortage of skilled workers reaches the supercritical stage in the next century, and to improve the image of the industry by creating a more high-tech look. As Shimizu states, robots can help relieve the poor image of the construction industry in Japan, popularly referred to as "3K"—*kitsui* (hard), *kitanai* (dirty), and *kiken* (dangerous); translated into English, it becomes "3D"—dirty, dangerous, and difficult.

Imagine a construction work site where unmanned vehicles deliver building components that will be unloaded and set in place by computer-programmed robots. The project manager, an electrical engineer with advanced degrees in computer technology, controls the entire construction cycle with the assistance of a personal computer and sophisticated software developed by his company. What may appear to be a far-fetched idea is being vigorously pursued by many Japanese construction companies, and Shimizu seems to be at the forefront of this movement.

Late in 1991, Shimizu announced a further development in construction robotics and computer-controlled construction processes—the SMART System, an acronym for *Shimizu Manufacturing by Advanced Robot Technology,* the culmination of years of research and the expenditure of millions of dollars. The SMART system technology encompasses the following phases of construction activity:

Construction management. A comprehensive, computerized site-command center where the process will be controlled and monitored

Initial ground structure. A roof-on-first completion phase that will permit work to proceed unaffected by weather; to be performed by automatic material-conveying and the optimum use of prefabricated construction components

Finishing and installation work.   To be performed via the utilization of automated material-conveying and the integration of equipment installation

Foundation work.   Will proceed simultaneously with the work on the superstructure, using newly developed industrialized methods of constructing underground structures, mechanizing excavation, and transporting the excavated materials to the surface by motorized conveyances, building each floor level on grade beginning with the roof level, and then jacking it into place so that the lower floor can be constructed, and so on until the entire structure has been completed

The SMART System is to be employed on the Nagoya Bank Project and will consist of a system of automated steel-erection and frame-welding, along with the automated installation of the precast floor planks and interior and exterior wall panels. Each of these components has been especially designed with simplified joints for ease of installation. The entire assembly sequencing will be orchestrated by instantaneous computer-control, resulting in a near-fully automated process.

Shimizu states that the heart of this process is in the jacking system and related components that were developed jointly with Mitsubishi Heavy Industries. A building schematic cut-away is shown in Figure 7.13, and the rendering of the completed structure is shown in Figure 7.14. Shimizu executives say that the development of SMART was three years in the making; however, its robotics research has been ongoing for the past 10 years in preparation for its incorporation into this system.

The process will work as follows: After excavation and subgrade foundation work has been completed, what will eventually end up as the top floor of the building will be constructed on-grade on top of four jacking towers. Control rooms will be housed within this top-floor level, and lifting equipment will be suspended from the structure in the area enclosed by the wide-band fascia. As a floor is completed, the cranes and winches contained in the top floor will move upward as jacking takes place; this lifting equipment then becomes available to lift steel framing members and precast plank into place on the lower floor level, now under construction. In effect, the entire building assumes a factory-like atmosphere.

The SMART System enables each floor under construction to be totally enclosed quite easily as it is being built on ground level. Any temporary protection required can be installed at grade, realizing dramatic labor savings. Shimizu states in one of its SMART brochures that each floor of this building can be built in eight days, and this schedule can

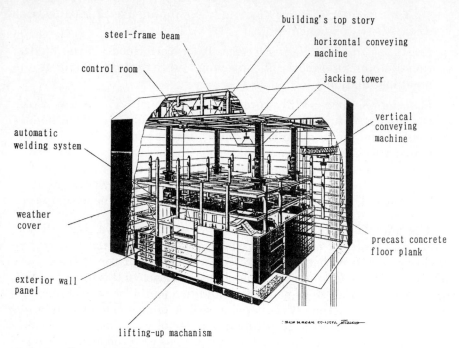

Figure 7.13 Cut-away of the SMART system.

be maintained because of the ability to control the elements. They have effectively created the controlled environment of a factory at a construction job site.

The SMART System components consist of:

Column assemblies.   Lifted in place to predesignated points automatically. Joining column to column requires redesign of connections to permit placement and securing by robots.

Beam assemblies.   Specially designed to set on and be fastened to columns by robots. These beams will be set in place by a hoisting rig that can rotate in vertical and horizontal planes.

Raising the SMART System.   Accomplished by hydraulic jacks; parts of the equipment will have the ability to open and close automatically to bypass previously installed components.

Monitor screens.   To display real-time progress of construction.

Control room.   Where all assembling and lifting operations are automatically controlled by computer command.

At Shimizu's Institute of Technology in the Koto ward of Tokyo, en-

Figure 7.14 Rendering of the Nagoya Bank building.

gineers and researchers had quietly been working on developing an automated building system, and they had actually completed the structural steel system for a small five-story building on the site without using any human steelworkers or welders. A newly designed system of columns with male and female socket-like connections, and beams with prewelded specially designed moment connections permitted computer-controlled lifting and welding devices to erect the simple, structural-steel framework for this building, which now serves as a laboratory at the Institute.

THE NAGOYA BANK SMART BUILDING PROJECT

Construction has already begun on the earthwork phase of the Nagoya Juroku Bank building in Nagoya, Japan, utilizing the experience Shimizu has gained in computer-assisted building construction and advanced-robotics technology.

The Nagoya Bank building's design is being completed by Nikken Sekkei, one of the country's largest architectural firms. The building will be a 20-story, 222,360-square-foot steel-frame structure and will employ Shimizu's version of the automated construction cycle being developed by each of the Big Six construction companies. Shimizu does not claim that this Nagoya Juroku SMART building-construction method is cost-effective. In fact, its contract with the bank is based upon conventional construction means and methods. But Shimizu has made giant strides from the erection of a simple, steel-frame building at its Institute a year or so ago to this much more complicated endeavor—and it is creating the future today.

TRY 2004

To mark the 200th anniversary of its company, in the year 2004 Shimizu intends to start construction of a futuristic, urban-construction concept named TRY 2004. This triangular-shaped "city in the air" (Fig. 7.15), when totally constructed, will have a base dimension of 9184 linear feet and will soar into the air to a height of 6573 feet at its apex. The Shimizu Corporation fully intends to commence construction of a one-triangle portion of this megastructure and add to it as time and money permit.

A closer look at TRY 2004 reveals a daring concept as set forth by Shimizu's architectural and engineering design team. Each unit within the final structure is composed of an octahedron, formed by combining two square pyramids having a perimeter measuring 1148 feet, and being the equivalent of an 821-foot-high building. The three-dimen-

Figure 7.15 Shimizu's 6573-foot-tall TRY 2004 building concept.

sional truss system will create an open environment where wind and sunlight will be everyday neighbors. High-rise office buildings and residential units will nestle in the octahedron unit (see Fig. 7.16), and the horizontal and diagonal shafts forming the octahedron, and connecting one unit to another, will contain mechanical and electrical distribution systems as well as communication and transportation facilities. The rigid horizontal shafts are to be constructed of lightweight materials such as carbon and glass fibers, and will measure 32.8 feet in diameter and 1148 feet in length. They will carry electrical and communications networks, and act as corridors and transportation systems. The diagonal tubes will be 52.5 feet wide and 1148 feet long, will act as plumbing and electrical conduits, and contain several high-speed elevators. The intersecting nodes (Fig. 7.17) will be enclosed in crystal globes measuring 164 feet in diameter, and will function as transportation foci.

This grandiose scheme envisions collecting and recycling waste water, and generating electricity from sunlight, wind, and from the incineration of garbage. Since each node will be self-sufficient, the growth of the entire complex can progress as new investors are found.

TRY 2004 really is the embodiment of its creator—bold, daring, innovative, and willing to assume risks for the sake of knowledge and future growth.

Figure 7.16 TRY 2004's octahedron trusses.

Figure 7.17 The glass-enclosed nodes in TRY 2004.

Chapter 8

Big Six Research and Development

Construction research in Japan is encouraged by the central government and scrupulously pursued in the private sector. Research and development activities in the Japanese construction industry appear to serve many functions:

- Provide a contractor with a unique product, system, design, or technology that acts as a marketing tool to retain existing clients and attract new ones

- Provide assurance that the contractor is providing the best possible product to his valued, long-term clients

- Permit a contractor to maintain and enhance its annual government rating, thereby gaining access to larger government projects

- Provide the industry with potential labor-saving devices better suited to the changing and shrinking nature of the limited pool of skilled workers in Japan

- Create designs and products tailored to the specific and geographic conditions that exist in Japan; i.e., frequent earthquakes, typhoons, unstable soils, coastal and marine conditions endemic to an island nation

- Create new products and designs to cope with changing demographics—the overcrowding of a few cities in a country where the resultant shortage of buildable sites drives the cost of land to astronomical proportions

- Promote a worldwide industry image of being on the cutting edge of building technology

According to statistics published by the U.S. National Science Foundation, Japan spends approximately 2.87 percent of its GNP on research and development, while the U.S. spends just slightly less, 2.75 percent. But the thrust and source of R&D funding in Japan is quite different from that in the United States where at least 50 percent of all available funds originate from the government—possibly because of the priority afforded defense-related projects. In Japan, by contrast, the government dispenses only 17 percent of the nation's R&D funds; the balance comes from private industry. Although the level of research and development in Japan may equal or surpass that of the United States in many areas, Japan is lagging in basic research, a fact that is becoming increasingly bothersome to its government and industry leaders. A glance at the list of Nobel Prize recipients in the last 50 years is telling. Since 1945, scientists and researchers in the United States have captured 51 Nobel Prizes in physics and 31 in chemistry; Japan has gathered only 3 in physics and 1 in chemistry.

But the Japanese are very adept at selecting those materials from the laboratory that show promise in industrial application. While the United States, the inventor of carbon fiber, used this material for Stealth technology, Japan was producing carbon-fiber-shafted golf clubs, tennis rackets, and fishing rods; and in the construction industry, this material was used to produce carbon-fiber-reinforced concrete-curtain-wall panels.

CONSTRUCTION INDUSTRY R&D

The Japanese construction industry as a whole typically invests one-half of one percent of its gross sales in research activities, while in the United States this figure is closer to one-tenth of one percent. There are thirty-six construction companies in Japan that own and operate research and development facilities, and 10 of these research institutes have 100 or more in staff. These same 10 contractors dedicate about one-percent of sales to R&D. The Big Six commitment to R&D can be seen at a glance just by looking at their 1991 budgets for R&D organizations:

Kajima	$180 (in millions)
Shimizu	$138
Taisei	$106
Obayashi	$98
Takenaka	$76
Kumagai Gumi	$37

The Japanese Management and Coordination Agency published a list of R&D investment shifts by industry between 1988 and 1989, and the construction industry posted a 24.7 percent increase that was surpassed only by publishing and printing with a 33 percent increase, and plastic products with a 32.8 percent increase. It would appear that construction has become one of those industries in Japan that is targeted for bigger and better things.

The government's role in R&D in the construction industry is carried out by the Ministry of Construction, an organization that has no counterpart in the United States. The MOC recognizes and rewards strong corporate research organizations by the way its annual contractor evaluation and rating system is structured. A construction company with considerable research activity in a specific field or endeavor may also be given preferential treatment when bids are being solicited for a project requiring that kind of expertise.

The way in which a construction company can obtain a special permit from the Ministry to use a new product or technology encourages corporations to promote R&D as a powerful marketing tool.

PUBLIC SECTOR CONSTRUCTION RESEARCH

In addition to its long-term planning activities for private- and public-sector construction work and development and in implementing a national building code, the Ministry of Construction also operates two research organizations, the *Building Research Institute* (BRI) and the *Public Works Research Institute* (PWRI). Both these organizations are located in the Tsukuba Science City, a newly created, research-oriented metropolis about 40 miles from Tokyo.

The Building Research Institute

The BRI operates with an annual budget slightly in excess of $15 million; its physical plant consists of 21 buildings situated on 51 acres located between the Public Works Research Institute and the Research Institute for High Energy Physics in Tsukuba (pronounced "Scuba").

The Institute employees 170 people, of which 118 are engineers and research technicians. BRI maintains a structural engineering department to study structural dynamics, aerodynamics, and geotechnical engineering. Its Housing and Building Economy Department is concerned with a multitude of housing construction problems, investigating life-cycle costs, and studying issues associated with the maintenance and rehabilitation of older housing stock. The separate Environment, Design and Fire Department addresses fire-protection technology and public safety issues and developments.

BRI's *International Institute of Seismology and Earthquake Engineering* (IISEE) reaches far beyond Japan's borders. IISEE annually trains about 20 engineers from earthquake-prone developing nations around the world, and this department sponsors joint earthquake research and engineering projects with the United States, Canada, France, and China.

The Public Works Research Institute

The PWRI facilities are spread over 330 acres in Tsukuba City among such neighbors as the Tsukuba Technology Center for Telegraph and Telephone Line Construction, the National Center for Disaster Prevention Science and Engineering, the University of Tsukuba, and the Geographical Survey Institute.

PWRI's 475-person staff is funded by the Ministry of Construction and has an annual budget in the $50 million range. At present there are 20 PhDs among the engineers and researchers at the Institute. The Public Works Research Institute deals with research for civil engineering projects related to water quality, dam construction, erosion control, bridge structures, road development, and earthquake disaster prevention.

Environmental research involving biotechnology to improve waste treatment processes and the use of "grey" water has become an ongoing research project at the Institute. Concrete, a material in wide use in most civil engineering projects, gets considerable attention at PWRI, where carbon fiber and high-performance concrete-technology research has been under way for several years.

THE BIG SIX RESEARCH AND DEVELOPMENT INSTITUTES

The Big Six R&D operations are highly sophisticated enterprises. The most modern equipment is housed in a series of well-planned, meticulously maintained buildings in campus settings. Staffed by experienced research engineers, many with advanced degrees, and funded by multimillion-dollar budgets, these research centers are looked upon as capstones in the corporation structure. Let's have a closer look at each one.

KaTRI—Kajima Technical Research Institute

In 1991 Kajima's corporate research and development budget was $180 million, with $72 million going directly to its two research institutes, the 6-acre Tobitakyu site and the 5.8-acre Nishichofu facility (Fig. 8.1). These combined facilities contain 19 buildings with a total floor area of 432,455-square feet, and are home to 440 employees, 280 of whom are engineers. The Tobitakyu complex has the following facilities: a radio-

(a)

(b)

Figure 8.1 Kajima's Research and Development complexes: (*a*) Tobitakyu, (*b*) Nishichofu.

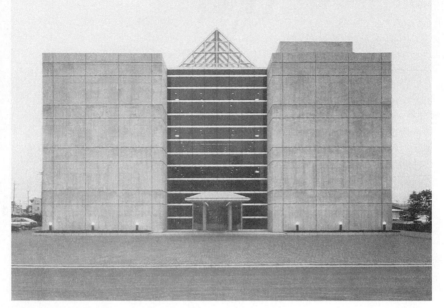

Figure 8.2 The Exhibit and Laboratory Building at KaTRI.

isotope lab, a material-testing lab, a large-structures-testing lab, a soil
mechanics and foundation lab, an oceanic and hydraulic lab, and assorted other research laboratories. At Nishichofu, there is a shaking
table, another large-structures-testing building, a second soil-mechan-
ics and foundation lab, a construction and fire-safety lab, an environ-
mental-engineering lab, and, at the gateway to the site, the Exhibit
and Laboratory Building (Fig. 8.2). Completed in 1989, this four-story
reinforced-concrete structure with a total floor area of 38,424 square
feet is a living laboratory that displays and tests many of the innovative products designed and developed by KaTRI, starting at the roof
and working downward:

- An 0.04-mm-thick stainless-steel roof membrane with continuously
  welded seams

- KUV (*Kajima Umpi Virtaus*) roof-drains utilizing a Finnish design
  to prevent air and rainwater from mixing, thereby enabling full-flow
  draining so that roof-leader piping can be reduced in diameter by
  one-half to one-third

- Ceramic-coated tile and concrete products for roof parapet copings
  and utility-roof-structures wall panels, assuring maximum weather-
  ing capability with virtually no maintenance

- Steel-fiber-reinforced concrete stairs that are lightweight and comfortable underfoot

- Carbon-fiber-reinforced concrete raised-access flooring 1.18 in. thick, capable of supporting a live load of 440 lb/sq ft

- Soundproof floor construction using rubber vibration-isolators under sleepers, particularly effective when aerobic and exercise rooms are placed over other work areas

- Long-span (59-ft) vinylon-fiber-reinforced precast-concrete floor planks, 19½ in. thick with 12 in. by 18 in. cores that can act as supply or return air ducts or as receptacles for ceiling-light fixtures.

- Low-radiation slim-line window blinds with a silvered exterior coating that keeps out the sun's rays but does not block a building occupant's view of the exterior

- A 24-in. square ceramic floor tile, ⁵⁄₁₆ in. thick, installed over a rubberized-asphalt-base sheet.

The testing equipment at KaTRI would be the envy of any first-class engineering university. The large-structures lab has a 39-foot-tall by 53-foot-long reaction wall constructed of 9.8-foot-thick prestressed concrete, capable of withstanding a load of 9.3 million pounds (Fig. 8.3). The 9576-foot-square reaction floor is 6.8 feet thick.

Figure 8.3 The reaction wall in Kajima's Large Structure Laboratory.

Kajima's 16-foot-square shaking table can support a 30-ton load and produce 2G acceleration levels in both horizontal and vertical directions. This piece of equipment is invaluable to a construction company that must test contemporary structures to assure aseismatic performance. All the Big Six labs have one.

Japan's marine environment provides many challenges for its builders, and Kajima has a hydraulic testing-lab with a wave basin 190 feet long and 66 feet wide that can replicate multidirectional waves of varying amplitudes. In another building there is a dynamic loading machine that can impose 100-ton and 50-ton loads on columns and beams, and test full-scale mock-ups to destruction.

Environmental testing has become very important in Japan and Kajima has a full range of labs for that purpose, including an anechoic-chamber reverberation room, an air-flow testing room, a heat-storage tank, and a biotechnology facility.

TAISEI CORPORATION TECHNOLOGY RESEARCH CENTER

Just a short taxi ride from the Higashi Totsuka railway station in Yokohama, the Technology Research Center occupies 8.9 acres across the street from the Kawakami Elementary School (see Fig. 8.4). On this site Taisei has a materials laboratory, a structural laboratory, an acoustics laboratory and a hydraulics laboratory, an environmental simulation chamber, and common experiment areas. The six buildings on the site, including an administration building, have a total floor area of 178,357 square feet. The Center's total staff is 354, and includes 129 researchers, 164 research assistants, 35 research support-staff, and 26 facilities-management assistants.

The Technical Research Department was established by Taisei in June 1958, and in August 1979 all functions moved to its present site in Totsuka-ku, where it became known as the Research Technology Center.

In 1990 Taisei budgeted a total of $83.85 million for corporate R&D, with $53 million going to the Technology Division and $30.85 million assigned to the Technology Research Center. The company's 1991 corporate budget increased to $106 million, of which the Center received $42 million. Taisei is proud of its offshore testing basin (Fig. 8.5), which incorporates a generator for regular and irregular waves that is essential to its investigation of hydrodynamic phenomena and responses of offshore structures to wave force, motion, scouring, and thermal diffusion. The Center's boundary layer wind tunnel (Fig. 8.6) can provide data on the wind pressure and flow, and the smoke and dust-dispersal effects of a proposed new building on the existing ones that surround it.

Figure 8.4 Taisei's Yokohama Research Center.

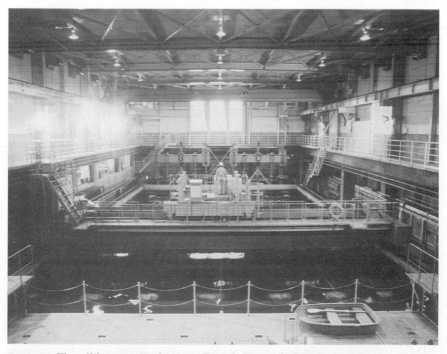

Figure 8.5 The offshore testing basin at Taisei's Research Center.

Figure 8.6 The Center's boundary layer wind tunnel.

OBAYASHI CORPORATION—TECHNICAL RESEARCH INSTITUTE

Obayashi established a research department at its Osaka main office in June 1948, and they opened a Tokyo-branch lab in 1957. In December 1965, both of these research operations were combined when the Kiyose, Tokyo, was opened.

The centerpiece of Obayashi's Technical Research Institute is its Energy Conservation Building, a four-story building incorporating state-of-the-art conservation measures such as double-skin walls, high-efficiency solar collectors for heating and cooling, photovoltaic cells, and vertical and underground heat-storage tanks; together, these won the company the 1984 ASHRAE Energy Award.

Another interesting building in the complex is the High Technology R&D Center, a working laboratory for Obayashi's base isolation technology, known as *menshin*. The R&D Center building foundation is separated from its superstructure by a series of base isolators (Fig. 8.7), which basically are rubber and steel-plate-layered columns that absorb horizontal seismic ground movement, thereby preventing most of it from being transmitted to the structure above.

The Institute, located on 18 acres in the Kiyose Ward of Tokyo, has

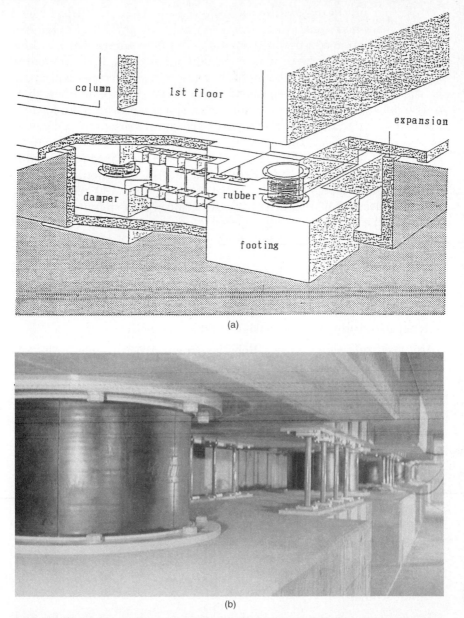

(a)

(b)

Figure 8.7 (*a*) Schematic design for Obayashi's Technology Building base isolation system. (*b*) Rubber dampers used in menshin.

15 buildings on the site, with a total floor area of 769,189 square feet, but Obayashi has some major expansion plans in mind. In September 1992, construction of a new fifteen-story, 171,000-square-foot building began, and together with a new 46,000-square-foot Environmental Engineering building now being built, these new structures will allow the company to relocate several existing labs on the site and demolish some older facilities to provide more open space now and room for further expansion in the future. Obayashi's corporate research and development budget reflects the intensity of its plans. In 1991 the company's R&D budget was $98 million, but in 1992 it was increased to $126 million, of which the Research Institute received $53.8 million.

There are 360 people at the Institute including 190 researchers. About 80 percent of the Institute's R&D projects originate from requests by the company's Construction Division. Eleven percent come from other corporate entities, and clients generate 9 percent of these research queries. The principal research work carried on by the various departments at the Institute is as follows:

Civil engineering.   Investigation of soils, rocks, seepage, stabilization of soil, design and construction methods of deeply embedded structures, tunneling technology, offshore structures

Architectural engineering.   Robotics, new-structure-materials research, performance evaluations, industrialized construction methods

Structural engineering.   Investigations of strengths, deformation characteristics, and design methods for high-rise structures, nuclear power plants, liquid natural gas (LNG) tanks, membrane and underground structures, foundation and diaphragm-wall construction

Soil and building foundation engineering.   Investigation of the bearing capacities of soils, setting, liquefaction countermeasures, physical properties of soils

Semismology and building vibration engineering.   Vibration hazards, elimination of microvibration, base isolation techniques, investigation of seismic effects

Environment technology.   Utilization of solar energy and heat storage, utilization of rainwater, clean air technologies, energy-conservation studies

Acoustic engineering.   Study of designs for studios, music halls, and chapels; sound insulation for buildings; noise prediction and countermeasures

Chemical engineering.   Investigation of materials, slurry properties, water and waste treatment, prevention of metal corrosion, concrete deterioration, and chemical pollution

Computational engineering. New uses for supercomputers in construction, including simulation static- and dynamic-testing analysis, response analysis of building structures

TAKENAKA TECHNICAL RESEARCH LABORATORY

In 1992 Takenaka set aside $76 million for corporate research, $38 million of which went to its research laboratories, including a small one in Osaka, and a much larger main branch, set back on a tree-lined site in Minamisuna, Koto-ku, Tokyo (Fig. 8.8). The Osaka labs are on the second floor of the company's head office, and include sound, vibration, and materials labs, a structure-testing lab, a concrete and chemical test lab, and mechanics and soils-testing facilities.

In Tokyo, there are five buildings housing a large-structure-testing lab, a boundary wind tunnel and a construction-equipment testing lab, a precision-controlled work-space lab, various construction-materials labs, a sound-testing lab, and an administration building. There is a combined staff of 280 at these two labs, 230 of which are research engineers.

Each year the company selects 16 employees with four to five years' tenure to be assigned to the Institute for two years as a part of Takenaka's overall corporate training program. The company has been doing this for 30 years and now 5 percent of all its engineers are "grad-

Figure 8.8 The Takenaka Technical Research Laboratory in Tokyo.

uates" of this program. Once a year, all employees attend a meeting where they are briefed on the current ongoing research projects at the Laboratory. Selected representatives from Headquarters take a two-day tour of the Laboratory each June, and researchers from the lab visit the company's Osaka office once a year and lecture on 60 ongoing research projects.

There is a small, six-story building on-site (Fig. 8.9), built specifically to test *active mass dampers* (AMDs) and to record the control these AMDs exercise in reducing building sway and motion during seismic events. On the top floor of this test building, an active-mass damper is connected to a hydraulically actuated arm. During a seismic event, sensors connected to a computer control the direction and throw of the hydraulic arm to move the mass damper so as to simulate a reaction to that which is created by an earthquake. Research such as this led Takenaka to design and install an AMD for a client using the building's penthouse ice-storage equipment as a mass damper (Fig. 8.10).

Figure 8.9 The active mass damper test building at Takenaka's laboratory.

(a)

Figure 8.10 (*a*) An ice-storage system used by Takenaka as the "mass" in its AMD system.

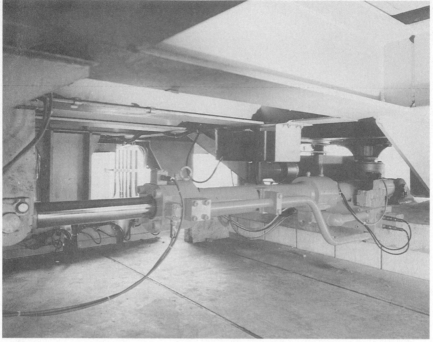

(b)

Figure 8.10 *(Continued)* *(b)* the hydraulic piston that positions the mass damper.

SHIMIZU'S INSTITUTE OF TECHNOLOGY

The Shimizu Corporation budgeted $123 million for corporate research in 1990 and upped that to $138 million in 1991. Its Research Institute received $73.8 million of these funds in 1990 and $82 million in 1991 to support its project commitments and the 400 researchers working on them at the Etchujima, Tokyo, facility (see Fig. 8.11). There are approximately 300 other research engineers assigned to other corporate divisions. Work at the Institute is divided into four areas: basic research, research and development work in conjunction with corporate projects, consigned research from outside groups, and consulting work in the open market.

About one-half of all Institute research projects are proposed by the researchers themselves. Thirty percent of all research projects originate with the design and construction departments and 20 percent of the Institute's projects result from contract work that originates with government or client requests. The Institute, like those of its other Big Six peers, has a full range of research and testing facilities, as reflected in its organizational chart (Fig. 8.12). In the 48 years that Shimizu has

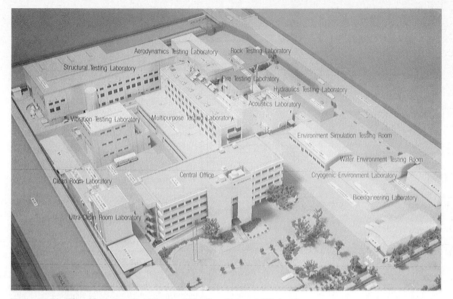

Figure 8.11 The Shimizu Institute of Technology at Etchujima.

maintained an R&D department, it has won 22 national awards from such prestigious organizations as the Japan Society of Civil Engineers, the Architectural Institute of Japan, the Japan Atomic Energy Society, and numerous industry leaders.

Shimizu's development of concrete placement and finishing robots, research on prefabrication and composite-construction methods, and computer-controlled mechatronics paved the way for the development of the Shimizu Manufacturing System by Advanced Robotics Technology, whereby an entire building can be assembled with minimal on-site staff. Figure 8.13 offers a schematic view of this system in action.

KUMAGAI GUMI AND ITS TSUKUBA SCIENCE CITY TECHNICAL R&D INSTITUTE

In 1988 Kumagai Gumi celebrated its fiftieth anniversary by opening its new Technical Research and Development Institute in Tsukuba Science City, a new metropolitan area established by the Japanese government solely for the purpose of creating an environment conducive to the advancement of science. The 104 researchers, biochemists, and administrative staff at the Institute avail themselves of the wide range of research seminars held by various government and private-industry organizations located in Tsukuba Science City. Mr. Hiromu Ikeda, deputy general manager of the Institute, states that the cross-pollination of

General Manager	Planning Department	
	General Affairs Department	

	Construction Engineering Department	•Construction Method •Architectural Performance •Material Properties •Concrete •Construction Management
	Structural Engineering Department	•Steel Structure •Earthquake Engineering •Building Structural Engineering •Civil Structural Engineering
	Underground Engineering Department	•Rock Mechanics •Ground water Hydrology •Soil Dynamics & Aseismic Engineering •Foundation Engineering •Soil Engineering
	Environmental Engineering Department	•Acoustics •Air Technology •Fluid Dynamics •Water Environment •Ocean Environmental Engineering •Human Science •Social Science
	Facility Engineering Department	•Facility Systems •HVAC •Electronic Facilities •Information Facilities
	Planning Engineering Department	•Fire Safety •Information Systems •Architectural Design Methods
	Advanced Technology Department	•Advanced Materials •Applied Biotechnology •Applied Physics & Radiation
	Special Programs	•New Prefabricated Houses •Soil Dynamics •Desert Environment •Next Generation Building Methods •Durability of Reinforced Concrete •Total Environmental Planning •Seawater Purification •Space Construction •Energy & Recycling
	Technology Development Engineering Department	•Applied Technology •Experimental Technology

Figure 8.12 The organizational chart of Shimizu's Institute of Technology.

ideas that takes place, both at these formal meetings and at the informal social gatherings between scientists living and working in Tsukuba, are invaluable; they reinforce the reasons for his company's decision to locate there. Eleven buildings, with a total floor area of 110,548 square feet on this tree-lined 12.8-acre site create an atmosphere of spaciousness, and allow plenty of room for future expansion (Fig. 8.14).

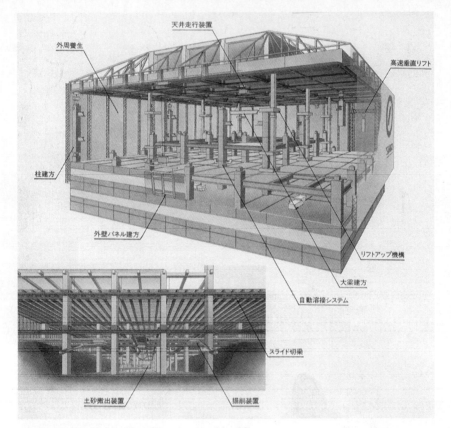

天井走行装置
外周養生
高速垂直リフト
柱建方
外壁パネル建方
リフトアップ機構
大梁建方
自動溶接システム
スライド切梁
土砂搬出装置
掘削装置

Figure 8.13 Shimizu's SMART automated building system.

The company's modern facilities, funded by a $37-million budget in 1991, run the gamut from soils mechanics labs, to vibration and structures labs, to acoustics and concretes labs, wind tunnels, and one of the world's largest and most modern marine-hydrodynamics facilities. It was in this laboratory that models of the immersed-tube tunnel were tested to determine how the strong tides of Hong Kong's Eastern Harbour would affect the towing-to-sea and sinking activities of those precast concrete sections.

While standing in this large structure, which contains a 131-foot-long by 65-foot-wide wave channel, the technician in charge activates the multidirectional wave generator. A model of an offshore structure has been placed in the middle of the basin, and this model is connected to a computer and a video screen which are mounted outside the basin. There are two TV cameras trained on the model, one on its east-west axis, and the second on its north-south axis. As the waves build in in-

Figure 8.14 Views of Kumagai Gumi's Tsukuba City Technical Research Institute.

tensity, the motion of the model structure is superimposed upon a grid system on the monitor, so that the effects of the simulated ocean waves in both directions can be observed while being recorded by the computer. The information gained in this manner will have a great deal of impact on the direction in which the final design of the actual structure is completed and the method by which the placement of the structure in its offshore environment will be effected.

A WORD ABOUT TSUKUBA SCIENCE CITY

In 1963 the Japanese government recognized a need to create a national center for advanced research and higher education to better equip the country for the challenges that lay ahead. The concept for Tsukuba Science City emerged. The government began to acquire parcels of land from 2300 owners in a rural area 40 miles northeast of Tokyo, and by 1973 had purchased 4447 of the proposed total 63,900 acres that would include the Science City district and the developing outskirts.

The idea behind Tsukuba was to centralize many government research facilities in one location, establish a series of technical institutes of higher learning, attract the research facilities of the country's leading industrial firms, and create a pleasant atmosphere with all of the facilities and amenities required to attract the best and brightest scientific minds.

Twenty-nine years after the Cabinet made its decision to proceed with this Science City concept, the results have exceeded all expectations. The tree-lined streets, convenient, bright, cheerful shopping areas, and 33 miles of bicycle paths and uncluttered pedestrian walkway areas have become a magnet to corporations and workers seeking a higher quality of life (see Fig. 8.15). The population of Tsukuba City now stands at about 166,000, about 32 percent less than its projected 220,000. As of 1991, 10,000 of these residents were students, 10,000 were researchers, 5000 are employed as research staff, and 2000 were international students, all working and living in the city.

The population and make-up of Science City's technological community is impressive. There are seven national research institutes, including one for metals, one for earth sciences, and another for inorganic materials and physical and chemical research. The National Space Development Agency of Japan also is in Tsukuba.

The Ministries of Education, Health and Welfare; Agriculture; Forestry and Fisheries; Transport; International and Agency Foreign Affairs; and the Public Service Corporation all have research facilities in Tsukuba—a total of 45, not counting the Ministry of Construction's four facilities.

Figure 8.15 Views of Tsukuba Science City.

The Japan Automobile Research Institute operates a three-mile-high speed test-track there, and the Nippon Agricultural Research Institute has an experimental farm complete with dairy and livestock herds. The Tsukuba Institute of the Japan Foundation for Shipbuilding has a large building on its site, with a rectangular water-tank and circulating water-channel to test new ship designs.

The University of Tsukuba and the Tsukuba College of Technology act as stimuli and role models to the students attending the seven kindergartens, six elementary schools, five junior high schools, and three high schools in the area.

Industry is represented by research facilities operated by Kobe Steel, Nippon Sheet Glass, Eisai (a pharmaceutical firm), Omran (a machine manufacturer conducting advanced automation research). Hitachi Chemical, Sumitomo, ICI Japan, Sanyo Electric, NTT, Takeda Chemical Industries, and about 15 other corporations. Toda Construction, one of Japan's "Little Six" construction companies, and another builder, Okumura Corporation, have their research facilities in Tsukuba Science City.

Tsukuba enters its third decade seeking to become more international in its scope and the center of research in the Asian community.

FROM RESEARCH TO ROBOTICS TO REALITY

"Mechatronics" is a term coined in Japan and represents the marriage of mechanical engineering to electronics engineering. Construction robots do not now, and probably never will, look or act like those glistening gold-tone Hollywood metal humanoids with flashing ruby red eyes and sonorous, synthetic voice systems. Many robots take the form of ordinary construction equipment with some added servo and black-box appendages, such as the concrete-floor-finishing or screeding robots or the rebar-placing robot of Kajima, which looks for all the world like a small backhoe with a clamp at the end of its boom.

When the writer visited Japan in 1988 and toured several construction research and development facilities including those of Kajima, Mitsui, and Obayashi, each company took pride in displaying some of its robots. There was the floor-finishing robot and an excavating robot, which was simply a computer-controlled arm from a Komatsu hydraulic backhoe. There was the exterior-wall-tile-integrity robot (a square box secured to a steel cable extending from a roof parapet) that traveled on the exterior surface of a building, tapping its way up and down to detect any hollow-sounding sections. However, the soil-compaction robot at Mitsui did seem to have a personality. A brightly colored box on wheels, standing maybe 2½ feet tall, measuring 3 feet across and 3½ feet long, it went about its self-powered way conducting full-time compaction tests on a small tract of land. A chime rang out as it proceeded along a magnetic-tape-guided boundary line, and when it reached the end of the line, the robot sounded a few double chirps, turned around, and chimed its way back to its operator.

But now, five years later, all of these seemingly disparate devices suddenly appear to fit into a much larger picture—one of a master plan to create a completely automated construction cycle.

THE IMPETUS BEHIND ROBOTICS AND AUTOMATED BUILDING SYSTEMS

There are strong cases to be made for the pursuit of construction robots and automated building systems: to free people from dirty, strenuous, and dangerous work; to make the industry more attractive to bright engineers just coming into the work force; to combat the hard, cold reality of the projections associated with the change in demographics, and to attain a highly mobile technology that is required for the coming age of borderless markets.

Construction in Japan had long been viewed as an unsafe, low-paying job without any particular charisma or glamour. This view may be a holdover from pre-war years when the contractor's main function was to secure the necessary labor force to build a building. The ways in which a labor pool of both domestic and foreign workers was recruited in those days, and the conditions in which they were housed on remote sites and made to work long hours, all bordered on indentured servitude.

In more modern times, the safety record of the construction industry in Japan was poor. In 1970 there were 2430 fatalities in the construction industry, a figure that equaled 40 percent of all industrial deaths. And by 1978, the building business accounted for 34 percent of all industrial accidents. Only with strenuous efforts by enlightened management and the strict enforcement of company safety programs did both of these figures drop dramatically in later years.

The development of robotics and automated building systems, contractors reasoned, would reduce the workers' exposure to dangerous operations and, hopefully, lower accident and fatality rates. These sophisticated systems would serve a secondary purpose, they reasoned, that of attracting newly graduated engineers to the construction industry rather than having them lured to the electronics field or other hi-tech businesses.

Japanese contractors began to pay attention to statistics about the changing demographics in their country. An aging work force and lack of adequate replacements would mean a shortage of skilled workers. Japan's work force is "greying," just like the labor market in the United States. In 1990, a survey conducted by the National Personnel Authority in Tokyo revealed that the average age of the management staff in Japan is 41 years. Japan's population of young people in the 15- to 19-age bracket peaked in 1990 and was expected to decline each year thereafter, which would lead to a labor shortage in years to come. Even in the short term, there would be problems.

In 1990, according to the Ministry of Labor, there was a shortage of 3 million skilled workers in the country, exceeding the shortage of 1.1 million workers reported for the previous year. With the unemployment rate in Japan estimated at 2.3 percent in 1991, contrasted with 5.5 to 6.5 percent in the United States, 5.9 percent in Germany, and 6.5 percent in Great Britain, any sustained growth in the Japanese economy would be hampered by a serious shortage of skilled workers. The labor situation in Japan is further exacerbated by that country's xenophobia, which prevents it from welcoming foreign labor. In fact, the government regularly conducts campaigns to round up and deport illegal workers from the country. However, the downturn in the world economy and the slowdown in Japan's industrial activity in 1992 may have delayed this impending labor shortage.

In the following paragraphs we discuss Big Six research and development projects.

THE FULLY AUTOMATED BUILDING CYCLE

Each Big Six contractor is embarking on a program to automate building construction. At Obayashi's research institute, a visitor can watch a video showing automated delivery-vehicles bringing materials to a twenty-first century construction site. Computer-controlled cranes lift steel columns and beams into place, and a robotic welder scurries back and forth tacking here, tacking there, orbitally welding a column before climbing up to the next level.

Takenaka used its roof push-up method to build the Yanagibashi Mitsui Building in 1991. Columns were alternately jacked up from below and lowered by crane from above. Exterior wall sections of *autoclaved lightweight concrete* (ALC), attached to cast-in-place floor slabs, and fitted out with windows, were lifted in place by a computer-controlled crane. The computer monitoring the lifting process took into account the jack loads, the torque action imposed on the columns, and the wind-loading effect. If nonacceptable limits were being approached at any of these critical points, an alarm would sound and action would cease.

●コンピュータによる管理
コンピュータによる総合管理システムの一環とし
て、自動施工の状況をリアルタイムにモニターす
るシステムです。

●柱、梁建方の自動化
柱や梁は、コンピュータ制御により所定の据付位
置へ自動搬送します。また、組み立て工程の効率
を高めるため、柱、梁のジョイント部の形状にも工
夫を凝らしています。

●装置リフトアップ自動化
1フロア分の建方が終わると、油圧ジャッキを利用して、装置全体を次のフロアに自動的にリフトアップ
します。

Figure 8.16 Shimizu's robot-controlled steel-erection process.

Shimizu, having successfully completed a robot-controlled structural-steel erection cycle on the ground of its research institute (Fig. 8.16), has now embarked on its first commercial application of this system. Taisei Corporation claims that their T-UP method (Fig. 8.17) reduces the construction time of a 900,000, 30-story building by 30 percent.

ULTRA-HIGH-RISE BUILDINGS

With the limited availability of buildable sites and the extremely high cost of land in the more desirable sections of Tokyo ($20,000 to $30,000 per square foot!) and in the country's other major cities, Japanese builders are spending a great deal of time and money on developing super-high-rise buildings and below-ground structures. The Big Six are at the forefront of these movements.

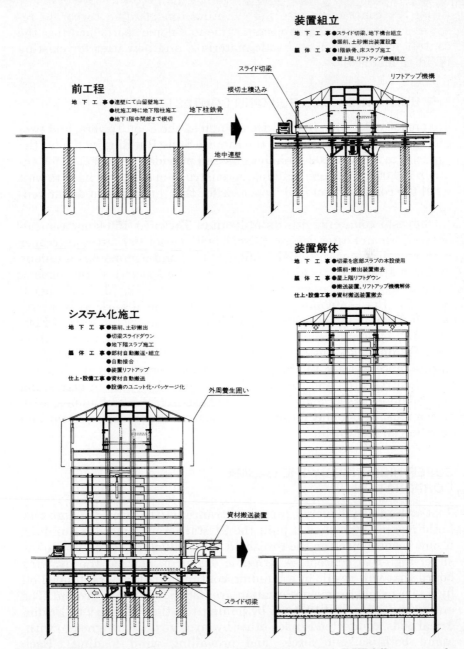

前工程
地 下 工 事 ●連壁にて山留壁施工
　　　　　　●杭施工時に地下階柱施工
　　　　　　●地下1階中間部まで根切

地中連壁
地下柱鉄骨

装置組立
地 下 工 事 ●スライド切梁、地下構台組立
　　　　　　●据削、土砂搬出装置設置
躯 体 工 事 ●1階鉄骨、床スラブ施工
　　　　　　●屋上階、リフトアップ機構組立

スライド切梁
根切土積込み
リフトアップ機構

システム化施工
地 下 工 事 ●据削、土砂搬出
　　　　　　●切梁スライドダウン
　　　　　　●地下階スラブ施工
躯 体 工 事 ●部材自動搬送・組立
　　　　　　●自動接合
　　　　　　●装置リフトアップ
仕上・設備工事 ●資材自動搬送
　　　　　　●設備のユニット化・パッケージ化

装置解体
地 下 工 事 ●切梁を底部スラブの本設使用
　　　　　　●据削・搬出装置撤去
躯 体 工 事 ●屋上階リフトダウン
　　　　　　●搬送装置、リフトアップ機構解体
仕上・設備工事 ●資材搬送装置撤去

外周養生囲い
資材搬送装置
スライド切梁

Figure 8.17 Schematic stages in the erection of Taisei Corporation's T-UP fully automated high-rise construction system.

Big Six contractors also are devoting considerable corporate resources to space-related projects, segmented-dome sports facilities, the control of seismic forces, exotic materials, and new uses for existing building materials.

THE ULTRA-HIGH-RISE BUILDING CONTEST

Takenaka's Sky City 1000, twice as high as the Sear Towers, and two-and-one-half times taller than the Empire State Building, will have the capacity to house 35,000 inhabitants and provide a work-space for another 100,000, all in one building. A construction start will have to wait until the company can find a sponsor for this multi-billion-dollar venture.

Obayashi counters with its Millenium Tower, a 150-story conical-shape Norman Foster design. Taisei has its Taisei 100 superskyscraper with four different sectional configurations, and Kajima has a unique design marking that company's entry into the space race. But none of these designs would have progressed much beyond the "dream" stage if these Big Six companies had not done their homework in basic research. Even if Japan were not positioned on the Pacific Ring of Fire, ultra-tall buildings would sway because of excessive and alternating wind-loadings; adding seismic considerations further complicates the design process. Each Big Six constructor has spent years on building-vibration research and control. They are world leaders in active and mass-damper research technology and base-isolation techniques, all of which must be not only feasible, but practical from an engineering and commercial standpoint.

SUPER-HIGH-RISE BY THE KAJIMA CORPORATION

Just as Kajima pioneered Japan's entrance into the world of high-rise buildings in 1968 when it built the 24-story Kasumigaseki Building, it now seems poised on the threshold of introducing the country to the super-high-rise concept. A dynamic design is now on the drawing board that will result in a building containing 200 floors, topped off by a glass and chrome observation area 2656 feet above ground. The entire structure will be built by joining together 50-story-tall cylindrical pods, connected to each other by large girders designed to withstand both seismic forces and prevailing wind loadings. Each 50-story-pod will be 164 feet in diameter, resulting in a per-floor area of 21,520 square feet. The structural trusses making up the outer walls of each pod will become part of its architectural curtain-wall system (see Fig. 8.18).

Figure 8.18 Kajima's ultra-high-rise building concept.

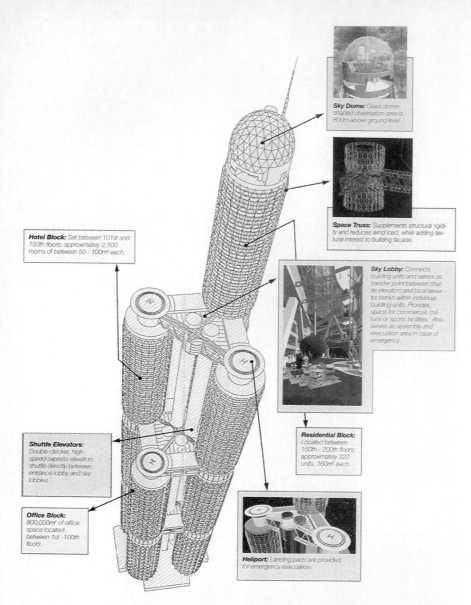

Sky Dome: Glass dome-shaped observation area is 800m above ground level.

Space Truss: Supplements structural rigidity and reduces wind load, while adding textural interest to building facade.

Hotel Block: Set between 101st and 150th floors; approximately 2,500 rooms of between 50 - 100m² each.

Sky Lobby: Connects building units and serves as transfer point between shuttle elevators and local elevator banks within individual building units. Provides space for commercial, cultural or sports facilities. Also serves as assembly and evacuation area in case of emergency.

Shuttle Elevators: Double-decker, high-speed express elevators shuttle directly between entrance lobby and sky lobbies.

Residential Block: Located between 150th - 200th floors; approximately 320 units, 160m² each.

Office Block: 800,000m² of office space located between 1st - 100th floors.

Heliport: Landing pads are provided for emergency evacuation.

Figure 8.18 (*Continued*) Kajima's ultra-high-rise building concept.

Kajima's ambitious scheme envisions the construction of 8.6 million square feet of office space on floors 1 through 100. A hotel with 2500 rooms will be located on floors 101 through 150, and approximately 320 residential units will be built on floors 150 through 200. Each of these apartments will contain about 1728 square feet, rather ample by Tokyo standards. Heliports located strategically on top of three of the lower pods will provide emergency evacuation capability in the unlikely event that a towering inferno occurs.

Each of the twelve 50-story building pods will have its own safety-management system, and each pod is compartmentalized so that if a fire emergency does take place, areas within the pod can be sealed off to prevent the further spread of the fire.

This structure will be an intelligent building with a full range of building-management systems and environment controls. Kajima's *active mass damper system* (AMD) will be connected to the building-management system and will assist the structure in responding to seismic forces and excessive wind-loading. A computerized, controlled, movable counterweight will be used to reposition the building's mass in response to forces created by earthquakes or wind. This AMD system also will control the normal sway that will occur in a tall structure such as this. Another product of KaTRI, the *active variable stiffness system* (AVS) will be employed in this building and will be used with a computer-assisted mechanism to adjust the rigidity of the structure so that resonant vibrations will not occur.

UNDERGROUND STRUCTURES

Takenaka, Kumagai Gumi, and Shimizu envision building underground structures to alleviate the congestion in heavily populated cities. These underground buildings can house infrastructure such as waste-treatment and water-treatment plants, along with parking garages, and even retail and commercial establishments. The tunneling and diaphragm slurry-wall-construction expertise that were developed in the laboratories of these contractors, and their considerable commercial success in using these techniques, can quite easily be transferred to other underground-structure concepts. Because of the hazardous conditions inherent in below-grade construction work the development of unmanned procedures was inevitable.

THE KAJIMA PNEUMATIC CAISSON

Excavating for deep caissons, especially where unstable soils are present, can be costly and hazardous. Kajima has developed a process whereby a caisson can be sunk into the ground without the need for any workers to be exposed to the dangers associated with this operation. With the automatic pneumatic-caisson system, the company developed a self-contained pressurized working chamber that is installed over the sheet piling around the proposed caisson's circumference. Compressed air is pumped into this chamber at pressures designed to counteract any underground water pressure, thereby eliminating ground water seepage into the excavation. Robotic excavators working in this pressurized environment load spoil onto a bucket that is raised through a tubelike shaft to the surface, where it can be removed from the site. Real-time monitoring of the robot-controlled operations via television cameras is performed by one operator stationed in a remote-control room on the surface. The addition of a second- or third-shift computer operator can extend the entire process to a round-the-clock operation with very little increase in overhead costs.

LESS EXOTIC RESEARCH PROJECTS

Not all R&D activity is devoted to such exotic end-uses as automated building systems or ultra-high-rise buildings. The overwhelming majority of Big Six clients are interested in more mundane matters such as durable and high-strength concrete that will yield more cost-effective and maintenance-free buildings. There are a number of ongoing research projects relating to concrete, such as high-strength formulations, super-durable concrete, roller-compacted concrete, methods to control the heat of hydration, new forming procedures, and the creation of intelligent concrete.

High-Strength Concrete

Japan appears to lag behind the United States in high-strength-concrete technology. Takenaka Corporation's bulletin on the timetable for high-strength-concrete development (Fig. 8.19) appears to be typical for the industry. For conversion purposes, one *MegaPascal* (MPa) is equal to 145 psi; therefore 40 MPa is equal to 5800 psi, 60 MPa is 8700 psi, 80 MPa is 11,600 psi, and 100 MPa is 14,500 psi.

Super-Durable Concrete

The following phenomena act to shorten the life of concrete:

1. Carbon dioxide in the atmosphere lowers the alkalinity, causing steel reinforcement to rust

2. As concrete cures, shrinkage and resulting cracks occur; harmful particles such as chloride ions can enter the material

3. In coastal areas, airborne sea salt can penetrate the concrete, causing deterioration of any steel reinforcing material

Although air entrainment helps in the freeze-thaw cycle, the microscopic voids created can contribute to carbonation. Takenaka has dis-

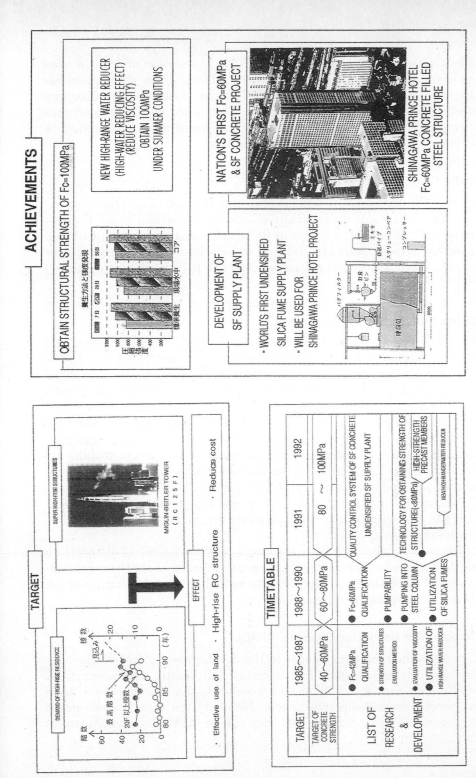

Figure 8.19 Takenaka's high-strength concrete development program.

covered a chemical compound, a glycol ether derivative, that makes concrete more dense, gives resistance to freeze-thaw action, and reduces shrinkage to half that of conventional concrete. The company claims that the use of these chemicals, combined with advanced concrete-placement technology and finishing operations, can produce a concrete structure that will last for 500 years.

Roller-Compacted Dam Concrete (RCD)

Where "fill dam construction" is required, the use of *roller-compacted concrete* (RCD) can dramatically shorten construction time. Kajima, along with Obayashi, a leader in RCD, envisions this technique being used on airport runways, factory foundations, and nuclear power plants. The construction sequence using the RCD method is displayed in Figure 8.20.

Controlling the Heat of Hydration

In the summer when ambient temperatures reach 90°F and above, the interior temperature of placed concrete can exceed 150°F due to the heat of hydration from within. To avoid thermal cracking, these internal temperatures need to be controlled. The Taisei Corporation has developed a vacuum cooling system that works by reducing the atmospheric pressure in a large vessel containing the aggregate used for ready-mix concrete. As the air is evacuated, the water on the surface of the aggregate evaporates, thereby lowering the temperature of the aggregate. When Taisei used this vacuum-cooling system in the construction of the Kodama Dam, a 334-foot-high by 918-foot-long structure, 68°F concrete was produced at 75°F ambient temperature. Without using this cooling process, the ready-mix would have been delivered by the batch plant at 83°F.

Takenaka calls its cooling process CRYOCRETE (Fig. 8.21), a method whereby liquid nitrogen is sprayed directly onto the coarse aggregate before batching, significantly reducing the temperature of the product during the mixing period.

Carbon-Fiber Reinforced Concrete (CFRC)

Kajima is the recognized leader in the development of carbon-fiber-reinforced concrete, a space-age material that creates exterior-curtain-wall panels that weigh 36 to 40 percent less than conventional steel-reinforced precast-concrete panels. Not only are these panels much stronger and more durable, but they can be cast into intricate architectural shapes.

Figure 8.20 Roller-compacted concrete and the Kajima construction cycle.

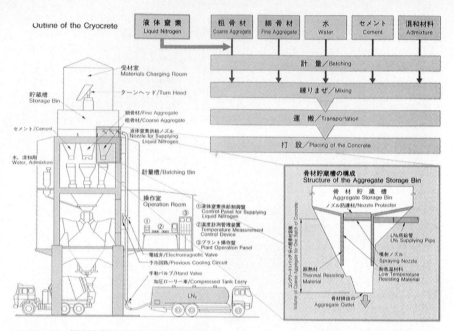

Figure 8.21 CRYOCRETE by Takenaka; the process for creating cooled aggregate.

The special properties of CFRC are vividly displayed in a Kajima photograph of an elephant standing on a plank made of this material (Fig. 8.22). Kajima has had so much commercial success with this product that it has established a subsidiary company, FRC Corporation, to manufacture and market carbon-fiber reinforced concrete products.

Intelligent Concrete

It is often difficult to verify the structural integrity of cast-in-place concrete by visual inspection alone. X-raying, chipping away to expose weak spots, or even total-destruction testing may be required to determine the health of a piece of concrete. Shimizu has taken a new approach to an old problem. It has developed a glass and carbon-fiber-reinforcing method for concrete, whereby the glass fibers perform the structural function and the carbon fibers can signal stress problems.

A composite reinforcing bar made of both glass and carbon fibers replaces the conventional steel rebar used in regular concrete construction, and as stress increases in the concrete structure over time, the carbon fibers break. The measure of electrical resistance through the conductive carbon fibers can be correlated to impose stress, and can warn of impending failure.

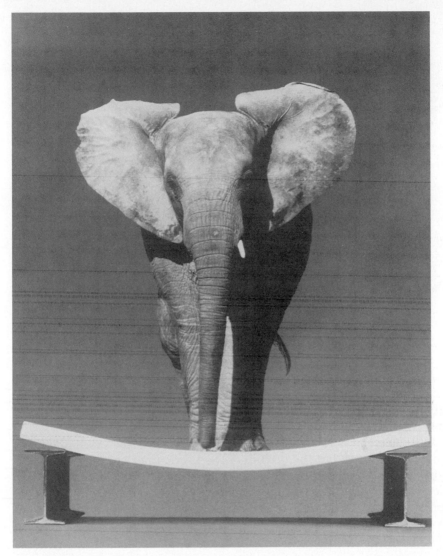

Figure 8.22 An elephant standing on a slab of Kajima carbon-fiber-reinforced concrete.

New Concrete-Forming Techniques

Not all concrete research is esoteric; Kumagai Gumi has developed a simple, but ingenious process that can create an architectural finish on cast-in-place concrete without any form liners, and can dramatically improve the appearance of concrete walls without the necessity to "rub" them after stripping the forms.

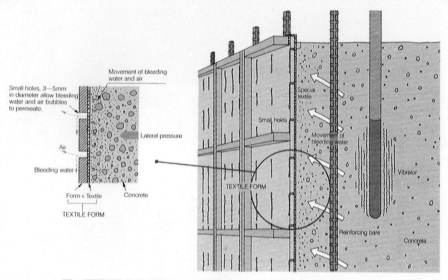

Figure 8.23 The TEXTILE FORM Method developed by Kumagai Gumi.

Kumagai Gumi's TEXTILE FORM Method (Fig. 8.23) uses a special textile liner behind a somewhat conventional wood form. Small, 3- to 5-mm-diameter holes are drilled through the surface of the wood form and combined with the fabric liner on the inside of the form. Air and water in the placed concrete are able to bleed through, eliminating the air pockets that cause craters to appear on the surface after the form has been stripped.

With the use of TEXTILE FORM, not only are these small and large voids eliminated, but the texture of the fabric liner actually imparts a fine-patterned surface to the face of the concrete wall. Other benefits accrue from using this system: concrete strength is greatly improved as the water-to-cement ratio is immediately decreased when the bleed-off occurs, and the surface of the concrete structure is denser and therefore more resistant to freeze-thaw cycles.

From the commonplace to the frontiers of construction research science, Kajima, Takenaka, Taisei, Obayashi, Shimizu, and Kumagai Gumi lead the pack. They don't have to look over their shoulders to see who is gaining on them, but rather to judge how far they have outpaced the competition.

Chapter 9

What Does It All Mean?

The United States and Japan are inextricably bound together, and for both countries to live up to their potential they must learn to work together harmoniously, borrowing the best from each other's culture. Akio Morita, chairman emeritus of the Sony Corporation, said this of the relationship between these two countries: "It is a bond we can never cut, and this might be the 'fatal attraction' between us." Morita, the co-author of the controversial book *The Japan That Can Say No* feels very strongly that an economic break between the United States and Japan would send shock waves around the world and create economic chaos.

Although our construction industries may be technically similar, the cultural differences between Japan and the United States manifest themselves in ways that result in dramatic contrasts in basic business philosophies:

- The long-term relationships between client, general contractor, and subcontractor in Japan as opposed to the "one-shot" relationships in the United States

- The reliance upon the intent of the contract in Japan, instead of the inviolacy of the written terms of an American construction contract

- The almost religious pursuit to achieve quality and on-time delivery of construction projects in Japan

- The synergistic effect of government and private industry working together in Japan

- The Japanese long-term view of business development, market share, and pay-backs resulting from research and development efforts

- The Japanese attitude toward nurturing both employees and subcontractors, resulting in lifelong relationships and company investments in training and education

The xenophobic Japan-bashing expressed in America from time to time, as yet another of our basic industries is assaulted by Japanese technology, leads to short-term solutions for deep-seated problems. Take, for example, the actions of the *Los Angeles County Transportation Commission* (LACTC) in January 1992. The LACTC solicited bids for 87 mass-transit cars and, after receiving a bid for $116.9 million from U.S. contractor Morrison-Knudsen Corp. (M-K), elected to make a tentative award to the Sumitomo Corporation of America, whose bid of $121.8 million was almost $5-million higher. The Transportation Authority reasoned that Sumitomo had successfully supplied cars to it for the first phase of its mass-transit system, and these cars were delivered "on time and on budget."

M-K, on the other hand, said officials of LACTC, lacked the experience to manufacture these cars and was going to have car parts made in several locations far from its main plant. The Sumitomo Corporation of America was awarded the contract for this equipment, only to have the Commission renege on the deal because of pressure to "buy American." When local politicians got into the act, a suggestion was made to have the county set up its own $49-million car-manufacturing plant. Cooler heads finally prevailed, and it was decided to lease these additional Metro Green light rail cars until a more long-term, rational approach could be ironed out.

Another, somewhat unrelated case was reported in the *New York Times* in January 1992. In Greece, New York (a suburb of Rochester), local government officials rejected the purchase of a used Komatsu backhoe that had been manufactured in Illinois at a plant owned jointly by Dresser Industries and Komatsu. Even though this excavator was $15,000 less expensive than a comparable model produced by John Deere, it was decided that they would run with the Deere. No one bothered to find out that the John Deere equipment was built in Japan, although it did have an American-made engine.

In basic philosophies, the United States and Japan see eye-to-eye on many important issues. Both countries desire peaceful relationships with their fellow nations, and both countries have a strong desire to elevate their citizenry, in both ethical and economic terms. Both countries value free world trade, but have different concepts on how it should be achieved. As best we can, we must deal with real issues and not be swayed too much by emotions that tend to run high around election time as politicians begin to beat the "trade issue" drum.

THE TRADE ISSUES

The annual trade deficit encountered by the United States in its dealings with Japan peaked at $56 billion in 1987 and declined to $41 billion in 1991 only to rise to an expected $50 billion in 1992. Although this trade deficit is a source of constant concern and reaches a fevered pitch at election time, in actuality, it is a two-edged sword. These multi-billion-dollar figures reflect a substantial outgo of U.S. dollars, but they also represent 30 to 40 percent of all products sold by Japan on the world market. So where would the Japanese economy be if sales to the United States nosedived? Japan's dependency on the U.S. market is obvious.

On the other side of the coin, Japan is one of America's best customers, spending approximately $17 billion annually on items such as aircraft, logs, lumber, computer chips and parts, agricultural products, tobacco, fish, and control instruments. Only two Japanese products—cars and computers—exacerbate the trade deficit problem each year, and at least on one count—automobiles—the American consumer does seem to gain some benefits by purchasing stylish and low-maintenance cars from Japan at reasonable prices.

The United States still possesses the world's largest economy. In 1990 the GNP of the United States was $5.05 trillion, almost double Japan's GNP of $2.8 trillion. The 12 combined nations of the new European Economic Community can challenge America in this respect, with their $4.9 trillion total output of goods and services.

JAPAN'S DIRECT INVESTMENT IN THE UNITED STATES

The United States represents a safe, stable place in which to invest, and during the last five years, Japan has been the source country for the largest number and dollar value of direct investments, due, in part, to the favorable yen-to-dollar conversion rate that existed in the early to mid-1980s. Table 9.1 shows the number of investments in the United States made by the leading foreign investors between 1985 and 1989, and what proportion of foreign investment in the United States it represents. Japan's investment in the United States is exceeded only by that of Great Britain with its $122.1 billion direct investment.

Doomsayers point to the fact that Japan has purchased billions of dollars of U.S. Treasury Bills and Notes, and that it could manipulate the value of the dollar by cashing in large blocks of these securities. Japanese purchases of T-Bills and Certificates have declined from a high of $26.4 billion in 1988 to $7.4 billion in 1991. Any attempt by the Japanese to depress the value of the U.S. dollar would backfire and have a devastating effect on its imports into this country, since a lowered dollar would result in substantially higher selling prices for their products.

TABLE 9.1   Number of Investments in the U.S. 1985–1989; Proportion of Total
Foreign Investment in the U.S., by Country

Source country	1985 No.	1985 %	1986 No.	1986 %	1987 No.	1987 %	1988 No.	1988 %	1989 No.	1989 %
Canada	101	11.1	114	10.8	122	9.2	86	7.9	88	8.0
France	61	6.7	45	4.3	69	5.2	66	6.0	49	4.4
Germany, FR	69	7.6	60	5.7	77	5.8	73	6.7	61	5.5
Japan	216	23.7	351	33.4	490	36.9	419	38.6	474	43.0
Netherlands	44	4.8	42	4.0	39	2.9	31	2.8	30	2.7
Switzerland	36	3.9	39	3.7	37	2.8	18	1.6	31	2.8
U.K.	176	19.3	176	16.7	248	18.7	213	19.6	163	4.8
All others	209	22.9	222	21.4	247	18.5	178	16.4	207	18.8
Total	912	100.0	1051	100.0	1328	100.0	1084	100.0	1103	100.0

SOURCE: U.S. Department of Commerce, International Trade Administration

JAPANESE INVESTMENT IN U.S. CONSTRUCTION COMPANIES

Japan was the only foreign power to invest in a U.S. construction firm in 1989 when Obayashi acquired New York builder E.W. Howell Company for $7 million. This, added to Japan's previous construction-related investments, is listed in Table 9.2, some of which were merely infusions of capital into their already-established U.S. subsidiaries.

THE BIG SIX AND THEIR U.S. PRESENCE

Each of the Big Six contractors has had a presence in the United States for many years: Kajima since 1964; Kumagai Gumi beginning in 1983; Obayashi 1972; Shimizu 1974; Taisei in 1983; and Takenaka for more than thirty years, having set up business here in 1960. The profiles of the Big Six represent not only a close look at six contractors of international stature, but also provide information about six potential competitors in the neighborhood.

One doesn't have to be a Top 100 contractor to feel the effects of this added competition. For example, in the writer's own marketing area, Fairfield County, Connecticut, and New York State's nearby Westchester County: Kajima International moved into Greenwich, Connecticut, in 1991 to begin work as a general contractor on The Daycroft School, a $10-million renovation project; in that same year, Takenaka discussed with Mitsubishi Paper plans to build a $4-million distribution center in Stamford, Connecticut; in Harrison, New York, one town away from White Plains, Shimizu joint-ventured with a New York contractor a few years back to build a private school.

On the larger playing field within the continental United States,

TABLE 9.2 Japanese Investments in U.S. Construction Companies

United States firm	Location	Investor	Value (if reported) (in millions)	Year invested
Woodland Hills Development Corp.	MD	Aoki Construction Co.		1979
Kuman Corp.	CA	Kumagai Gumi		1980
PanPacific Development	HI	Tokyo Construction Co.		1980
Kajima International	CA	Kajima Corp.		1980
Toda America	CA	Toda Construction Co.		1980
Toda Construction of California	CA	Toda Construction Co.		1982
Hazama Gumi	CA	Hazama Gumi, Ltd.		1983
JDH America Group	FL	Japan Der & Construction Co.	$.5	1984
Sumico Development Co.	TX	Sumitomo Construction Co., Ltd.		1985
Citadel Corporation	GA	Obaysahi Corp.		1985
Shimizu America Corp.	HI	Shimizu Construction Co., Ltd.		1985
K.G. Corp.	HI	Kumagai Gumi Co., Ltd.		1985
Geo-Con Inc.	PA	Taisei Corp.		1985
Sunrise Corp.	CA	Mitsubishi Estate Co., Ltd.	$10	1986
N.V.E., Inc.	CA	Dai Nippon Construction Co., Ltd.		1986
Doric/Mitsui JV	CA	Mitsui & Co., Ltd.—Joint Venture		1987
IDM/Kowa Bussan JV	CA	Kowa Bussan—Joint Venture		1987
Ray Wilson Corp.	CA	Tokyo Group	$2.5	1988

these Japanese contractors have been making their mark in countless other urban, suburban, and rural areas, not only as contractors for their Japanese clients, but as competitive bidders in both the public and private sectors.

So, do we learn to live and work with these foreign builders, or do we legislate against them as we did in 1988 when the Brooks-Murkowski Amendment was passed by Congress, or when Section 301 of the Trade and Competitiveness Act of 1988 was invoked?

Many politicians, and possibly several major U.S. international contractors, may believe that the latter approach is fair play, since the Japanese government seemingly has made it so difficult for American contractors and designers to penetrate the "electronics curtain." Since 1965, no U.S. firm had been awarded a major prime construction contract in Japan until Houston-based Brown and Root landed a $7-billion contract award in Japan from the Sanpo Land Industrial Company, Ltd., in late-1991. Brown and Root, who hadn't even kept its Japanese contractor's license current, will begin to build a huge resort complex on an island in Ise Bay near the city of Nagoya. The project will include condominiums, a hotel, two golf courses, a private airport, and other amenities. Other U.S. firms have also met with success in finding work in Japan in recent years by entering into joint-venture agreements with local contractors.

Doubtless, there is some validity to both arguments. In the eyes of the Japanese, Japan's domestic market is not exclusionary, but simply must be played by a certain set of rules. The U.S. contractors' response to that argument is that the "old boy" network in Japan does a very good job of keeping outsiders where they belong—out.

In this rapidly shrinking world of ours, the trend toward globalization has had an effect on most major industries, including the contracting business, and a more long-term approach to market share will require that contractors from all over the globe try to work with each other and thus reap the benefits that such cross-pollination ultimately will create. But first we need to create an atmosphere that is conducive to working together.

U.S.-JAPANESE RELATIONS IN THE CONSTRUCTION INDUSTRY

Construction-related matters between the United States and Japan have been strained for years. While Japanese contractors have had almost total access to the $350- to $400-million American construction market, roadblocks to U.S. builders thrown up by the Japanese government ostensibly have prevented them from gaining any significant share of the lucrative domestic construction market in Japan. When international construction markets dried up in the past as they did back in 1986, the Japanese contractors looked to their domestic market to shore up volume, and they wanted this market for themselves. That was when the image of "Japan, Incorporated" struck the eyes of foreign concerns attempting to gain a foothold in that country's markets.

U.S. ATTEMPTS TO LEGISLATE
OPEN MARKETS

On December 21, 1987, Senator Frank Murkowski of Alaska and Representative Jack Brooks of Texas tacked the Brooks-Murkowski Amendment onto a defense authorization bill. The passage of this bill allowed Congress and the U.S. trade representative to determine which foreign countries denied American companies fair market opportunities for products or services in their countries, and then to authorize the trade representative to take action against those countries.

One immediate effect of this law was to ban Japanese construction companies in the United States from bidding on federally funded work. And it worked. The U.S. subsidiary of Kajima pulled in its horns at that time, and Obayashi, who had submitted a very competitive bid on one phase of work for the Metro subway system in Washington, D.C., withdrew its proposal. Although Japan specifically was mentioned as one of the countries denying access to U.S. builders, Senator Murkowski wanted to make sure his message got across, so he tacked an amendment onto the Airport and Airways Improvement Act that was being reviewed in Congress in early 1988. This amendment made participation in the $25-billion-plus airport construction and improvement program contingent upon reciprocal opportunities for U.S. firms in foreign markets.

On May 25, 1988, the then Department of Commerce Secretary C. William Verity exchanged a series of letters with Japanese Ambassador Noburo Matsunaga that formed the basis of nondiscriminatory procurement practices to be enacted by the Japanese government with respect to foreign contractor participation in proposed projects in Japan worth $15 billion. These letters exhibiting good faith on the part of Japan effectively suspended the exclusion of Japanese contractors in the United States from bidding on publicly funded projects in this country.

As late as May 1991, the U.S.-Japanese construction pot was being stirred again by Trade Representative Carla Hill, who threatened to bar Japanese contractors for 30 days from bidding on certain types of federally funded projects if U.S. firms continued to be denied a fair chance to obtain domestic Japanese contracts for design or construction. Ambassador Hill had the authority to carry out this threat by invoking the provisions of Section 301 of the 1974 Trade Act.

This may not have posed much of a threat to Japanese contractors. Federally funded work in the United States represented $14 billion of the $435-billion total construction market in this country in 1990, while the Japanese domestic public works construction market was estimated at $38 billion, rising to $40.1 billion in 1991. Japan was planning to increase the funding of its infrastructure from 6.5 to 7.3 percent of GNP in 1992, so the threat of exclusion for the U.S. market may not have had the full effect it was meant to have. Making it difficult for foreigners to obtain work in Japan would leave this lucrative market to the Big Six.

Between 1988 and 1991, a few U.S. contractors were able to gain access to the domestic Japanese construction market as Schal, Bechtel, Fluor, Turner, and Tishman, among others, were awarded contracts, some on the basis of joint-venture agreements. During this time, according to the U.S. Department of Commerce, American contractors were awarded $473 million in contracts for work in Japan. Japanese builders operating in the U.S. between 1988 and 1991 captured contracts worth $564 million.

As a requisite for doing business in Japan each of these U.S. builders had to obtain a license under the Japanese construction business licensing provisions, which, until they were modified slightly in 1988, made licensing of foreign concerns almost impossible. A Catch-22 situation existed whereby in order to obtain a license an applicant was required to show proof of experience in similar projects, which meant, ostensibly, prior work in Japan.

THE MPA (MAJOR PROJECT ARRANGEMENT)

A major project arrangement agreement was reached in mid-1991 after Secretary of Commerce Robert A. Mosbacher met with Japanese Ambassador Ryohei Murata and a review was made of the guidelines contained in the 1988 Matsunaga-Verity exchange of letters. According to Secretary Mosbacher, *the major project arrangement,* referred to as MPA, contained a clear indication that Japan had taken effective steps to open her domestic market to foreign firms by instituting special policies and procedures for licensing and bid preparation, including a review and adjustment of that government's contractor rating system.

The entire text of the MPA Statement of Policies of the agreement can be summed up in the first paragraph of the document:

> It has been and will continue to be the policy of the Government of Japan to maintain open, transparent, competitive and non-discriminatory procedures in the procurement of public works, and to treat foreign firms no less

favorably than domestic firms, including providing information in a non-discriminatory manner. The Government of Japan believes that international competition should be facilitated in major projects procurement by all entities, public and private. The Government of Japan welcomes the entry of foreign firms into the Japanese market and will, as a general principle, undertake positive steps to promote and facilitate the entry of foreign firms into the Japanese construction market.

WE HAVE MET THE ENEMY AND HE MAY BE US

The philosopher George Santayana said, "Those who cannot remember the past are condemned to repeat it," and this thought might be borne in mind as we look at the present state of the automobile industry in this country, some of the reasons why it is where it is today, and how this situation may relate to the construction industry.

The U.S. automobile industry shares many similarities with the construction industry. Both industries are key elements in the economy: the construction industry employs more than five million people while the car business accounts for about 800,000 employees. But these figures tell only a part of the story. When residential and commercial construction is at its peak, so are sales at the local furniture store; by the same token, when auto sales are up, the 5000 automotive-component suppliers throughout the country have a good year, not to mention such basic industries as steel, glass, plastics, and rubber.

Both industries rely heavily upon engineering skills, and both industries assemble a complex product composed of thousands of individual parts. The auto industry manufacturing plant is climate-controlled and highly systematized, while the construction industry, in contrast, produces its product in an open air "factory," subject to all the vagaries of the weather. Unlike the car industry, where a certain number of standard parts and assembly techniques are used over and over again in a repetitive process, most construction projects are "one-off" products.

A similarity between the two industries that casts a long, dark shadow is the challenge mounted by the Japanese, whose auto manufacturers changed the face of that U.S. industry. The challenge to U.S. contractors that Japanese builders have been mounting so far has been documented more clearly in the international construction market.

In 1955, Ford, General Motors, and Chrysler dominated the domestic automobile scene, manufacturing 95 percent of all cars sold in this country. Now, just 36 years later, the Japanese share of the U.S. market continues to grow, from 28 percent in 1990 to 31 percent in 1991. Toyota became the largest seller of foreign cars in the country, selling

1 million units in 1990, which surpassed the sales of the Chrysler Corporation if the latter's trucks and minivans were excluded.

A close look at the top international contractor lists over the years reveals a similar trend toward dominance as Japanese builders can be observed slowly moving up through the pack; in 1991 they ran neck-and-neck with the U.S. builder, Fluor Corporation, for the Number 1 international spot; the Japanese remain firmly established in positions 2, 3, 4, and 5.

Remember that we are not talking about construction companies operating halfway around the world. We're talking about aggressive, well-financed companies operating possibly in your backyard. We're talking about each of Japan's Big Six and several others, sometimes referred to as the "Little Six," a somewhat lower sales-volume-tier of contractors, such as Toda Construction, Mitsui, and Daiwa, but still classed as billion-dollar builders.

Big Six contractors have offices and bases of operations in New York; Chicago; San Francisco; Los Angeles; Dallas; Atlanta, Norcross, and Marietta, Georgia; Louisville, Kentucky; Portland, Oregon; and in Florida, New Jersey, Puerto Rico, and several other cities and states in between. Hawaii may represent the largest concentrated operational base for the Big Six. Japanese investment in our fiftieth state exceeded $11.6 billion during the period from 1970 to 1990.

WHAT CAN BUILDERS LEARN FROM CARMAKERS?

The automobile industry in America was revolutionized by Henry Ford when he developed the assembly line and changed the industry from one where skilled craftsmen fitted every part to an automobile to one where less-skilled workers performed simple, repetitive operations before passing the next task on to another worker. If something didn't fit quite right, rather than stop the line, the car was shuttled off to a "re-work" area when it came off the assembly line, and at that point a team of skilled workers tried to make the fit right. Sometimes it took quite a bit of muscle to re-work an ill-fitting part, but the continuous flow of the assembly line was considered sacrosanct, and it was left to others off the line to perform what has now been termed "quality control."

Directives and orders from management to labor, rather than communication between the two groups, was the rule of the day and the adversarial relationship that existed in so many industries soon found another home on the assembly line.

It seems rather ironic that one of America's great strengths during and after World War II—mass production—contributed in large part to the down-turn of the automobile industry in this country later. The very high capital investment in the auto industry in America, including complex assembly lines and costly dies and tools, required a new car model to have a 10-year life-cycle. During the life of the model, cosmetic and minor sheet-metal changes were made each year to create the appearance of a new product, but the basic components and body panels remained basically the same.

THE JAPANESE METHOD OF AUTOMAKING

Starting with a clean slate in 1945, the Japanese took notice of the U.S. car industry and was in awe of its capacity to produce automobiles—as many as 7 million during the peak year of 1955. Primarily because of its lack of capital, the Japanese created a system of just-in-time inventory-control, where suppliers would be obliged to deliver car parts when needed, often on a daily or hourly basis. This practice eliminated many logistical problems and substantially reduced the automakers' cash requirements.

Dies required to form sheet-metal body parts for a new model are expensive and generally not produced until the body design has been completed, a cycle that required two years in Detroit. The Japanese devised a system whereby the designer and diemaker worked together from the early stages of design on through the final design. This resulted in a one-year cycle from the time the block of die steel was ordered to the die's completion. The concept of working together and closely communicating with each other not only allowed the Japanese to "fast-track" the die process, but also gave them the added advantage of being able to modify the design rapidly and introduce new models more quickly.

The Japanese assembly line is designed so that any worker can stop the line any time a problem arises, such as to correct a poorly fitting component. When this procedure was first initiated in Japan, the line stopped frequently, and teams of workers would analyze the problem to trace it back to its source. This method of dealing with quality control, observing the problem, and tracing it back to its source for correction finally resulted in an assembly line that ran all day, uninterrupted. The automobile that came off the line required almost no re-work. This was the "Quality Circle," which, strangely enough, was devised by an American, W. Edwards Deming, whose lectures to industrialists in the United States in the 1950s and 1960s fell on deaf ears.

The Japanese also pioneered the concept of "walking around" management, where top managers are visible on the factory floor and can observe the work process they have been charged to manage. Divisions between worker and manager in the Japanese factory become blurred as both boss and worker park in a parking lot with no reserved spaces and eat in the same company dining room while wearing similar company-furnished jackets.

The nurturing atmosphere in Japanese business life manifests itself in its auto industry in the relationship between the parts supplier and the automaker. Japanese car makers create "performance specifications" for their parts and select suppliers that can meet these requirements; in the United States, however, car makers go through the ritual of writing complex specifications for various components and then seeking competitive bids for these parts. An added benefit of the Japanese process is that it removes valuable and costly engineering work from the manufacturer and shifts it to the supplier.

HOW DOES ALL OF THIS RELATE TO CONSTRUCTION?

There are three key elements in the successful operation of the Japanese automobile manufacturing process—communication, quality control, and the nurturing of employees, subcontractors, and suppliers. Each of these elements has ready application in the construction industry.

Communication

What builder hasn't experienced a better relationship with a client and design team when the contractor, the owner, the architect, and the engineer all sit around a table, roll up their sleeves, and discuss the common goals necessary for creating an efficient, economical structure that best suits the client's needs? When the start of this "team" effort or "partnering" begins in the conceptual design stage and good communication is maintained throughout the project, chances are that all parties will be satisfactorily rewarded in the end.

Good communication between managers within the company and the office and field staff is essential in the building business as revisions, changes, updates to schedules, and work in progress must be accurately and quickly disseminated to all concerned parties. Good communication between the contractor and subcontractor will ensure that both parties are working with the same set of documents, with the result that time, money, and tempers are saved.

Quality Control

The problem of the re-work area at the end of the automobile assembly line, where mistakes are corrected after the product is completed, can be easily adopted in the construction process. Quality control in the construction industry may run on tracks parallel to those of a successful carmaker. If a builder does not correct an out-of-plumb steel-stud-framed wall quickly, correcting it later after applying sheetrock, or possibly millwork or expensive wall coverings will require more time and result in much higher costs. QC in the construction cycle should begin in the design stage, where drawings are created with details that can be built in the field and quality levels acceptable to designer, contractor and client can be attained.

Not only are job satisfaction and client goodwill the end-products of a well-planned quality-control program, but completion of a project with little or no defects or punch-list items is more economical. Less time and money is spent on rework, and final payments and job close-outs occur more rapidly.

Nurturing

Relationships between the general contractor and subcontractor can be amicable or adversarial. It has often been said that a general contractor is no better or worse than the assemblage of subcontractors engaged to work on his project.

In this competitive world of "low bidder," there is a strong temptation to award a contract based upon price alone, with no regard for the subcontractor's expertise, financial stability, and the quality of its work. Such an award often has disastrous results.

But when general contractor and subcontractor work together to solve their mutual problems rather than firing off barrages of inflammatory letters, work usually progresses more satisfactorily. If a subcontractor appears lacking in, say, proper contract administration procedures, more positive results will accrue if the general contractor assists the subcontractor in the proper method of submitting requisitions rather than returning invoices as incorrect. If a particularly difficult detail is indicated on the contract drawings, and if the general contractor can help the subcontractor by suggesting a simpler method of installation, why not do so? This, in effect, is nurturing, a part of the "give and take" relationship that many general contractors pursue with their subcontractors.

THE CHANGING NATURE OF THE BUSINESS

Remember the days when a deal was closed with a handshake, and one of the highest compliments that could be paid to a contractor was, "His word is his bond"? Hands are shaken less frequently these days and the spector of liability has put the cabosh on many informal commitments.

The day-to-day demands of an ever-increasingly competitive construction marketplace leave little room for error; with profit margins becoming minuscule, builders may be more concerned with survival than they are with good communication, quality control, and nurturing. But the foreign competitors in the auto industry have been able to provide innovative, quality products at very competitive prices, and still survive. Is there any reason to believe that foreign contractors won't follow suit?

HOW JAPAN AND THE UNITED STATES COMPARE IN CONSTRUCTION TECHNOLOGY

The Office of Technology Assessment is an investigative arm of the U.S. Congress, and in 1987 it conducted a study to determine how the American engineering and construction community fared in international markets. Their report stated, "Today, foreign contractors often have technology as good as—in some cases, better than—American firms. European and Japanese contractors have pioneered new approaches to tunneling and reinforced-concrete construction. South Korean construction companies learned their trade in Vietnam and the Middle East during the 1960s and 1970s, often working alongside American firms."

The U.S. position in construction technology at the time of this 1987 report was as follows:

- U.S. holds a lead in

  Computer software: CAD, engineering design, database

  Data-acquisition technology

  Construction-management systems

  High-rise building structures

- U.S. is falling behind in

  Physical construction systems

  Concrete technology

  Welding and pipe prefabrication

  Tunneling

  Advanced methods in earthwork

  Material technology

  Petrolift technology

Daniel Halpin, head of the Division of Construction Engineering and Management at Purdue University, assisted in the preparation of this report. He published a list of technologies where the United States is particularly strong, and also where other countries are gaining or, in fact lead the United States. The following shows where the United States maintains strong technology:

Technology	Nearest Competitor
Steel offshore platforms	United Kingdom
Bridge piers	Japan
Pile foundations	Belgium, The Netherlands
Precast concrete manufacture	The Netherlands
Massive earthwork	No near-competitor
High-rise buildings	Australia
Sunken-tube tunneling	Denmark, The Netherlands
Pavements, concrete	France, Italy
Concrete dams	Italy
Submarine pipe-laying	Italy, France

The following shows technologies where other countries lead the United States:

Technology	Leader
Structural-steel fabrication	Japan
Coastal protection	The Netherlands
Concrete offshore structures	Norway, France
Concrete buildings	France, Germany
Concrete bridges	France, Germany
Industrialized buildings, precast	The Netherlands
Tunneling in hard ground	Sweden, Austria, Norway
Soft-ground tunneling	Japan
Dredging	The Netherlands

Halpin, in a study entitled "The International Challenge in Design and Construction," published in 1991, stated that there are four basic reasons why foreign contractors have been successful in developing and implementing new technologies:

1. Many countries receive government support for research and development activities

2. The design-construction approach employed in many of these countries reduces the adversarial relationship

3. Foreign clients are more prone to share the risk with their design-build teams

4. Contractors in other countries are more willing to seek and use generic solutions to problems

THE U.S.-JAPAN ALLIANCE

A worthy goal for the balance of the twentieth century might be to begin to forge a stalwart alliance with our friends from the East. With the formation of the European Economic Community, even with its past cultural ties to Europe, American businesspeople and American contractors may face a tough time penetrating that market.

On the other side of the globe, Asia represents a rapidly expanding market for most goods and services. A United States alliance with Japan that draws upon each other's strong cultural ties with various sectors of the world could yield great dividends for both countries.

An exchange of ideas and technology could have a positive effect on both countries' economies, yielding the highest quality infrastructure at the lowest possible cost to their citizens, providing more affordable housing, and building high-caliber commercial and industrial structures with optimum life-cycle costs.

FORMULATION OF A RATIONAL POLICY

The United States and Japan should formulate rational economic plans for government and industrial policies that allow them to compete as well as collaborate with each other.

More cultural exchanges should be instituted and domestic markets should be opened to the most qualified builders so that joint ventures in all areas can be fostered and encouraged.

How This Could Affect Both Countries' Construction Industries

Obviously, we can learn a great deal from each other. The Japanese unabashedly admit they have learned a great deal from us. Just stop for a moment and consider the annual rating system for contractors in Japan. Would a modified contractor's annual rating system be such a bad thing to adopt in this country? Most public works projects in the United States require a contractor to submit a qualification statement and a bid bond to qualify for placement on a bidder's list for government projects.

And when the bids are opened and the low bid is so far below the agency's estimate and so far below all of the other bids, a warning sign should be waved. Has this low bidder worked on similar projects in the past? What is its reputation in the construction community? Has it been involved in considerable litigation? Many times, these questions are never considered when an award is made, often with tragic results.

Most contractors don't really mind competent competition. That's part of what the construction business is all about. It just makes one sharpen one's pencil a little more. But what these contractors do object to is knowing that the low bidder doesn't even own a pencil!

If American and Japanese governments encourage participation in each other's construction markets and allow the cross-breeding of ideas, techniques, and cultures, they may better position themselves for work in all parts of the world. U.S. contractors allied with Japanese contractors could present a formidable team, whether participating in the burgeoning Asian and Pacific Rim market, the EEC, or the unlimited potential of Eastern European expansion once those countries obtain the wherewithal to pay for their investments.

HOW CAN WE START THE PROCESS?

The joining of hands and minds could begin by having construction companies on both sides of the Pacific offer summer internships to promising university students and exchange programs of longer duration to construction professionals and managers already in the work force.

The major construction companies in both countries could contribute annually to a fund that would be used to select and send applicants from small and mid-sized companies to international seminars and symposiums offering material that could improve their company's performance.

Establish an East-West construction research and development institute funded by government and private industry that would act as a clearinghouse, a central databank, with fully equipped and staffed laboratory facilities that could actively pursue projects and technologies of worldwide concern. Japanese and American engineers and researchers working side by side could attack energy conservation issues, devise universal testing procedures and material and product analysis, investigate erosion-control problems, seismic and life-safety concerns, environmental issues, and conduct basis research.

Set up an international joint venture registry for general contractors and subcontractors of all nations seeking to join up with partners on international projects. What better way to transfer technology, improve management skills, broaden the horizons of company executives, and get to know and understand that foreign neighbor a little better.

And consider the creation of an international association of contractors and subcontractors to further disseminate information and provide training seminars in the world's latest and most sophisticated design-construct means and methods.

Create an annual award to be presented to the construction company contributing the most to a better international understanding among countries, and add to this another award for the company making the most outstanding contribution to the industry-at-large during the same period of time. The United States is still the world's richest and most competitive economy, although other countries are quickly gaining on us.

In the rapidly changing world in which we live, it is not so much what we did yesterday but what we are capable of doing tomorrow that counts.

Index

ABOUT THE AUTHOR

Sidney M. Levy, senior vice president of a major construction firm in Connecticut, has more than 30 years of experience in the construction industry, including service as construction manager on residential, commercial, and industrial projects. He is the author of the best-selling book *Project Management in Construction,* also published by McGraw-Hill. Mr. Levy resides in Woodbridge, Connecticut.